P9-CQM-976

The Adult Learner:
A Neglected Species
Third Edition

Gulf Publishing Company
Book Division
Houston, London, Paris, Tokyo

The Adult Learner:
A Neglected Species

Third Edition

Malcolm Knowles

Building Blocks of Human Potential
Leonard Nadler, Series Editor

The Adult Educator—A Handbook for Staff Development by H. G. Miller and
J. R. Verduin
The Adult Learner: A Neglected Species/3rd edition by M. S. Knowles
Clients and Consultants: Meeting and Exceeding Expectations/
2nd edition by C. R. Bell and L. Nadler
The Conference Book by L. Nadler and Z. Nadler
Creative Worklife by D. N. Scobel
Handbook of Creative Learning Exercises by H. Engel
Handbook of Training Evaluation and Measurement Methods by J. Phillips
Human Resource Development: The European Approach by H. E. Frank
How to Delegate: A Guide to Getting Things Done by H. Engel
Managing Cultural Differences by P. Harris and R. Moran
Managing Cultural Synergy by R. Moran and P. Harris
The Winning Trainer: Winning Ways to Involve People in Learning by J. Eitington

The Adult Learner: A Neglected Species/Third Edition

Copyright© 1973, 1978, 1984 by Gulf Publishing Company,
Houston, Texas. All rights reserved. Printed in the United States
of America. This book, or parts thereof, may not be reproduced in
any form without permission of the publisher.

First Edition, February 1973
Second Printing, September 1974
Third Printing, February 1975
Fourth Printing, September 1976
Second Edition, August 1978
Second Printing, January 1980
Third Printing, September 1981
Third Edition, August 1984
Second Printing, January 1986

Library of Congress Cataloging in Publication Data

Knowles, Malcolm Shepherd, 1913-
The adult learner.

(Building blocks of human potential series)
Bibliography: p.
Includes indexes.
1. Adult education. I. Title. II. Series: Building
blocks of human potential.
LC5215.K59   1984   374   83-22642
ISBN 0-87201-005-8

Contents

C.2- 77393

Foreword

Welcome to the Third Edition of what has become a classic in the field of adult learning (that is, Human Resource Development and Adult Education). You, the reader, will find some significant changes in this edition, as Malcolm has updated it with some of the more recent work in the field of adult learning and in related fields.

On reading this manuscript, several thoughts occurred to me that I would like to share with you. The first relates to his style. If you have heard him, you will hear his voice coming through the pages. For the most part, this is written as he speaks. It is not addressed to a general audience but rather to individuals. As you read this book, you will begin to feel that it is addressed to you.

We have somehow developed the idea that for material to be good it must be impersonal, difficult to read, and not enjoyable. Why should that be? In this book, the author is writing for the individual reader (many of them) so do not be too surprised if you feel that you are involved in a dialogue. At times, I am sure, you will feel like responding to some of the ideas and experiences he shares.

You may not agree with everything he has written. That is all right too. I know that there were times, as I read the manuscript, when I wanted to pick up the phone, call him, and get involved in a discussion. I still look forward to doing that the next time we get together.

When you read the book, you may feel the same way. If you do, by all means, make a note of your questions, and the next time you are at a workshop or similar activity that Malcolm is conducting, ask him.

You are not getting just Malcolm Knowles in this book. True, you will be able to share the almost half-century that he has spent in the field of adult learning. But it is more than just a personal document. This book is one of the few resources that contains, in one place, the wide range of research related to the field of adult learning.

He has provided rich appendices to supplement the points he has made. These are not just fillers, so be sure to read them in conjunction with his discussions in the book.

I know that some forewords are designed to march the reader through the book on a chapter-by-chapter basis. I have written some of those. Somehow, I did not feel that was the way to go with this book. I prefer that you walk with Malcolm.

Read, enjoy, and learn—that is what this book is about.

Leonard Nadler
Series Editor
Washington, DC

The Adult Learner:
A Neglected Species
Third Edition

1

Exploring the World of Learning Theory

Why Explore Learning Theory?

A good question. Perhaps you shouldn't. If you have no questions about the quality of Human Resources Development* in your organization, if you are sure it's the best it can be, I'd suggest you cancel your reservation and get a refund.

But if you are a policy-level executive, you may have such questions as these: Are our HRD activities based on assumptions about human nature and organizational life that are congruent with the assumptions on which our management policies are based? Is our HRD program contributing to long-run gains in our human capital, or only short-run cost reduction? Why are our HRD personnel making the decisions they are concerning priorities, activities, methods and techniques, materials, and the use of outside resources (consultants, package pro-

---

*Human Resources Development (HRD) is used in this book with the broadest possible meaning and includes adult and continuing education in educational institutions, business and industry, government agencies, health agencies, voluntary organizations, religious institutions, labor unions, mass media, and by commercial providers.

grams, hardware, software, and university courses)? Are these the best decisions? How can I assess whether or not or to what degree the HRD program is producing the results I want?

If you are an HRD administrator, to use the breakdown of the roles of the human resource developer presented by Nadler in the foundational book in this series [Nadler, 1970, p. 151], you may have all of the above questions plus such others as: Which learning theory is most appropriate for which kind of learning, or should our entire HRD program be faithful to a single learning theory? How do I find out what learning theories are being followed by the various consultants, package programs, and other outside resources available to us? What difference might their theoretical orientation make in our HRD program? What are the implications of the various learning theories for our program development, selection and training of instructional personnel, administrative policies and practices, facilities, and program evaluation?

If you are a learning specialist (instructor, curriculum builder, methods and materials developer), you may have some of the above questions plus such others as: How can I increase my effectiveness as a learning specialist? Which techniques will be most effective for particular situations? Which learning theories are most congruent with my own view of human nature and the purpose of education? What are the implications of the various learning theories for my own role and performance?

If you are a consultant (advocate, expert, stimulator, change agent), you may have some of the above questions plus such others as: Which learning theory should I advocate under what circumstances? How shall I explain the nature and consequences of the various learning theories to my clients? What are the implications of the various learning theories for total organizational development? Which learning theory is most congruent with my conception of the role of consultant?

A good theory should provide both explanations of phenomena and guidelines for action. But theories about human behavior also carry with them assumptions about human nature, the purpose of education, and desirable values. The better you understand the various theories, therefore, the better decisions you will be able to make regarding learning experiences that will achieve the ends you wish to achieve.

What Is a Theory?

Webster's Seventh New Intercollegiate Dictionary gives five definitions: (1) the analysis of a set of facts in their relation to one another; (2) the general or abstract principles of a body of fact, a science, or an art; (3) a plausible or scientifically acceptable general principle or body of principles offered to explain phenomena; (4) a hypothesis assumed for the sake of argument or investigation; (5) abstract thought. Learning theorists use all five of these definitions in one way or another, but let me give you a taste of the wide variations in their usages:

First, here are some definitions-by-usage-in-context. It is my observation that most writers in this field don't expressly define the term, but expect their readers to get its meaning from the way it is used.

The research worker needs a set of assumptions as a starting point to guide what he does, to be tested by experiment or to serve as a check on observations and insights. Without any theory his activities may be as aimless, as wasteful as the early wanderings of the explorers in North America. . . .Some knowledge of theory always aids practice. [Kidd, 1959, pp. 134-135]

A scientist, along with the desire to satisfy his curiosity about the facts of nature, has a predilection for ordering his facts into systems of laws and theories. He is interested not only in verified facts and relationships, but in neat and parsimonious ways of summarizing these facts. [Hilgard and Bower, 1966, pp. 1-2]

Every managerial act rests on assumptions, generalizations, and hypotheses—that is to say, on theory. [McGregor, 1960, p. 6]

The word "theory" conveys a sense of intangibility which is forbidding to some students. To others, theory is associated with a sense of impracticality and unrealism which prompts negative initial reaction. Yet nearly everyone, whether teacher, parent, employer, or college student, has and believes his own theory of learning, even though he may not have stated it in so many words. [Kingsley and Garry, 1957, p. 82]

It is easy enough to use one's chosen theory for explaining modifications in behavior as an instrument for describing growth; there are so many aspects of growth that any theory can find something that it can explain well. [Bruner, 1966, pp. 4-5]

We can now understand why the term "model" is sometimes used as a synonym for "theory," especially one which is couched in the postulational style. . . .In my opinion, this sort of usage of the term "model" is of dubious worth, methodologically speaking. If "model" is co-extensive with "theory," why not just say "theory," or if need be, "theory in postulational form"? In a strict sense, not all theories are in fact models: in general, we learn something about the subject-matter *from* the theory, but not by investigating properties *of* the theory . . . Consider, for instance, the difference between the theory of evolution and a model which a geneticist might construct to study mathematically the rate of diffusion in a hypothetical population of a characteristic with specified survival value. [Kaplan, 1964, pp. 264-265]

There are some psychologists who don't believe in theories at all. Gagne, for example, writes, "I do not think learning is a phenomenon which can be explained by simple theories, despite the admitted intellectual appeal that such theories have." [Gagne, 1965, p. v] He goes on to explain, however, that a number of useful generalizations can be made about eight distinguishable classes of performance change which he describes as conditions of learning.

Skinner objects to theories on the score that the hypothesis-formulation-and-testing procedures they generate are wasteful and misleading. "They usually send the investigator down the wrong paths, and even if the scientific logic makes them self-correcting, the paths back are strewn with discarded theories." [Hilgard, 1966, p. 143] Skinner believes that the end result of scientific investigation is a "described functional relationship demonstrated in the data." After reviewing the classical theories he comes to the conclusion that "such theories are now of historical interest only, and unfortunately much of the work which was done to support them is also of little current value. We may turn instead to a more adequate analysis of the changes which take place as a student learns." [Skinner, 1968, p. 8]

Where does all this leave us in answering the question, What is a theory? Perhaps the only realistic answer is that a theory is what a given author says it is: if you want to understand his thinking you have to go along with his definitions. So here is mine: *A theory is a comprehensive, coherent, and internally consistent system of ideas about a set of phenomena.*

What Is Learning?

One of our most distinguished contemporary interpreters of learning theory, Ernest Hilgard, maintains that there is no basic disagreement about the definition of learning between the theories.

> While it is extremely difficult to formulate a satisfactory definition of learning so as to include all the activities and processes which we wish to include and eliminate all those which we wish to exclude the difficulty does not prove to be embarrassing because it is not a source of controversy as between theories. The controversy is over fact and interpretation, not over definition. [Hilgard and Bower, 1966, p. 6]

This generalization appears to hold with regard to those learning theorists who dominated the field until recently, although there are striking variations in the degree of precision among them. Let's start with three definitions by different authors in the same book. [Crow and Crow, 1963]

> Learning involves change. It is concerned with the acquisition of habits, knowledge, and attitudes. It enables the individual to make both personal and social adjustments. Since the concept of change is inherent in the concept of learning, any change in behavior implies that learning is taking place or has taken place. Learning that occurs during the process of change can be referred to as the *learning process*. [Crow and Crow, 1963, p. 1]

> Learning is a change in the individual, due to the interaction of that individual, and his environment, which fills a need and makes him more capable of dealing adequately with his environment. [Burton, 1963, p. 7]

> There is a remarkable agreement upon the definition of learning as being reflected in a change in behavior as the result of experience. [Haggard, 1963, p. 20]

This last notion that we don't know what learning is directly, but can only infer it is supported by Cronbach's statement, "Learning is shown by a change in behavior as a result of experience." [Cronbach, 1963, p. 71] Harris and Schwahn go back to, "Learning is essentially change due to experience," but then go on to distinguish among *learning as product* (which emphasizes the end result or outcome of the learning experience), *learning as process* (which emphasizes what happens during the course of a learning experience in attaining a given learning product or outcome), and *learning as function* (which emphasizes certain critical aspects of learning, such as motivation, retention, and transfer, which presumably make behavioral changes in human learning possible). [Harris and Schwahn, 1961, pp. 1-2]

Other definers take care to distinguish between planned learning and natural growth.

> Learning is a change in human disposition or capability, which can be retained, and which is not simply ascribable to the process of growth. [Gagne, 1965, p. 5]

> Learning is the process by which an activity originates or is changed through reacting to an encountered situation, provided that the characteristics of the change in activity cannot be explained on the basis of native response tendencies, maturation, or temporary states of the organism (e.g., fatigue, drugs, etc.). [Hilgard and Bower, 1966, p. 2]

Two concepts lie at the heart of Skinner's treatment of learning: (1) *control* ("Recent improvements in the conditions which control behavior in the field of learning are of two principal sorts. The Law of Effect has been taken seriously; we have made sure that effects *do* occur under conditions which are optimal for producing changes called learning") and (2) *shaping* ("Once we have arranged the particular type of consequence called a reinforcement, our techniques

permit us to shape the behavior of an organism almost at will").
[Skinner, 1968, p. 10]

It is clear that these learning theorists (and most of their precur-
sors and many of their contemporaries) see learning as a process by
which behavior is changed, shaped, or controlled. Other theorists
prefer to define learning in terms of growth, development of competencies, and fulfillment of potential. Jerome Bruner, for example,
observes, "It is easy enough to use one's chosen theory for explaining modifications in behavior as an instrument for describing
growth; there are so many aspects of growth that any theory can
find something that it can explain well." He then lists these
"benchmarks about the nature of intellectual growth against which
to measure one's efforts at explanation":

1. Growth is characterized by increasing independence of response
   from the immediate nature of the stimulus.
2. Growth depends upon internalizing events into a "storage system"
   that corresponds to the environment.
3. Intellectual growth involves an increasing capacity to say to oneself
   and others, by means of words or symbols, what one has done or
   what one will do.
4. Intellectual development depends upon a systematic and contingent interaction between a tutor and a learner.
5. Teaching is vastly facilitated by the medium of language, which
   ends by being not only the medium for exchange but the instrument
   that the learner can then use himself in bringing order into the environment.
6. Intellectual development is marked by increasing capacity to deal
   with several alternatives simultaneously, to tend to several sequences during the same period of time, and to allocate time and
   attention in a manner appropriate to these multiple demands.
   [Bruner, 1966, pp. 4-6]

Other theorists feel that even this emphasis on growth, with its
focus on cognitive development, is too narrow to explain what
learning is really about. Jones objects to Bruner's underemphasis on
emotional skills; his exclusive attention to extra-psychic stimuli; the
equating of symbolism with verbalism; and his preoccupation with
the processes of concept attainment to the seeming exclusion of the

processes of concept formation or invention. [Jones, 1968, pp. 97-104]

Nevertheless, Bruner is moving away from the perception of learning as a process of controlling, changing, or shaping behavior and putting it more in the context of competency-development. One of the most dynamic and prolific developments in the field of psychology, *humanistic psychology*, has recently exploded on the scene (the Association of Humanistic Psychology was founded in 1963) and has carried this trend of thought much farther. One of its exponents is Carl Rogers.

> Let me define a bit more precisely the elements which are involved in such significant or experiential learning. *It has a quality of personal involvement*—the whole person in both his feeling and cognitive aspects being *in* the learning event. *It is self-initiated.* Even when the impetus or stimulus comes from the outside, the sense of discovery, of reaching out, of grasping and comprehending, comes from within. *It is pervasive.* It makes a difference in the behavior, attitudes, perhaps even the personality of the learner. *It is evaluated by the learner.* He knows whether it is meeting his need, whether it leads toward what he *wants* to know, whether it illuminates the dark area of ignorance he is experiencing. The locus of evaluation, we might say, resides definitely in the learner. *Its essence is meaning.* When such learning takes place, the element of meaning to the learner is built into the whole experience. [Rogers, 1969, p. 5]

Maslow sees the goal of learning to be self-actualization, ". . . the full use of talents, capacities, potentialities, etc." [Maslow, 1970, p. 150] He conceives of growth toward this goal as being determined by the relationship of two sets of forces operating within each individual.

> One set clings to safety and defensiveness out of fear, tending to regress backward, hanging on to the past. . . . The other set of forces impels him forward toward wholeness to Self and uniqueness of Self, toward full functioning of all his capacities . . . . We grow forward when the delights of growth and anxieties of safety are greater than the anxieties of growth and the delights of safety. [Maslow, 1972, pp. 44-45]

Building on the notion that "recent insights from the behavioral sciences have expanded the perception of human potential, through a re-casting of the image of man from a passive, reactive recipient, to an active, seeking, autonomous, and reflective being," Sidney Jourard develops the concept of *independent learning*.

> ... That independent learning is problematic is most peculiar, because man always and only learns by himself. . . .Learning is not a task or problem; it is a way to be in the world. Man learns as he pursues goals and projects that have meaning for him. He is always learning something. Perhaps the key to the problem of independent learning lies in the phrase "the learner has the need and the capacity to assume responsibility for his own continuing learning." [Jourard, 1972, p. 66]

Other educational psychologists question the proposition that learning can be defined as a single process. For example, Gagne identifies five *domains of the learning process*, each with its own praxis.

(1) *Motor skills*, which are developed through practice.
(2) *Verbal information*, the major requirement for learning being its presentation within an organized, meaningful context.
(3) *Intellectual skills*, the learning of which appears to require prior learning of prerequisite skills.
(4) *Cognitive strategies*, the learning of which requires repeated occasions in which challenges to thinking are presented.
(5) *Attitudes,* which are learned most effectively through the use of human models and "vicarious reinforcement." [Gagne, 1972, pp. 3-4]

Tolman distinguished six "types of connections or relations" to be learned: (1) cathexes, (2) equivalence beliefs, (3) field expectancies, (4) field-cognition modes, (5) drive discriminations, and (6) motor patterns. [Hilgard and Bower, 1966, pp. 211- 213] Bloom and his associates identified three domains of educational objectives: (1) cognitive, "which deal with the recall or recognition of knowledge and the development of intellectual abilities and skills;"

(2) affective, "which describe changes in interest, attitudes, and values, and the development of appreciations and adequate adjustment;" and (3) psychomotor. [Bloom, 1956, p. 7]

A distinction is frequently made between *education* and *learning*. For example, Wright says

> Education is an activity undertaken or initiated by one or more agents that is designed to effect changes in the knowledge, skill, and attitudes of individuals, groups, or communities. The term *education* emphasizes the educator, the agent of change who presents stimuli and reinforcement for learning and designs activities to induce change.
> The term *learning,* in contrast, emphasizes the person in whom the change occurs or is expected to occur. Learning is the act or process by which behavioral change, knowledge, skills, and attitudes are acquired. [Boyd, Apps, et al, 1980, pp. 100-101]

The difficulty of defining learning is summarized by Smith in these words:

> It has been suggested that the term *learning* defies precise definition because it is put to multiple uses. Learning is used to refer to (1) the acquisition and mastery of what is already known about something, (2) the extension and clarification of meaning of one's experience, or (3) an organized, intentional process of testing ideas relevant to problems. In other words, it is used to describe a product, a process, or a function. [Smith, 1982, p. 34]

It is certainly clear by now that learning is an elusive phenomenon. And, as we shall see next, the way people define it greatly influences how they theorize and go about causing it to occur. Until recently, educators of adults have been wallowing around in this same morass, and after wallowing around in it a bit more ourselves, we'll see how adult-educators are beginning to extricate themselves.

2

Theories of Learning

We know more about how animals (especially rodents and pigeons) learn than about how children learn; and we know much more about how children learn than about how adults learn. Perhaps this is because the study of learning was early taken over by experimental psychologists whose canons require a rigid control of variables. And it is obvious that the conditions under which animals learn are more controllable than those under which children learn; and the conditions under which children learn are much more controllable than those under which adults learn.

The fact is that all of the scientific theories of learning have been derived from the study of learning by animals and children.

Propounders and Interpreters

In general, there are two types of literature about learning theory: that produced by propounders of theories (who tend to be dogmatic and argumentative), and that produced by interpreters of theories (who tend to be reconciliatory). Just so you'll have a perspective on this literature, I have extracted from the sources I have been studying a list of the major propounders and major interpreters and displayed them in Table 2-1. To provide a sense of historical development, they are listed more or less in the order of

Table 2-1
Propounders and Interpreters of Learning Theory

Propounders	Interpreters
Ebbinghaus (1885)	
Thorndike (1898)	
Angell (1896)	
Dewey (1896)	
Pavlov (1902)	
Woodworth (1906)	
Watson (1907)	
Judd (1908)	
Freud (1911)	
Kohler (1917)	
Tolman (1917)	
Wertheimer (1923)	
Koffka (1924)	Kilpatrick (1925)
Pressey (1926)	
Guthrie (1930)	Rugg (1928)
Skinner (1931)	Hilgard (1931)
Hall (1932)	
McGeoch (1932)	
Lewin (1933)	
Piaget (1935)	
Miller (1935)	
Spence (1936)	
Mowrer (1938)	
Katona (1940)	Bode (1940)
Maslow (1941)	Melton (1941)
Festinger (1942)	Cronbach (1943)
Rogers (1942)	Brunner (1943)
Estes (1944)	Lorge (1944)
Krech (1948)	
McClelland (1948)	
Sheffield (1949)	
Underwood (1949)	
Dollard (1950)	Schaie (1953)
Tyler (1950)	Garry (1953)
	Koch (1954)
	McKeachie (1954)
	Birren (1954)
Bloom (1956)	Getzels (1956)

Table 2-1. Continued

Propounders	Interpreters
Bruner (1956)	Bugelski (1956)
Erikson (1959)	Kuhlen (1957)
Crowder (1959)	Kidd (1959)
Lumsdaine (1959)	Botwinick (1960)
Combs and Snygg (1959)	Miller (1960)
Ausubel (1960)	Glaser (1962)
Glaser (1962)	Flavell (1963)
Gagne (1963)	
	Hill (1963)
	Gage (1963)
	McDonald (1964)
Jourard (1964)	Goldstein (1965)
Suchman (1964)	Reese and Overton (1970)
Crutchfield (1969)	Goble (1971)
Freire, 1970	
Knowles, 1970	
Tough, 1971	
Houle, 1972	
Dave, 1973	
Loevinger, 1976	
Cross, 1976	
Botwinick, 1977	Howe, 1977
Gross, 1977	Knox, 1977
Srinivasan, 1977	
Cropley, 1980	Chickering, 1981

their appearance in the evolving body of literature. To keep the list within reasonable bounds, I have defined major as those who have made the greatest impact on the thinking of others as I sense the literature.

It must be admitted that the distinction between propounders and interpreters is not absolute. Some theorists, such as Pressey, Estes, Lorge, Gagne, Hilgard and Kuhlen, made contributions of both sorts and have been placed in the column representing their major work. It is interesting to note that the bulk of the theory-production occurred in the first half of the century and that the bulk of the interpretation has appeared since 1950. Perhaps we have entered an era of integration. It is also interesting to note that both the theorists and interpreters from 1970 on have been concerned almost exclusively with adult learners.

Types of Theories

The proliferation of propounders has presented a major challenge to the interpreters in their quest to bring some sort of order into the system. In perhaps the most comprehensive interpretive work to date, Hilgard and Bower organize their review according to eleven categories.

Thorndike's Connectionism

Pavlov's Classical Conditioning

Guthrie's Contiguous Conditioning

Skinner's Operant Conditioning

Hull's Systematic Behavior Theory

Tolman's Sign Learning

Gestalt Theory

Freud's Psychodynamics

Functionalism

Mathematical Learning Theory

Information Processing Models

They then share their frustration in arranging these disparate categories into a pattern.

Learning theories fall into two major families: *stimulus-response* theories and *cognitive* theories, but not all theories belong to these two families. The stimulus-response theories include such diverse members as the theories of Thorndike, Pavlov, Guthrie, Skinner, and Hull. The cognitive theories include at least those of Tolman and the classical gestalt psychologists. Not completely and clearly classifiable in these terms are the theories of functionalism, psychodynamics, and the probabilistic theories of the model builders. The lines of cleavage between the two families of theories are not the only cleavages within learning theories: there are other specific issues upon which theories within one family may differ. [Hilgard and Bower, 1966, p. 8]

McDonald breaks the theories down into six categories in his analysis:

Recapitulation (Hull)
Connectionism (Thorndike)
Pragmatism (Dewey)
Gestalt and field theory (Ogden, Hartman, Lewin)
Dynamic psychology (Freud)
Functionalism (Judd) [McDonald, 1964, pp. 1-26]

Gage identifies three families of learning theories: (1) conditioning, (2) modeling, and (3) cognitive. [Gage, 1972, p. 19] Kingsley and Garry, two sets: (1) association or stimulus-response (Thorndike, Guthrie, and Hull), and (2) field theories (Lewin, Tolman, and the gestalt psychologists). [Kingsley and Garry, 1957, p. 83] Taba agrees with the two-family set, but uses different labels: (1) associationist or behaviorist theories, and (2) organismic, gestalt, and field theories. [Taba, 1962, p. 80]

Obviously, the interpreters had not succeeded up to this point in organizing the field of learning theories in a really fundamental way—at least not in a way that satisfied most of them, and certainly not me. Then, in 1970, two developmental psychologists, Hayne W. Reese and Willis F. Overton, presented a way of conceptualizing the theories in terms of larger models, and the mist began to clear.

The Concept of Mechanistic and Organismic Models of Development

Reese and Overton start with the proposition, "Any theory presupposes a more general model according to which the theoretical concepts are formulated." The most general models are the world views or metaphysical systems which constitute basic models of the essential characteristics of man and indeed of the nature of reality. [Reese and Overton, 1970, p. 117]

Two systems which have been pervasive in both the physical and the social sciences are the *mechanistic* world view, the basic metaphor of which is the machine, and the *organismic* world view, the basic metaphor of which is the organism—the living, organized system presented to experience in multiple forms.

The *mechanistic model* represents the universe as a machine composed of discrete pieces operating in a spatio-temporal field. These pieces—elementary particles in motion—and their relations form the basic reality to which all other more complex phenomena are ultimately reducible. When forces are applied in the operation of the machine a chain-like sequence of events results; and, since these forces are the only immediate efficient or immediate causes of the events, complete prediction is possible—in principle. As Reese and Overton point out, "A further characteristic of the machine, and consequently of the universe represented in this way, is that it is eminently susceptible to quantification." [*Ibid.*, p. 131]

When applied to the sphere of epistemology and psychology, this world view results in a *reactive*, passive, robot or empty-organism *model of man*. The organism is inherently at rest; activity is viewed as the resultant of external forces. Psychological functions, such as thinking, willing, wishing, and perceiving, are seen as complex phenomena that are reducible to more simple phenomena by *efficient causes*. Change in the products or behavior of the organism is not seen as resulting from change in the structure of the organism itself.

> The appearance of qualitative changes is considered either as epiphenomenal (caused by another phenomenon) or as reducible to quantitative change, since the organism, like the elementary particles of classical physics, does not exhibit basic qualitative changes. [*Ibid.*, pp. 131-132]

The *organismic model* represents the universe as a unitary, interactive, developing organism. The essence of substance it perceives to be activity, rather than the static elementary particle proposed by the mechanistic model.

> From such a point of view, one element can never be like another, and as a consequence, the logic of discovering reality according to the analytical ideal of reducing the many qualitative differences to the one is repudiated. In its place is substituted a search for unity among the many; that is, a pluralistic universe is substituted for a monistic one, and it is the diversity which constitutes the unity. . .Thus, unity is found in multiplicity, being is found in becoming, and constancy is found in change. [*Ibid.*, p. 133]

The whole is therefore organic rather than mechanical in nature. "The nature of the whole, rather than being the sum of its parts, is presupposed by the parts and the whole constitutes the condition of the meaning and existence of the parts." [*Ibid.*] Accordingly, efficient cause is replaced by formal cause—cause by the essential nature of the form. Thus, the possibility of a predictive and quantifiable universe is precluded.

When applied to the sphere of epistemology and psychology, this world view results in an inherently and spontaneously *active organism model of man*. It sees man as an active organism rather than a reactive organism, as a *source* of acts, rather than as a collection of acts initiated by external forces. It also represents man as an organized entity.

> . . .a configuration of parts which gain their meaning, their function, from the whole in which they are imbedded. From this point of view, the concepts of psychological structure and function, or means and ends, become central rather than derived. Inquiry is directed toward the discovery of principles of organization, toward the explanation of the nature and relation of parts and wholes, structures and functions, rather than toward the derivation of these from elementary processes. [*Ibid.*, pp. 133-134]

> The individual who accepts this model will tend to emphasize the significance of processes over products, and qualitative change over quantitative change. . . . In addition, he will tend to emphasize the significance of the role of experience in facilitating or inhibiting the course of development, rather than the effect of training as the source of development. [*Ibid.*, p. 134]

With this and the preceding set of concepts as a frame of reference, let us turn to a brief examination of the theories about learning derived from the study of learning in animals and children.

Theories Based on a Mechanistic Model

The first systematic investigation in this country of the phenomenon we call learning was conducted by Edward L. Thorndike. It was a study of learning in animals, first reported in his *Animal Intelligence*, published in 1898.

Thorndike conceived learners to be empty organisms who responded to stimuli more or less randomly and automatically. A specific response is *connected* to a specific stimulus when it is rewarded. In this situation the stimulus, *S*, is entirely under the control of the experimenter (or teacher), and in large measure so is the response, *R*, for all the experimenter has to do to connect the particular *R* to a particular *S* is to reward the *R* when the organism happens to make it. This association between sense impressions and impulses to action came to be known as a bond or a connection. Thus, Thorndike's system has sometimes been called *bond psychology* or *connectionism*, and was the original stimulus-response (or S-R) psychology of learning.

Thorndike developed three laws which he believed governed the learning of animals and human beings: (1) the law of readiness (the circumstances under which a learner tends to be satisfied or annoyed, to welcome or to reject); (2) the law of exercise (the strengthening of connections with practice); and (3) the law of effect (the strengthening or weakening of a connection as a result of its consequences). In the course of a long and productive life (he died in 1949), and with help from many collaborators, both friendly and critical, Thorndike's system of thought became greatly refined and elaborated, and provided the subfoundation of the behaviorist theories of learning.

Soon after Thorndike started his work on connections in this country the Russian physiologist, Ivan Pavlov (1849-1936), inaugurated his experiments which resulted in the concept of conditioned reflexes. Hilgard describes his classical experiment.

> When meat powder is placed in a dog's mouth, salivation takes place; the food is the *unconditioned* stimulus and salivation is the *unconditioned* reflex. Then some arbitrary stimulus, such as a light, is combined with the presentation of the food. Eventually, after repetition and if time relationships are right, the light will evoke salivation independent of the food; the light is the *conditioned stimulus* and the response to it is the *conditioned reflex*. [Hilgard and Bower, 1966, p. 48]

Pavlov developed several concepts and accompanying techniques which have been incorporated into the behaviorist system. One was *reinforcement*, in which a conditioned reflex becomes fixed by following the conditioned stimulus repeatedly by the unconditioned stimulus and response at appropriate time intervals. Another was *extinction*: when reinforcement is discontinued and the conditioned stimulus is presented alone, unaccompanied by the unconditioned stimulus, the conditioned response gradually diminishes and disappears. Another was *generalization*, in which a conditioned reflex evoked to one stimulus can also be elicited by other stimuli, not necessarily similar to the first. A fourth basic concept was *differentiation*, in which the initial generalization is overcome by the method of contrasts in which one of a pair of stimuli is regularly reinforced and the other is not; in the end, the conditioned reflex occurs only to the positive (reinforced) stimulus and not to the negative (nonreinforced) stimulus. Pavlov's system has been termed *classical conditioning* to distinguish it from later developments in *instrumental conditioning* and *operant conditioning*.

John B. Watson (1878-1958) is generally credited with being the father of behaviorism.

> The behaviorists, then and now, had and have in common the conviction that a science of psychology must be based upon a study of that which is overtly observable: physical stimuli, the muscular movements and glandular secretions which they arouse, and the environmental products that ensue. The behaviorists have differed among themselves as to what may be inferred in addition to what is measured, but they all exclude self-observation. [Hilgard and Bower, 1966, p. 75]

Watson placed emphasis on kinesthetic stimuli as the integrators of animal learning and, applying this concept to human beings, conjectured that thought was merely implicit speech—that sensitive enough instruments would detect tongue movements or other movements accompanying thinking.

Edwin R. Guthrie (1886-1959) built on the works of Thorndike, Pavlov, and Watson and added the principle of contiguity of cue and response. His one law of learning, "from which all else about learning is made comprehensible," was stated as follows: "A combination of stimuli which has accompanied a movement will on its recurrence tend to be followed by that movement." [Hilgard and Bower, 1966, p. 77] In his later work, Guthrie placed increasing emphasis on the part played by the learner in selecting the physical stimuli to which it would respond; hence, the importance of the attention or *scanning* behavior that goes on before association takes place.

Guthrie's system of thought was further clarified and formalized by his students, Voeks and Sheffield, but the next major advance in behaviorist psychology was the result of the work of B.F. Skinner and his associates. It is from their work that the current educational technology of programmed instruction and teaching machines has been derived. Rather than trying to summarize Skinner's rather complex system of thought in the text, I include as Appendix A a more detailed description of his ideas and their applications to training by one of his advocates, John R. Murphy. (It is also a good example of the sarcasm and name-calling used by advocates of one school of thought when referring to another school of thought, to which I alluded earlier.)

Another development in behaviorist psychology occurring during the middle decades of the century was the construction of Clark L. Hull's *systematic behavior theory* and its elaboration by Miller, Mowrer, Spence, and others. Hull's theory is a conceptual descendant of Thorndike's, inasmuch as he adopted reinforcement as an essential characteristic of learning. Hull constructed an elaborate "mathematico-deductive" theory revolving around the central notion that there are intervening variables in the organism which influence what response will occur following the onset of a stimulus. He developed sixteen postulates regarding the nature and operation of these variables, and stated them in such precise terms that they were readily subjected to quantitative testing. Hilgard's assessment of the effect of Hull's work follows.

> It must be acknowledged that Hull's system, for its time, was the best there was—not necessarily the one nearest to psychological reality, not necessarily the one whose generalizations were the most likely to endure—but the one worked out in the greatest detail, with the most conscientious effort to be quantitative throughout and at all points closely in touch with empirical tests. . . .Its primary contribution may turn out to lie not in its substance at all, but rather in the ideal it set for a genuinely systematic and quantitative psychological system far different from the *schools* which so long plagued psychology. [Hilgard and Bower, p. 187]

His work also no doubt stimulated the rash of mathematical models of learning which were developed after 1950 by Estes, Burke, Bush, Mosteller and others—it should be pointed out that these are not themselves learning theories, but mathematical representations of substantive theories.

Theories Based on an Organismic Model

The first direct protest against the mechanistic model of the associationists was made by John Dewey in 1896. Although his work falls into the category of educational philosophy rather than learning theory, his emphasis on the role of interest and effort and on the child's motivation to solve his own problems became the starting point for a line of theorizing that has been given the label *functionalism*. Translated into schoolroom practices, functionalism provided the conceptual basis for progressive education, which, as Hilgard states, "at its best was an embodiment of the ideal of growth toward independence and self-control through interaction with an environment suited to the child's developmental level." [Hilgard and Bower, 1966, p. 299]

The spirit of experimentalism fostered by functionalism is reflected in the work of such learning theorists as Woodworth, Carr, McGeogh, Melton, Robinson, and Underwood. The flavor of functionalism is summarized by Hilgard.

1. The functionalist is tolerant but critical.
2. The functionalist prefers continuities over discontinuities or typologies.
3. The functionalist is an experimentalist.
4. The functionalist is biased toward associationism and environmentalism. [Hilgard and Bower, 1966, pp. 302-304]

Edward C. Tolman (1886-1959) in a sense represents a bridge between the mechanistic and the organismic models. His system was behavioristic in that he rejected introspection as a method for psychological science, but it was *molar* rather than *molecular* behaviorism—an act of behavior has distinctive properties all its own, to be identified and described irrespective of the muscular, glandular, or neural processes that underlie it. But most importantly, he saw behavior as purposive—as being regulated in accordance with objectively determined ends. Purpose is, of course, an organismic concept. He rejected the idea that learning is the association of particular responses to particular stimuli. In contrast to the associationists, who believed that it is the response or sequence of responses resulting in reward that is learned, Tolman believed it is the route to the goal that is learned. He believed that organisms, at their respective levels of ability, are capable of recognizing and learning the relationships between signs and desired goals; in short, they perceive the significance of the signs. [Kingsley and Garry, 1957, p. 115] Tolman called his theory *purposive behaviorism,* but Hilgard referred to it as *sign learning* and Kingsley and Garry as *Sign-Gestalt-Expectation Theory.*

The most complete break with behaviorism occurred at the end of the first quarter of the century with the importation of the notion of *insight learning* in the gestalt theories of the Germans Wertheimer, Koffka, and Kohler. They took issue with the proposition that all learning consisted of the simple connection of responses to stimuli, insisting that experience is always structured, that we react not to just a mass of separate details, but to a complex pattern of stimuli. And we need to perceive stimuli in organized wholes, not in disconnected parts. The learner tends to organize his perceptual field according to four laws.

1. *The law of proximity.* The parts of a stimulus pattern that are close together or near to each other tend to be perceived in groups; therefore, the proximity of the parts in time and space affects the learner's organization of the field.

2. *The law of similarity and familiarity.* Objects similar in form, shape, color, or size tend to be grouped in perception; and familiarity with an object facilitates the establishing of a figure-ground pattern. (Related to this law is the Gestaltists' view of memory as the persistence of *traces* in the brain which allows a carry-over from previous to present experiences. They view these traces not as static, but as modified by a continual process of integration and organization.)

3. *The law of closure.* Learners try to achieve a satisfying end-state of equilibrium; incomplete shapes, missing parts, and gaps in information are filled in by the perceiver. (Kingsley and Garry observe that "closure is to Gestalt psychology what reward is to association theory.") [1957, p. 109]

4. *The law of continuation.* Organization in perception tends to occur in such a manner that a straight line appears to continue as a straight line, a part circle as a circle, and a three-sided square as a complete square.

Gestalt psychology is classified by most interpreters as within the family of *field theories*—theories which propose that the total pattern or field of forces, stimuli, or events determine learning. Kurt Lewin (1890-1947) developed what he referred to specifically as a *field theory*. Using the topological concepts of geometry, Lewin conceptualized each individual as existing in a *life space* in which many forces are operating. The life space includes features of the environment to which the individual is reacting—material objects he encounters and manipulates, people he meets, and his private thoughts, tensions, goals, and fantasies. Behavior is the product of the interplay of these forces, the direction and relative strength of which can be portrayed by the geometry of vectors. Learning occurs as a result of a change in cognitive structures produced by changes in two types of forces: (1) change in the structure of the cognitive field itself, or (2) change in the internal needs or motivation of the individual. Because of its emphasis on the immediate field of forces, field theory places more emphasis on motivation than any of the preceding theories. Lewin felt that success was a more potent motivating force than reward and gave attention to the concepts of ego-involvement and level of aspiration as forces affecting success. He saw change in the relative attractiveness of one goal over another, which he called *valence,* as another variable affecting motivation. Since some of the strongest forces affecting an individual's psychological field are other people, Lewin became greatly interested in group and institutional dynamics; and, as we shall see later, it is in this dimension of education that his strongest influence has been felt.

The most recent development in the field theoretical approach has appeared under several labels: phenomenological psychology, perceptual psychology, humanistic psychology, and third-force psychology. Since the bulk of the work with this approach has been with adults, major attention to it will be reserved for a later section. But two phenomenologists, Arthur Combs and Donald Snygg, have focused on the learning of children and the education of teachers of children so recently (1959) that their theories are not treated in most books on learning theory.

Since phenomenologists are concerned with the study of the progressive development of the mind—or, as our contemporaries would insist, the person—they see man as an organism forever seeking greater personal adequacy. The urge for self-actualization is the driving force motivating all of man's behavior.

> The adequate personality is one that embodies positive percepts of self, a clearly developing concept of self, a growing acceptance of self and identification with others, and finally a rich, varied, available perceptive field of experience. [Pittenger and Gooding, 1971, p. 107]

The flavor of Combs and Snygg's system of thought can be caught from statements from Pittenger and Gooding, 1971.

- Man behaves in terms of what is real to him and what is related to his self at the moment of action. [p. 130]
- Learning is a process of discovering one's personal relationship to and with people, things, and ideas. This process results in and from a differentiation of the phenomenal field of the individual. [p. 136]
- Further differentiation of the phenomenological field occurs as an individual recognizes some inadequacy of a present organization. When a change is needed to maintain or enhance the phenomenal self, it is made by the individual as the right and proper thing to do. The role of the teacher is to facilitate the process. [p. 144]
- Given a healthy organism, positive environmental influences, and a nonrestrictive set of percepts of self, there appears to be no forseeable end to the perceptions possible for the individual. [pp. 150-151]
- Transfer is a matter of taking current differentiations and using them as first approximations in the relationship of self to new situations. [p. 157]
- Learning is permanent to the extent that it generates problems that may be shared by others and to the degree that continued sharing itself is enhancing. [p. 165]

Two other contemporary psychologists, Piaget and Bruner, have had great impact on thinking about learning although they are not literally learning theorists. Their focus is on cognition and the theory of instruction. Piaget has conceptualized the process of the development of cognition and thought in evolutionary stages. According to him, the behavior of the human organism starts with the organization of sensory-motor reactions and becomes more intelligent as coordination between the reactions to objects becomes progressively more interrelated and complex. Thinking becomes possible after language develops—and with it a new mental organization. This development involves the following evolutionary periods:

1. *The formation of the symbolic or semiotic function* (ages two to seven or eight)—which enables the individual to represent objects or events that are not at the moment perceptible by evoking them through the agency of symbols or differentiated signs.
2. *The formation of concrete mental operations* (ages seven or eight to eleven or twelve)—linking and dissociation of classes, the sources of classification; the linking of relations; correspondences, etc.
3. *The formation of conceptual thought* (or formal operations) (ages eleven or twelve through adolescence)—"This period is characterized by the conquest of a new mode of reasoning, one that is no longer limited exclusively to dealing with objects or directly representable realities, but also employs 'hypotheses' . . . " [Piaget, 1970, pp. 30-33]

Some reservations have been expressed about the rigid age scale and minimization of individual differences in Piaget's schema, but his conception of evolutionary stages adds a dimension that is not generally given much attention in the established learning theories.

Jerome Bruner has also been interested in the process of intellectual growth, and his benchmarks were described on pages 8 and 9. But his main interest has been in the structuring and sequencing of knowledge and translating this into a *theory of instruction.* But he does have a basic theory about the *act of learning,* which he views as involving three almost simultaneous processes: (1) acquisition of new information, often information that runs counter to or is a replacement of what the person has previously known, but which at the very least is a refinement of previous knowledge; (2) transformation, or the process of manipulating knowledge to make it fit new tasks; and (3) evaluation, or checking whether the way we have manipulated information is adequate to the task. [Bruner, 1960, pp. 48-49] We shall return to this theory of instruction in a later chapter.

The main criticism of Piaget, Bruner and other cognitive theorists by other adherents to the organismic model is that they are unbalanced in their overemphasis on cognitive skills at the expense of emotional development; that they are preoccupied with the aggressive, agentic, and autonomous motives to the exclusion of the homonymous, libidinal, and communal motives; and that they concern themselves with concept attainment to the exclusion of concept formation or invention. [Jones, 1968, p. 97]

In recent years new frontiers have been opened in such learning-related fields of inquiry as *neurophysiology* (K.H. Pribram, G.A. Miller, J.F. Delafresnaye, H.F. Harlow, D.P. Kimble, W.G. Walter, D.E. Wooldridge, J.Z. Young); *mathematical modeling* (R.C. Atkinson, R.R. Bush, W.K. Estes, R.D. Luce, F. Restle); *information processing and cybernetics* (H. Borko, E.A. Feigenbaum, B.F. Green, W.R. Reitman, K.M. Sayre, M. Yovitts, J. Singh, K.O. Smith); *creativity* (J.P. Guilford, R.P. Crawford, J.E. Drevdahl, A. Meadow, S.J. Parnes, J.W. Getzels, P.W. Jackson); and *ecological psychology* (R.G. Barker, P.V. Gump, H.F. Wright, E.P. Willems, H.L. Raush). But to date these lines of investigation have resulted in knowledge that can be applied to existing theories about learning rather than producing comprehensive learning theories of their own.

3

A Theory of Adult Learning: Andragogy

Considering that the education of adults has been a concern of the human race for a very long time, it is curious that there has been so little thinking, investigating, and writing about adult learning until recently. The adult learner has indeed been a neglected species.

Although many of the ancient great Chinese, Hebrew, Greek, and Roman teachers taught adults, philosophized about the aims of adult education, and invented techniques especially for adults (such as case-method parables and the Socratic dialogue), I can find little evidence in their writings of any interest in the *processes* of adult learning. They had theories about the *ends* of adult education but none about the *means* of adult learning. They presumably made the assumption that adults learned in precisely the same way that children learned (or, better, in the same way that they believed children learned).

These assumptions and beliefs (and blindspots) persisted through the ages well into the twentieth century. There was only one theoretical framework for all of education, for children and adults alike—pedagogy; in spite of the fact that pedagogy literally means the art and science of teaching children.

Starting shortly after the end of World War I, there began emerging both in this country and in Europe a growing body of notions about the unique characteristics of adults as learners. But only in the last two decades have these notions evolved into a comprehensive theory of adult learning. It is fascinating to trace this evolutionary process in this country.

Two Streams of Inquiry

Two streams of inquiry are discernible beginning with the founding of the American Association for Adult Education in 1926 and the provision of substantial funding to it for research and publications by the Carnegie Corporation of New York. One stream we might call the scientific stream and the other the artistic stream. The scientific stream, which seeks to discover new knowledge through rigorous (and often experimental) investigation, was launched by Edward L. Thorndike with the publication of his *Adult Learning* in 1928. The title is misleading, however, for Thorndike was not concerned with the processes of adult learning but rather with learning ability. His studies demonstrated that adults could learn, and this was important, for it provided a scientific foundation for a field that had previously been based on the mere faith that adults could learn. Additions to this stream in the next decade included Thorndike's *Adult Interests* in 1935 and Herbert Sorenson's *Adult Abilities* in 1938. By the onset of World War II, therefore, adult educators had scientific evidence that adults could learn and that they possessed interests and abilities that were different from those of children.

It was the artistic stream, which seeks to discover new knowledge through intuition and the analysis of experience, that was concerned with *how* adults learn. This stream was launched with the publication of Eduard C. Lindeman's *The Meaning of Adult Education* in 1926. Strongly influenced by the educational philosophy of John Dewey, Lindeman laid the foundation for a systematic theory about adult learning with such insightful statements as these:

> . . . the approach to adult education will be via the route of situations, not subjects. Our academic system has grown in reverse order: subjects and teachers constitute the starting-point, students are secondary. In conventional education the student is required to adjust himself to an established curriculum; in adult education the curriculum is built around the student's needs and interests. Every adult

person finds himself in specific situations with respect to his work, his recreation, his family-life, his community-life, et cetera—situations which call for adjustments. Adult education begins at this point. Subject matter is brought into the situation, is put to work, when needed. Texts and teachers play a new and secondary role in this type of education; they must give way to the primary importance of the learners. [Lindeman, 1926, pp. 8-9]

. . . the resource of highest value in adult education is the *learner's experience*. If education is life, then life is also education. Too much of learning consists of vicarious substitution of someone else's experience and knowledge. Psychology is teaching us, however, that we learn what we do, and that therefore all genuine education will keep doing and thinking together. . . . Experience is the adult learner's living textbook. [*Ibid.*, pp. 9-10]

Authoritative teaching, examinations which preclude original thinking, rigid pedagogical formulae—all these have no place in adult education. . . . Small groups of aspiring adults who desire to keep their minds fresh and vigorous; who begin to learn by confronting pertinent situations; who dig down into the reservoirs of their experience before resorting to texts and secondary facts; who are led in the discussion by teachers who are also searchers after wisdom and not oracles: this constitutes the setting for adult education, the modern quest for life's meaning. [*Ibid.*, pp. 10-11]

Adult education presents a challenge to static concepts of intelligence, to the standardized limitations of conventional education and to the theory which restricts educational facilities to an intellectual class. Apologists for the status quo in education frequently assert that the great majority of adults are not interested in learning, are not motivated in the direction of continuing education; if they possessed these incentives, they would, naturally, take advantage of the numerous free educational opportunities provided by public agencies. This argument begs the question and misconceives the problem. We shall never know how many adults desire intelligence regarding themselves and the world in which they live until education once more escapes the patterns of conformity. Adult education is an attempt to discover a new method and create a new incentive for learning; its implications are qualitative, not quantitative. Adult learners are precisely those whose intellectual aspirations are least likely to be aroused by the rigid, uncompromising requirements of authoritative, conventionalized institutions of learning. [*Ibid.*, pp. 27-28]

Adult education is a process through which learners become aware of significant experience. Recognition of significance leads to evaluation. Meanings accompany experience when we know what is happening and what importance the event includes for our personalities. [*Ibid.,* p. 169]

Two excerpts from other Lindeman writings elaborate on these ideas:

I am conceiving adult education in terms of a new technique for learning, a technique as essential to the college graduate as to the unlettered manual worker. It represents a process by which the adult learns to become aware of and to evaluate his experience. To do this he cannot begin by studying "subjects" in the hope that some day this information will be useful. On the contrary, he begins by giving attention to situations in which he finds himself, to problems which include obstacles to his self-fulfillment. Facts and information from the differentiated spheres of knowledge are used, not for the purpose of accumulation, but because of need in solving problems. In this process the teacher finds a new function. He is no longer the oracle who speaks from the platform of authority, but rather the guide, the pointer-out who also participates in learning in proportion to the vitality and relevance of his facts and experiences. In short, my conception of adult education is this: a cooperative venture in nonauthoritarian, informal learning, the chief purpose of which is to discover the meaning of experience; a quest of the mind which digs down to the roots of the preconceptions which formulate our conduct; a technique of learning for adults which makes education coterminous with life and hence elevates living itself to the level of adventurous experiment. [Gessner, 1956, p. 160]

One of the chief distinctions between conventional and adult education is to be found in the learning process itself. None but the humble become good teachers of adults. In an adult class the student's experience counts for as much as the teacher's knowledge. Both are exchangeable at par. Indeed, in some of the best adult classes it is sometimes difficult to discover who is learning most, the teacher or the students. This two-way learning is also reflected by shared authority. In conventional education the pupils adapt themselves to the curriculum offered, but in adult education the pupils aid in formulating the curricula. . . . Under democratic conditions authority is of the group. This is not an easy lesson to learn, but until it is learned democracy cannot succeed. [*Ibid.,* p. 166]

I am tempted to quote further from this pioneering theorist, but these excerpts are sufficient to portray a new way of thinking about adult learning. Lindeman here identifies several of the key assumptions about adult learners that have been supported by later research and that constitute the foundation stones of modern adult learning theory:

1. Adults are motivated to learn as they experience needs and interests that learning will satisfy; therefore, these are the appropriate starting points for organizing adult learning activities.
2. Adults' orientation to learning is life-centered; therefore, the appropriate units for organizing adult learning are life situations, not subjects.
3. Experience is the richest resource for adults' learning; therefore, the core methodology of adult education is the analysis of experience.
4. Adults have a deep need to be self-directing; therefore, the role of the teacher is to engage in a process of mutual inquiry with them rather than to transmit his or her knowledge to them and then evaluate their conformity to it.
5. Individual differences among people increase with age; therefore, adult education must make optimal provision for differences in style, time, place, and pace of learning.

It is interesting to note that Lindeman did not dichotomize adult versus youth education, but rather adult versus "conventional" education, thus implying that youth might learn better, too, when their needs and interests, life situations, experience, self-concepts, and individual differences are taken into account.

The artistic stream of inquiry which Lindeman had launched in 1926 flowed on through the pages of the *Journal of Adult Education,* the quarterly publication of the American Association for Adult Education, which between February, 1929, and October, 1941, provided the most distinguished body of literature yet produced in the field of adult education. The following excerpts from its articles reveal the growing collection of insights about adult learning gleaned from the experience of successful practitioners.

By Lawrence P. Jacks, principal of Manchester College, Oxford, England:

> Earning and living are not two separate departments or operations in life. They are two names for a continuous process looked at from opposite ends. . . . A type of education based on this vision of *continuity* is, obviously, the outstanding need of our times. Its outlook will be lifelong. It will look upon the industry of civilization as the great "continuation school" for intelligence and for character, and its object will be, not merely to fit men and women for the specialized vocations they are to follow, but also to animate the vocations themselves with ideals of excellence appropriate to each. At the risk of seeming fantastic I will venture to say that the final objective of the New Education is the gradual transformation of the industry of the world into the university of the world; in other words, the gradual bringing about of a state of things in which "breadwinning" and "soulsaving" instead of being, as now, disconnected and often opposed operations, shall become a single and continuous operation. [*Journal of Adult Education I,* 1 (February, 1929), pp. 7-10]

By Charles R. Mann, director of the American Council on Education, Washington, D.C.:

> The most significant fact in American industrial and professional life at present is this steady transformation of industry and the professions into educational institutions. The American people seem to realize that their greatest material success depends upon the degree to which each worker finds the right opportunity for self-education on the job. (*Ibid.,* p. 56)

By David Snedden, professor of education, Teachers College, Columbia University:

> Surely between ages twelve and eighteen schools can, if they will, greatly *idealize* practices of self-education to be systematically entered upon when full-time attendance ceases.

> Surely large proportions of the programs of adult education provided by public, philanthropic, or private agencies can in a degree be so constructed as to throw upon the learning individual *considerably greater responsibilities for educative effort on his own behalf than is now the case.* . . .

And why not, in schools attended by young persons from thirteen to eighteen, offer six weeks' courses occasionally under the caption "Short Unit Course M (or N or P)—Training in Powers of Self-Education? . . ."

And should not similar short unit courses be available as a part of a program of adult education, designed to push the *personal* teacher into the background, to push forward the learner's own powers of self-help, and to emphasize also the libraries, bibliographies, analyses and the like upon which these can work? [*Ibid.,* II, 1 (January, 1930), p. 37]

By Robert D. Leigh, president of Bennington College:

At the other end of the traditional academic ladder the adult educational movement is forcing recognition of the value and importance of continuing the learning process indefinitely. . . . But among the far-seeing leaders of the movement in the United States it is recognized not so much as a substitute for inadequate schooling in youth as an educational opportunity superior to that offered in youth—superior because the learner is motivated not by the artificial incentives of academic organization, but by the honest desire to know and to enrich his experience, and because the learner brings to his study relevant daily experience, and consequently the new knowledge "takes root firmly, strikes deep, and feeds on what the day's life brings it."

There is gradually emerging, therefore, a conception of education as a lifelong process beginning at birth and ending only with death, a process related at all points to the life experiences of the individual, a process full of meaning and reality to the learner, a process in which the student is active participant rather than passive recipient. [*Ibid.,* II, 2 (April, 1930), p. 123]

By David L. Mackaye, director of the Department of Adult Education, San Jose, California, public schools:

A person is a good educator among adults when he has a definite conviction about life and when he can present intelligent arguments on behalf of it; but primarily he does not qualify as an adult educator at all until he can exist in a group that collectively disputes, denies, or ridicules his conviction, and continues to adore him because he rejoices in them. That is tolerance, an exemplification of Proudhon's contention that to respect a man is a higher intellectual feat than to love him as one's self. . . .

. . . there is positive evidence that no adult education system will ever make a success of collegiate methods of instruction to adults in the cultural fields. Something new in the way of content and method must be produced as soon as possible for adult education, and probably it will have to grow up in the field. No teacher-training-college hen can lay an adult education egg. [*Ibid.,* III, 3 (June, 1931), pp. 293-294]

By Anne E.M. Jackson, executive secretary, Lecture Division, Extension Department, University of California:

Agencies for adult education might profitably spend a large part of their time and resources on establishing forums and discussion groups; not for rudderless discussion, but for planned and directed thinking under trained leaders, using every available source for the acquisition of true knowledge. . . . We have indeed many groups modeled on the New School of Social Research scattered around the country in which, under trained leaders, men may discuss trends and theories. These men are not so much being educated as educating themselves. [*Ibid.,* III, 4 (October, 1931), p. 438]

By James E. Russell, dean emeritus, Teachers College, Columbia University:

It can not be pointed out too often that all education is self-education. Teachers may help define procedure, collect equipment, indicate the most propitious routes, but the climber must use his own head and legs if he would reach the mountaintop. . . . The best method of teaching adults yet hit upon is undoubtedly group discussion. [*Ibid.,* X, 4 (October, 1938), pp. 385-386]

By Maria Rogers, volunteer worker, New York City Adult Education Council:

"Come and be educated," says the adult education institution. "We have knowledge; you want it. Come and we will give it to you." By the millions, Americans respond. . . .

But millions do *not* respond. Most adult educators are conscious of this fact, and they strive constantly to improve their methods in order to reach more people. . . .

One type of adult education merits particular consideration and wider use by educators seeking new methods. Though meagerly publicized, it has proved effective in numerous instances. It has undertaken a far more difficult task than that assumed by the institutions for adult education which confine their concept of method to the sequence of procedure established for adults who enter classrooms to learn something already set up to be learned. Its prime objective is to make the group life of adults yield educational value to the participants. . . .

The educator who uses the group method of education takes ordinary, gregarious human beings for what they are, searches out the groups in which they move and have their being, and then helps them to make their group life yield educational values. [*Ibid.*, pp. 409-411]

By Mildred J. Wiese, specialist in curriculum and teacher education, and G.L. Maxwell, assistant director, Education Division, Works Progress Administration:

Teachers want help in planning courses and units of study; in setting up definite objectives consistent with the needs of their students; in keeping their courses flexible and adapted to the developing interests of their students. They want to know how to bring the experiences of their students' daily lives into the framework of a course of study; how to take advantage of spontaneous and unpredictable educational opportunities; how to cut across "subjects" in dealing with the ways of thinking and of acting that are characteristic of everyday adult life.

Teachers want to understand and master the methods of group work and study; to learn how to lead a group without dominating; how to provide opportunity for democratic participation; how to get students increasingly to accept responsibility for planning their own programs of study and activity; how to help students to broaden their interests; how to conduct the work of a group so that it shall be reflected in the life of the community. . . .

Teacher education at all times should exemplify and demonstrate the teaching methods found most effective with adult groups. Because of the variety of needs to be served, a teacher-education program will give opportunity to utilize many teaching methods: group discussion to solve common problems; discussion by a panel, composed of representatives of community welfare; forums to supply information on public affairs. Group projects, observation, individual study, and lectures may be employed in appropriate situations. If the use of each method is preceded by an examination of its potential values and is followed by an analysis of its effectiveness, every lesson will not only serve its own specific purpose, but will also demonstrate a technique of teaching. [*Ibid.,* XI, 2 (April, 1939), pp. 174-175]

By Ruth Merton, director of the Education Department, Milwaukee Y.W.C.A.:

In a day school, where the students are usually children or young adolescents, a learned teacher-ignorant pupil relationship is almost inevitable, and frequently it has its advantages. But in a night school the situation is entirely different. Here, so far as the class is concerned, the teacher is an authority upon one subject only, and each of the students has, in his own particular field, some skill or knowledge that the teacher does not possess. For this reason, there is a spirit of give-and-take in a night-school class that induces a feeling of comradeship in learning, stimulating to teacher and students alike. And the quickest way to achieve this desirable state is through laughter in which all can join.

And so I say again that, if we are really wise, we teachers in night schools will, despite taxes or indigestion, teach merrily! [*Ibid.,* p. 178]

By Ben M. Cherrington, chief of the Division of Cultural Relations, United States Department of State:

Authoritarian adult education is marked throughout by regimentation demanding obedient conformity to patterns of conduct handed down from authority. Behavior is expected to be predictable, standardized. . . . Democratic adult education employs the method of self-directing activity, with free choice of subject matter and free choice in determining outcomes. Spontaneity is welcome. Behavior cannot with certainty be predicted and therefore is not standardized. Individual, critical thinking is perhaps the best description of the democratic method and it is here that the gulf is widest between democracy and the authoritarian system. [*Ibid.,* XI, 3 (June, 1939), pp. 244-245]

By Wendell Thomas, author of *Democratic Philosophy* and a teacher of adult education teachers in New York City:

On the whole, adult education is as different from ordinary schooling as adult life, with its individual and social responsibilities, is different from the protected life of the child. . . . The adult normally differs from the child in having both more individuality and more social purpose.

Adult education, accordingly, makes special allowance for individual contributions from the students, and seeks to organize these contributions into some form of social purpose. [*Ibid.,* XI, 4 (October, 1939), pp. 365-366]

By Harold Fields, acting assistant director of Evening Schools, Board of Education, New York City:

Not only the content of the courses, but the method of teaching also must be changed. Lectures must be replaced by class exercises in which there is a large share of student participation. "Let the class do the work" should be adopted as a motto. There must be ample opportunity for forums, discussions, debates. Newspapers, circulars, and magazines as well as textbooks should be used for practice in reading. Extracurricular activities should become a recognized part of the educational process. . . . These are some of the elements that must be incorporated in a program of adult education for citizens if it is to be successful. [*Ibid.,* XII, 1 (January, 1940), pp. 44-45]

By 1940 most of the elements required for a comprehensive theory of adult learning had been discovered, but they had not yet been brought together into a unified theory; they remained as isolated insights, concepts, and principles. During the 1940s and 1950s these elements were clarified, elaborated on, and added to in a veritable explosion of knowledge from the various disciplines in the human sciences. (It is interesting to note that during this period there was a gradual shift in emphasis in research away from the highly quantitative, fragmentary, experimental research of the 1930s and 1940s to more holistic longitudinal case studies with, in my estimation, a higher yield of useful knowledge).

Contributions from the Social Sciences

Some of the most important contributions to learning theory have come from the discipline of psychotherapy. After all, psychotherapists are primarily concerned with reeducation, and their subjects are overwhelmingly from the adult population.

Sigmund Freud has influenced psychological thinking more than any other individual, but he did not formulate a theory of learning as such. His major contribution was no doubt in identifying the influence of the subconscious mind on behavior. Some of his concepts such as anxiety, repression, fixation, regression, aggression, defense mechanism, projection, and transference (in blocking or motivating learning) have had to be taken into account by learning theorists. Freud was close to the behaviorists in his emphasis on the animalistic nature of man, but he saw the human being as a dynamic animal which grows and develops through the interaction of biological forces, goals, purposes, conscious and unconscious drives, and environmental influences—a conception more in keeping with the organismic model.

Carl Jung advanced a more holistic conception of human consciousness, introducing the notion that it possesses four functions— or four ways of extracting information from experience and achieving internalized understanding—sensation, thought, emotion, and intuition. His plea for the development and utilization of all four functions in balance laid the groundwork for the concepts of the balanced personality and the balanced curriculum.

Erik Erikson provided the "eight ages of man," the last three occurring during the adult years, as a framework for understanding the stages of personality development:

1. Oral-sensory, in which the basic issue is trust vs. mistrust.
2. Muscular-anal, in which the basic issue is autonomy vs. shame.
3. Locomotion-genital, in which the basic issue is initiative vs. guilt.
4. Latency, in which the basic issue is industry vs. inferiority.
5. Puberty and adolescence, in which the basic issue is identity vs. role confusion.
6. Young adulthood, in which the basic issue is intimacy vs. isolation.
7. Adulthood, in which the basic issue is generativity vs. stagnation.
8. The final stage, in which the basic issue is integrity vs. despair.

In fact, the central role of self-concept in human development (and learning) received increasing reinforcement from the entire field of psychiatry as it moved away from the medical model toward an educational model in its research and practice. (See especially the works of Erich Fromm and Karen Horney).

But it is the clinical psychologists, especially those who identify themselves as *humanistic,* who have concerned themselves most deeply with problems of learning. The humanistic psychologists speak of themselves as "third force psychologists." In Goble's words, "By 1954 when Maslow published his book *Motivation and Personality,* there were two major theories dominant" in the behavioral sciences, Freudianism and behaviorism, in which "Freud placed the major motivational emphasis on deep inner drives (and) urges and the behaviorists placed the emphasis on external, environmental influences." But "like Freud and like Darwin before him, the behaviorists saw man as merely another type of animal, with no essential differences from animals and with the same destructive, anti-social tendencies." [Goble, 1971, pp. 3-8.] Third force psychologists are concerned with the study and development of *fully functioning persons* (to use Rogers' term) or *self-actualizing persons* (to use Maslow's). They are critical of the atomistic approach common in physical science and among the behaviorists, breaking things down into their component parts and studying them separately.

> Most behavioral scientists have attempted to isolate independent drives, urges, and instincts and study them separately. This Maslow found to be generally less productive than the holistic approach which holds that the whole is more than the sum of the parts. [*Ibid.,* p. 22]

> Growth takes place when the next step forward is subjectively more delightful, more joyous, more intrinsically satisfying than the previous gratification with which we have become familiar and even bored; that the only way we can ever know that it is right for us is that it feels better subjectively than any alternative. The new experience validates *itself* rather than by any outside criterion. [Maslow, 1972, p. 43]

Maslow placed special emphasis on the role of safety, as becomes clear in the following formulation of the elements in the growth process:

1. The healthily spontaneous [person], in his spontaneity, from within out, reaches out to the environment in wonder and interest, and expresses whatever skills he has.
2. To the extent that he is not crippled by fear, to the extent that he feels safe enough to dare.

3. In this process, that which gives him the delight-experience is fortuitously encountered, or is offered to him by helpers.

4. He must be safe and self-accepting enough to be able to choose and prefer these delights, instead of being frightened by them.

5. If he can choose these experiences which are validated by the experience of delight, then he can return to the experience, repeat it, savor it to the point of repletion, satiation, or boredom.

6. At this point, he shows the tendency to go on to richer, more complex experiences and accomplishments in the same sector (if he feels safe enough to dare).

7. Such experiences not only mean moving on, but have a feedback effect on the Self, in the feeling of certainty ("This I like; that I don't for *sure*"); of capability, mastery, self-trust, self-esteem.

8. In this never ending series of choices of which life consists, the choice may generally be schematized as between safety (or, more broadly, defensiveness) and growth, and since only that [person] doesn't need safety who already has it, we may expect the growth choice to be made by the safety-need gratified [individual].

9. In order to be able to choose in accord with his own nature and to develop it, the [individual] must be permitted to retain the subjective experiences of delight and boredom, as *the* criteria of the correct choice for him. The alternative criterion is making the choice in terms of the wish of another person. The Self is lost when this happens. Also this constitutes restricting the choice to safety alone, since the [individual] will give up trust in his own delight-criterion out of fear (of losing protection, love, etc.).

10. If the choice is really a free one, and if the [individual] is not crippled, then we may expect him ordinarily to choose progression forward.

11. The evidence indicates that what delights the healthy [person], what tastes good to him, is also, more frequently than not, "best" for him in terms of far goals as perceivable by the spectator.

12. In this process the environment (parents, teachers, therapists) is important in various ways, even though the ultimate choice must be made by the individual.

    a. it can gratify his basic needs for safety, belongingness, love and respect, so that he can feel unthreatened, autonomous, interested and spontaneous and thus dare to choose the unknown;

    b. it can help by making the growth choice positively attractive and less dangerous, and by making regressive choice less attractive and more costly.

13. In this way the psychology of Being and the psychology of Becoming can be reconciled, and the [person], simply being himself, can yet move forward and grow. [Maslow, 1972, pp. 50-51]

Carl R. Rogers, starting with the viewpoint that "in a general way, therapy is a learning process," [1951, p. 132] developed nineteen propositions for a theory of personality and behavior which were evolved from the study of adults in therapy [*Ibid.*, pp. 483-524] and then sought to apply them to education. This process led him to conceptualize *student-centered teaching* as parallel to *client-centered therapy*. [*Ibid.*, pp. 388-391]

Rogers' student-centered approach to education was based on five "basic hypotheses," the first of which was: *We cannot teach another person directly; we can only facilitate his learning.* This hypothesis stems from the propositions in his personality theory that "Every individual exists in a continually changing world of experience of which he is the center," and "The organism reacts to the field as it is experienced and perceived." It requires a shift in focus from what the teacher does to what is happening in the student.

His second hypothesis was: *A person learns significantly only those things which he perceives as being involved in the maintenance of, or enhancement of, the structure of self.* This hypothesis underlines the importance of making the learning relevant to the learner, and puts into question the academic tradition of required courses.

Rogers grouped his third and fourth hypotheses together: *Experience which, if assimilated, would involve a change in the organization of self tends to be resisted through denial or distortion of symbolization,* and *The structure and organization of self appear to become more rigid under threat; to relax its boundaries when completely free from threat. Experience which is perceived as inconsistent with the self can only be assimilated if the current organization of self is relaxed and expanded to include it.* These hypotheses acknowledge the reality that significant learning is often threatening to an individual, and suggest the importance of providing an acceptant and supportive climate, with heavy reliance on student responsibility.

Rogers' fifth hypothesis extends the third and fourth to educational practice: *The educational situation which most effectively promotes significant learning is one in which (a) threat to the self of the learner is reduced to a minimum, and (2) differentiated perception of the field is facilitated.* He points out that the two parts of this hypothesis are almost synonymous, since differentiated perception is most likely when the self is not being threatened.

(Rogers defined undifferentiated perception as an individual's "tendency to see experience in absolute and unconditional terms, to anchor his reactions in space and time, to confuse fact and evaluation, to rely on ideas rather than upon reality-testing," in contrast to differentiated perception as the tendency "to see things in limited, differentiated terms, to be aware of the space-time anchorage of facts, to be dominated by facts, not concepts, to evaluate in multiple ways, to be aware of different levels of abstraction, to test his inferences and abstractions by reality, in so far as possible." [*Ibid.*, p. 144])

Rogers sees learning as a completely internal process controlled by the learner and engaging his whole being in interaction with his environment as he perceives it. But he also believes that learning is as natural—and required—a life process as breathing. His Proposition IV states: *The organism has one basic tendency and striving— to actualize, maintain, and enhance the experiencing organism.* [*Ibid.*, p. 497] This central premise is well summarized in the following statement:

> Clinically I find it to be true that though an individual may remain dependent because he has always been so, or may drift into dependence without realizing what he is doing, or may temporarily wish to be dependent because his situation appears desperate. I have yet to find the individual who, when he examines his situation deeply, and feels that he perceives it clearly, deliberately chooses dependence, deliberately chooses to have the integrated direction of himself undertaken by another. When all the elements are clearly perceived, the balance seems invariably in the direction of the painful but ultimately rewarding path of self-actualization and growth. [*Ibid.*, p. 490]

Both Maslow and Rogers acknowledge their affinity with the work of Gordon Allport (1955, 1960, 1961) in defining growth not as a process of "being shaped," but a process of becoming. The essence of their conception of learning is captured in this brief statement by Rogers:

> I should like to point out one final characteristic of these individuals as they strive to discover and become themselves. It is that the individual seems to become more content to be a *process* rather than a *product*. [1961, p. 122]

The discipline of developmental psychology has contributed a growing body of knowledge about changes with age through the life span in such characteristics as physical capabilities, mental abilities, interests, attitudes, values, creativity, and life styles. Pressey and Kuhlen (1957) pioneered in the collection of research findings on human development and laid the foundation for a new field of specialization in psychology—life-span developmental psychology—which has been built on by such contemporary scholars as Bischof (1969) and Goulet and Baltes (1970). Havighurst (1961) identified the developmental tasks associated with different stages of growth which give rise to a person's readiness to learn different things at different times and create "teachable moments." My own adaptation of Havighurst's concept of developmental tasks (or life problems) is given in Appendix B. A popular portrayal of the "Predictable Crises of Adult Life" was provided by Sheehy (1974) and a more scholarly summary of research findings on adult development and learning by Knox (1977) (see also: Stevens-Long, 1979; Stokes, 1983). Closely related to this discipline is gerontology, which has produced a large volume of research findings regarding the aging process in the later years (Birren, 1964; Botwinick, 1967; Donahue and Tibbitts, 1957; Grabowski and Mason, 1974; Gubrium, 1976; Kastenbaum, 1964 and 1965; Maas and Kuypers, 1975; Neugarten, 1964 and 1968; Woodruff and Birren, 1975).

The disciplines of sociology and social psychology have contributed a great deal of new knowledge about the behavior of groups and larger social systems, including the forces which facilitate or inhibit learning and change (Argyris, 1964; Bennis, 1966; Bennis, Benne and Chin, 1968; Bennis and Slater, 1968; Etzioni, 1961 and 1969; Hare, 1969; Knowles and Knowles, 1973; Lewin, 1951; Lippitt, 1969; Schein and Bennis, 1965; Zander, 1982) and about environmental influences, such as culture, race, population characteristics, and density, on learning (Jensen, *et al,* 1964, pp. 113-175; Harris and Moran, 1979; Moran and Harris, 1982).

Contributions from Adult Education

Most scholars in the field of adult education itself have dealt with the problem of learning by trying to adapt theories about child learning to the "differences in degree" among adults. (For example, Brunner, 1959; Kidd, 1959; Kempfer, 1955; Verner and Booth, 1964.)

Howard McClusky followed this line for the most part, but began to map out directions for the development of a "differential psychology of the adult potential" in which the concepts of *margin* (the power available to a person over and beyond that required to handle his load), *commitment, time perception, critical periods,* and *self concept* are central. A summary of McClusky's emergent theory is presented in Appendix D, which you may wish to turn to at this point.

Cyril O. Houle began a line of investigations in the 1950s at the University of Chicago that has been extended by Allen Tough at the Ontario Institute for Studies in Education which promises to yield better understanding about the process of adult learning. Their approach was a study through in-depth interviews of a small sample of adults who were identified as *continuing learners.*

Houle's study of twenty-two subjects was designed to discover primarily *why* adults engage in continuing education, but it sheds some light also on *how* they learn. Through an involved process of the analysis of the characteristics uncovered in the interviews, he found that his subjects could be fitted into three categories. As Houle points out, "These are not pure types; the best way to represent them pictorially would be by three circles which overlap at their edges. But the central emphasis of each subgroup is clearly discernible." [Houle, 1961, p. 16] The criterion for typing the individuals into subgroups was the major conception they held about the purposes and values of continuing education for themselves. The three types are:

1. The *goal-oriented* learners, who use education for accomplishing fairly clear-cut objectives. These individuals usually did not make any real start on their continuing education until their middle twenties and after—sometimes much later.

The continuing education of the goal-oriented is in episodes, each of which begins with the realization of a need or the identification of an interest. There is no even, steady, continuous flow to the learning of such people, though it is an ever-recurring characteristic of their lives. Nor do they restrict their activities to any one institution or method of learning. The need or interest appears and they satisfy it by taking a course, or joining a group, or reading a book or going on a trip. [*Ibid.,* p. 18]

2. The *activity-oriented,* who take part because they find in the circumstances of the learning a meaning which has no necessary connection—and often no connection at all—with the content or the announced purpose of the activity. These individuals also begin their sustained participation in adult education at the point when their problems or their needs become sufficiently pressing.

All of the activity-oriented people interviewed in this study were course-takers and group-joiners. They might stay within a single institution or they might go to a number of different places, but it was social contact that they sought and their selection of any activity was essentially based on the amount and kind of human relationships it would yield. [*Ibid.,* pp. 23-24]

3. The *learning-oriented,* who seek knowledge for its own sake. Unlike the other types, most learning-oriented adults have been engrossed in learning as long as they can remember.

What they do has a continuity, a flow and a spread which establish the basic nature of their participation in continuing education. For the most part, they are avid readers and have been since childhood; they join groups and classes and organizations for educational reasons; they select the serious programs on television and radio; when they travel . . . they make a production out of it, being sure to prepare adequately to appreciate what they see; and they choose jobs and make other decisions in life in terms of the potential for growth which they offer. [*Ibid.,* pp. 24-25]

Tough's investigation was concerned not only with what and why adults learn, but how they learn and what help they obtain for learning. Tough found that adult learning is a very pervasive activity.

Almost everyone undertakes at least one or two major learning efforts a year, and some individuals undertake as many as 15 or 20. . . . It is common for a man or woman to spend 700 hours a year at learning projects. . . . About 70% of all learning projects are planned by the learner himself, who seeks help and subject matter from a variety of acquaintances, experts, and printed resources. [Tough, 1979, p. 1]

Tough found that his subjects organized their learning efforts around "projects . . . defined as a series of related episodes, adding up to at least seven hours. In each *episode* more than half of the person's total motivation is to gain and retain certain fairly clear knowledge and skill, or to produce some other lasting change in himself." [*Ibid.*, p. 6]

He found that in some projects the episodes may be related to the desired knowledge and skill. For example, the learner may want to learn more about India: in one episode he reads about the people of India; in another episode he discusses the current economic and political situation with an Indian graduate student; in a third he watches a television program describing the life of an Indian child. Or the episodes can also be related by the use to which the knowledge and skill will be put: one person might engage in a project consisting of a number of learning experiences to improve his competence as a parent; another project might consist of episodes aimed at obtaining the knowledge and skill necessary for building a boat.

Tough was interested in determining what motivated adults to begin a learning project, and found that overwhelmingly his subjects anticipated several desired outcomes and benefits to result, as summarized in Figure 3-1. Some of the benefits are immediate: satisfying a curiosity, enjoying the content itself, enjoying practicing the skill, enjoying the activity of learning; others are long-run: producing something, imparting knowledge or skill to others, understanding what will happen in some future situation, etc. Clearly pleasure and self-esteem were critical elements in the motivation of Tough's subjects.

Tough came to the conclusion that an adult learner proceeds through several phases in the process of engaging in a learning project, and speculated that helping them gain increased competence in dealing with each phase might be one of the most effective ways of improving their learning effectiveness.

The first phase is deciding to begin, in which Tough identified twenty-six possible steps the learner might take, including setting an action goal, assessing his interests, seeking information on certain opportunities, choosing the most appropriate knowledge and skill, establishing a desired level or amount, estimating the cost and benefits.

A second phase is choosing the planner, which may be himself, an object (e.g., programmed text, workbook, tape recordings), an in-

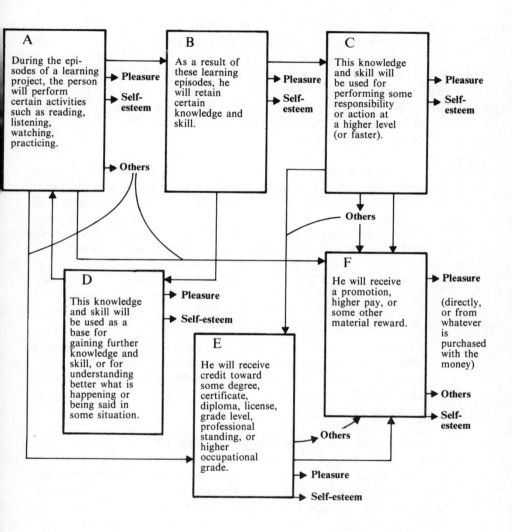

Figure 3-1. The relationships among the benefits that a learner may expect from a learning project. [Tough, 1979, p. 48]

dividual *learning consultant* (instructor, counselor, resource person), or a group. Competence in choosing a planner and using him *proactively* rather than *reactively,* collaboratively rather than dependently, were found to be crucial in this phase.

Finally, the learner engages in learning episodes sketched out in the planning process, the critical elements here being the variety and richness of the resources, their availability and the learner's skill in making use of them.

Tough emerged from his study with this challenging vision regarding future possibilities in adult learning:

> The last 20 years have produced some important new additions to the content of adult learning projects. Through group and individual methods, many adults now set out to increase their self-insight, their awareness and sensitivity with other persons and their interpersonal competence. They learn to "listen to themselves," to free their body and their conversations from certain restrictions and tensions, to take a risk, to be open and congruent. Attempting to learn this sort of knowledge and skill seemed incredible to most people 20 years ago. Great changes in our conception of what people can and should set out to learn have been created by T-groups, the human potential movement, humanistic psychology, and transpersonal psychology.
>
> Perhaps the next 20 years will produce several important additions to what we try to learn. In 1990, when people look back to our conception of what adults can learn, will they be amused by how narrow it is? [Tough, 1979, pp. 43-44]

Tough's prediction in the final paragraph is being borne out. In the decade-and-half since he made it, a rising volume of research on adult learning has been reported. Most of this research builds on, reinforces, and refines the research of Tough's "last 20 years," especially in regard to the developmental stages of the adult years. Two significant new thrusts in the research pertain to learning style and the physiology of learning, as epitomized in the "right-brain, left-brain" metaphor. The most comprehensive recent overview of this research is in K. Patricia Cross's *Adults As Learners,* 1980. My own prediction is that the major new discoveries in the next decade will be related to the physiology and chemistry of learning, with special implications for the acceleration of learning and the efficiency of information processing.

The Roots of Andragogy—An Integrative Concept

Attempts to bring the isolated concepts, insights, and research findings regarding adult learning together into an integrated framework began as early as 1949, with the publication of Harry Overstreet's *The Mature Mind,* and continued with my own *Informal Adult Education* in 1950, Edmund Brunner's *Overview of Research in Adult Education* in 1954, J.R. Kidd's *How Adults Learn* in 1959, J.R. Gibb's chapter on "Learning Theory in Adult Education" in the *Handbook of Adult Education in the U.S.* in 1960, and Harry L. Miller's *Teaching and Learning in Adult Education* in 1964. But these turned out to be more descriptive listings of concepts and principles than comprehensive, coherent, and integrated theoretical frameworks. What was needed was an integrative and differentiating concept.

Such a concept had been evolving in Europe for some time—the concept of a unified theory of adult learning for which the label *andragogy* had been coined to differentiate it from the theory of youth learning, *pedagogy.* I was first introduced to the concept and the label in 1967 by a Yugoslavian adult educator, Dusan Savicevic, and introduced them into our American literature with my article, "Androgogy, Not Pedagogy," in *Adult Leadership* in April, 1968. (Note my misspelling of the word until I was corrected through correspondence with the publishers of Merriam-Webster dictionaries). Since this label has now become widely adopted in our literature, it may be worthwhile to trace the history of its use.

A Dutch adult educator, Ger van Enckevort, has made an exhaustive study of the origins and use of the term andragogy, and I shall merely summarize his findings.* The term (Andragogik) was first coined, so far as he could discover, by a German grammar school teacher, Alexander Kapp, in 1833. Kapp used the word in a description of the educational theory of the Greek philosopher Plato, although Plato never used the term himself. A few years later the better-known German philosopher Johan Friedrich Herbart acknowledged the term by strongly opposing its use. Van Enckevort observes that "the great philosopher had more influence than the

---

*Ger van Enckevort, "Andragology: A New Science," Nederlands Centrum Voor Volksontwikkeling, Amersfoort, The Netherlands, April, 1971 (mimeographed.)

simple teacher, and so the word was forgotten and disappeared for nearly a hundred years."

Van Enckevort found the term being used again in 1921 by the German social scientist Eugen Rosenstock, who taught at the Academy of Labor in Frankfort. In a report to the Academy in 1921 he expressed the opinion that adult education required special teachers, special methods, and a special philosophy. "It is not enough to translate the insights of education theory [or pedagogy] to the situation of adults . . . the teachers should be professionals who could cooperate with the pupils; only such a teacher can be, in contrast to a "pedagogue," an "andragogue." Incidentally, Rosenstock believed that he invented the term until 1962, when he was informed of its earlier use by Kapp and Herbart. Van Enckevort reports that Rosenstock used the term on a number of occasions, and that it was picked up by some of his colleagues, but that it did not receive general recognition.

The Dutch scholar next finds the term being used by a Swiss psychiatrist, Heinrich Hanselmann, in a book published in 1951, *Andragogy: Nature, Possibilities and Boundaries of Adult Education,* which dealt with the nonmedical treatment or reeducation of adults. Only six years later, in 1957, a German teacher, Franz Poggeler, published a book entitled *Introduction to Andragogy: Basic Issues in Adult Education.* About this time the term started being used in other than German-speaking countries. In 1956 M. Ogrizovic published a dissertation in Yugoslavia on "penological andragogy" and in 1959 a book entitled *Problems of Andragogy.* Soon other leading Yugoslavian adult educators, including Samolovcev, Filipovic, and Savicevic, began speaking and writing about andragogy, and faculties of andragogy offering doctorates in adult education were established at the universities of Zagreb and Belgrade in Yugoslavia and the universities of Budapest and Debrecen in Hungary.

Andragogy started being used in the Netherlands by Professor T.T. ten Have in his lectures in 1954, and in 1959 he published the outlines for a science of andragogy. Since 1966 the University of Amsterdam has had a doctorate for andragogues, and in 1970 a department of pedagogical and andragogical sciences was established in the faculty of social sciences. In the current Dutch literature a distinction is made among "andragogy," which is any intentional and professionally guided activity that aims at a change in adult persons; "andragogics," which is the background of methodological and ideological systems that govern the actual process of andragogy; and "andragology," which is the scientific study of both andragogy and andragogics.

During the past decade andragogy has come into increasing use by adult educators in France (Bertrand Schwartz), England (J.A. Simpson), Venezuela (Felix Adam), and Canada (a Bachelor of Andragogy degree program was established at Concordia University in Montreal in 1973).

In this country, to date four major expositions of the theory of andragogy and its implications for practice have appeared; [Knowles, 1970, rev. 1980; Ingalls and Arceri, 1972; Knowles, 1973 and 1975] a number of articles have appeared in periodicals reporting on applications of the andragogical framework to social work education, religious education, undergraduate and graduate education, management training, and other spheres; and an increasing volume of research on hypotheses derived from andragogical theory is being reported. There is a growing evidence, too, that the use of andragogical theory is making a difference in the way programs of adult education are being organized and operated, in the way teachers of adults are being trained, and in the way adults are being helped to learn. There is even evidence that concepts of andragogy are beginning to make an impact on the theory and practice of elementary, secondary, and collegiate education. I am preparing a new book, *Andragogy in Action,* that will provide case descriptions of a variety of programs based on the andragogical model.

The field of adult education has long sought a glue to bind its diverse institutions, clienteles, and activities into some sense of unity; perhaps andragogy will give it at least a unifying theory. And, extended in its application to the concept of lifelong education, perhaps andragogy will provide a unifying theme for all of education.

"Andragogy" is not yet a word that appears in any dictionary. But apparently its time is coming.

An Andragogical Theory of Adult Learning

For more than three decades I have been trying to formulate a theory of adult learning that takes into account what we know from experience and research about the unique characteristics of adult learners.

Originally (in *Informal Adult Education,* 1950), I organized my ideas around the notion that adults learn best in informal, comfortable, flexible, nonthreatening settings. Then, in the mid-1960's I was exposed to the term *andragogy* by a Yugoslavian adult educator who was attending a summer session workshop at Boston University, and it seemed to me to be a more adequate organizing concept—for it meant, as I understood it then, the art and science of helping adults learn.

When I first started constructing an andragogical model of education I saw it as the antithesis of the pedagogical model. In fact, the subtitle of the 1970 edition of *The Modern Practice of Adult Education* was "Andragogy Versus Pedagogy." So, I need to explore the meaning of pedagogy a bit before elaborating on the meaning of andragogy.

First There Was Pedagogy

"Pedagogy" is derived from the Greek words *paid,* meaning "child" (the same stem from which "pediatrics" comes) and *agogus,* meaning "leader of." Thus, pedagogy literally means the art and science of teaching children. The pedagogical model of education is a set of beliefs—indeed, as viewed by many traditional teachers, an ideology—based on assumptions about teaching and learning that evolved between the seventh and twelfth centuries in the monastic and cathedral schools of Europe out of their experience in teaching basic skills to young boys. As secular schools started being organized in later centuries, and public schools in the nineteenth century, this was the only model in existence. And so our entire educational enterprise, including higher education, was frozen into the pedagogical model. When adult education began being organized systematically in this country after World War I, it was the only model teachers of adults had to go on. As a result, adults have by and large been taught as if they were children until fairly recently.

The pedagogical model assigns to the teacher full responsibility for making all decisions about what will be learned, how it will be learned, when it will be learned, and if it has been learned. It is teacher-directed education, leaving to the learner only the submissive role of following a teacher's instructions. It is thus based on these assumptions about learners:

1. *The need to know.* Learners only need to know that they must learn what the teacher teaches if they want to pass and get promoted; they do not need to know how what they learn will apply to their lives.
2. *The learner's self-concept.* The teacher's concept of the learner is that of a dependent personality; therefore, the learner's self-concept eventually becomes that of a dependent personality.

Let me elaborate on this point a bit. I speculate, with growing support from research [see Bruner, 1961; Erikson, 1950, 1959, 1964; Getzels and Jackson, 1962; Bower and Hollister, 1967; Iscoe and Stevenson, 1960; White, 1959] that as individuals mature, their *need* and *capacity* to be self-directing, to utilize their experience in learning, to identify their own readinesses to learn, and to organize their learning around life problems, increases steadily from infancy to pre-adolescence, and then increases rapidly during adolescence.

In Figure 3-2 this rate of natural maturation is represented as a decrease in dependency, as represented by the solid line. Thus, pedagogical assumptions are realistic—and pedagogy is practiced appropriately—because of the high degree of dependency during the first year, but they become decreasingly appropriate in the second, third, fourth, and so on, years—as represented by the area with the vertical lines. But it is my observation that the American culture (home, school, religious institutions, youth agencies, governmental systems) assumes—and therefore permits—a growth rate that is much slower, as represented by the broken line. Accordingly, pedagogy is practiced increasingly inappropriately as represented by the shaded area between the solid and broken lines. The problem is that the culture does not nurture the development of the abilities required for self-direction, while the need to be increasingly self-directing continues to develop organically. The result is a growing gap between the need and the ability to be self-directing, and this produces tension, resistance, resentment, and often rebellion in the individual.

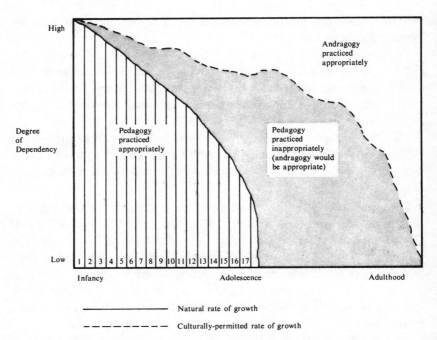

Figure 3-2. The natural maturation toward self-direction as compared with the culturally-permitted rate of growth of self-direction.

3. *The role of experience.* The learner's experience is of little worth as a resource for learning; the experience that counts is that of the teacher, the textbook writer, and the audio-visual aids producer. Therefore, transmittal techniques—lectures, assigned readings, etc., are the backbone of pedagogical methodology.

4. *Readiness to learn.* Learners become ready to learn what the teacher tells them they must learn if they want to pass and get promoted.

5. *Orientation to learning.* Learners have a subject-centered orientation to learning; they see learning as acquiring subject-matter content. Therefore, learning experiences are organized according to the logic of the subject-matter content.

6. *Motivation.* Learners are motivated to learn by external motivators—grades, the teachers' approval or disapproval, parental pressures.

And Then Came Andragogy

Before describing the andragogical assumptions about learners and learning, it is helpful to look at what we mean by "adult." As I see it, there are four definitions of "adult." First, the *biological* definition: we become adult biologically when we reach the age at which we can reproduce—which at our latitude is in early adolescence. Second, the *legal* definition: we become adult legally when we reach the age at which the law says we can vote, get a driver's license, marry without consent, and the like. Third, the *social* definition: we become adult socially when we start performing adult roles, such as the role of full-time worker, spouse, parent, voting citizen, and the like. Finally, the *psychological* definition: we become adult psychologically when we arrive at a self-concept of being responsible for our own lives, of being self-directing. From the viewpoint of learning, it is the psychological definition that is most crucial. But it seems to me that the process of gaining a self-concept of self-directedness starts early in life (I was almost completely self-directing in learning to use my leisure time by age five) and grows cumulatively as we become biologically mature, start performing adult-like roles (I was a magazine salesman and pa-per-route entrepreneur in high school), and take increasing responsibility for making our own decisions. So we become adult by degree as we move through childhood and adolescence, and the rate of increase by degree is probably accelerated if we live in homes, study in schools, and participate in youth organizations that foster our taking increasing responsibilities. But most of us probably do not have full-fledged self-concepts of self-directedness until we leave school or college, get a full-time job, marry, and start a family.

The Andragogical Model

The andragogical model is based on several assumptions that are different from those of the pedagogical model:

1. *The need to know.* Adults need to know why they need to learn something before undertaking to learn it. Tough (1979) found that when adults undertake to learn something on their own

they will invest considerable energy in probing into the benefits they will gain from learning it and the negative consequences of not learning it. Consequently, one of the new aphorisms in adult education is that the first task of the facilitator of learning is to help the learners become aware of the "need to know." At the very least, facilitators can make an intellectual case for the value of the learning in improving the effectiveness of the learners' performance or the quality of their lives. When I think of all the courses I have taken in school and college, I can think of very few in which I understood the need to know what the teacher was teaching me; I was taking the courses to get credits toward a diploma or degree. And I am sure that I would have learned more from those courses if the teachers had shown me how I would be able to use the learnings in real life. But even more potent tools for raising the level of awareness of the need to know are real or simulated experiences in which the learners discover for themselves the gaps between where they are now and where they want to be. Personnel appraisal systems, job rotation, exposure to role models, and diagnostic performance assessments are examples of such tools. Paolo Freire, the great Brazilian adult educator, has developed an elaborate process for what he calls the "consciousness-raising" of peasants in developing countries in his *The Pedagogy of the Oppressed* (1970).

2. *The learners' self-concept.* Adults have a self-concept of being responsible for their own decisions, for their own lives. Once they have arrived at that self-concept they develop a deep psychological need to be seen by others and treated by others as being capable of self-direction. They resent and resist situations in which they feel others are imposing their wills on them. But this presents a serious problem to us in adult education: the minute they walk into an activity labeled "education" or "training" or any of their synonyms, they harken back to their conditioning in their previous school experience, put on their dunce hats of dependency, fold their arms, sit back, and say "Teach me." I have experienced over and over again adults who are obviously self-directing in every other aspect of their lives putting pressure on me to tell them what to do. The problem occurs when we assume that this is really where they are

coming from and start treating them like children, for then we create a conflict within them between their intellectual model—learner equals dependent—and the deeper, perhaps subconscious psychological need to be self-directing. And the way most people deal with psychological conflict is to try to flee from the situation causing it—which probably accounts in part for the high dropout rate in much voluntary adult education. As we have become aware of this problem, adult educators have been working at creating learning experiences in which adults are helped to make the transition from dependent to self-directing learners. My little book, *Self-Directed Learning: A Guide for Learners and Teachers* (1975) is a collection of such experiences.

3. *The role of the learners' experience.* Adults come into an educational activity with both a greater volume and a different quality of experience from youths. By virtue of simply having lived longer, they have accumulated more experience than they had as youths. But they also have had a different kind of experience. When I was 15, I had not had the experience of being a full-time worker, a spouse, a parent, a voting citizen; when I was 30, I had had all those experiences. This difference in quantity and quality of experience has several consequences for adult education.

For one, it assures that in any group of adults there will be a wider range of individual differences than is the case with a group of youths. Any group of adults will be more heterogeneous—in terms of background, learning style, motivation, needs, interests, and goals—than is true of a group of youths. Hence, the great emphasis in adult education on individualization of teaching and learning strategies.

For another, it means that for many kinds of learning the richest resources for learning reside in the adult learners themselves. Hence, the greater emphasis in adult education on experiential techniques—techniques that tap into the experience of the learners, such as group discussion, simulation exercises, problem-solving activities, case method, and laboratory methods—over transmittal techniques. Hence, also, the greater emphasis on peer-helping activities.

But the fact of greater experience also has some potentially negative effects. As we accumulate experience, we tend to develop mental habits, biases, and presuppositions that tend to cause us to close our minds to new ideas, fresh perceptions, and alternative ways of thinking. Accordingly, adult educators are trying to discover ways of helping adults to examine their habits and biases and open their minds to new approaches. Sensitivity training, value clarification, meditation, and dogmatism scales are among the techniques that are used to tackle this problem.

There is another, more subtle reason for emphasizing the utilization of the experience of the learners; it has to do with the learners' self-identity. Young children derive their self-identity largely from external definers—who their parents, brothers, sisters, and extended families are; where they live; and what churches and schools they go to. As they mature, they increasingly define themselves in terms of the experiences they have had. To children, experience is something that happens to them; to adults, their experience is *who they are*. For example, when I was 10, if I had been asked who I am, I probably would have replied, "My name is Malcolm Knowles; my father is Dr. A.D. Knowles, a veterinarian; I live at 415 Fourth Street, Missoula, Montana; I attend Roosevelt Grammar School on Sixth Street; and I am a member of the Sunday School at the Presbyterian Church on Fifth Street. If someone had asked me at age 30 who I was I would have replied, "My name is Malcolm Knowles; I was a delegate to the World Boy Scout Jamboree in Berkinhead, England in 1929; I studied international law at Harvard College, graduating in 1934; I was director of training for the National Youth Administration of Massachusetts from 1935 to 1940, and so on. I derived my self-identity from my experiences. The implication of this fact for adult education is that in any situation in which adults' experience is ignored or devalued, they perceive this as not rejecting just their experience, but rejecting them as persons.

4. *Readiness to learn.* Adults become ready to learn those things they need to know and be able to do in order to cope effectively with their real-life situations. An especially rich source of "readiness to learn" is the developmental tasks associated with

moving from one developmental stage to the next. The critical implication of this assumption is the importance of timing learning experiences to coincide with those developmental tasks. For example, a sophomore girl in high school is not ready to learn about infant nutrition or marital relations, but let her get engaged after graduation and she will be very ready. Bench workers are not ready for a course in supervisory training until they have mastered doing the work they will be supervising and decided that they are ready for more responsibility.

It is not necessary to sit by passively and wait for readiness to develop naturally, however. There are ways to induce readiness through exposure to models of superior performance, career counseling, simulation exercises, and other techniques.

5. *Orientation to learning.* In contrast to children's and youths' subject-centered orientation to learning (at least in school), adults are life-centered (or task-centered or problem-centered) in their orientation to learning. Adults are motivated to devote energy to learn something to the extent that they perceive that it will help them perform tasks or deal with problems that they confront in their life situations. Furthermore, they learn new knowledge, understandings, skills, values, and attitudes most effectively when they are presented in the context of application to real-life situations.

This point is so critical that I would like to reinforce it with three illustrations.

For many years, we sought to reduce illiteracy in this country by teaching courses in reading, writing, and arithmetic, and our record was terribly disappointing. The dropout rate was high, motivation to study was low, and achievement scores were poor. When researchers started trying to discover what was wrong in the early 1970's, they quickly discovered that the words presented in the standard vocabulary lists in the reading and writing courses were not the words these people used in their life situations and that the mathematical problems presented in their arithmetic courses were not the problems they had to be able to solve when they went to the store, the bank, or the shop. As a result, new curriculums organized around life situations and the acquisition of coping skills (e.g., coping with the world of work, of local government and community services, of health, of the family, of consuming) were constructed. Many of the problems encountered in the traditional courses disappeared or were greatly reduced.

A second example is from university extension. For many years it was the practice of universities to offer late afternoon or evening courses for adults that were exactly the same courses taught to teenagers in the day. Then in the 1950s I began noticing the evening programs changing. A course titled "Composition I" in the day program became "Writing Better Business Letters" in the evening program; "Composition II" became "Writing for Pleasure and Profit"; and "Composition III" became "Improving Your Professional Communications." And it wasn't just the titles that changed; the way they were taught also changed. While students in "Composition I" still memorized rules of grammar, students in "Writing Better Business Letters" started right off writing business letters and then extracted principles of grammatical writing from an analysis of what they had written.

A third example comes from my own personal experience with trying to learn to use a computer for writing letters, articles, and books, keeping my accounts, maintaining mailing lists, and the like. In December 1981 I bought myself one of the more popular personal computers, set it up in my study, and started reading the instruction manual with enthusiastic anticipation. The instruction manual started right off making me memorize commands. After memorizing about three pages' worth, I had to go off on a short trip, and when I returned I dashed up to my study to practice the commands I had memorized. Lo and behold, after retrieving three or four commands, I couldn't remember the others. It occurred to me that I was being asked to learn something for its own sake without knowing how I would use it to perform the tasks I wanted the computer to perform for me. So I decided to ignore the manual and teach myself how to make the computer write letters for me. It was a struggle, and the manual wasn't very helpful, but after several months I was using the computer for most of my correspondence, and in June I wrote my first article on it. It became clear to me that the computer company could have saved me a lot of time if its software producers and manual writers understood that adults are task-centered in their learning and had taught me the commands in the context of using them to write letters or perform other tasks I wanted to perform. Some months later I wrote an article for *Training and Development Journal* in which I included a "Memo to the Computer Industry" (see Appendix D) as an example of the application of the andragogical model to computer instruction.

This assumption is strongly supported by the studies of adults' time perspective described by McClusky in Appendix C and by Tough's studies of adult learning projects described earlier in this chapter. In fact, I now prefer Tough's concept of learning projects as a basis of organizing adult educational programs to my earlier concept of problem areas.

6. *Motivation.* While adults are responsive to some external motivators (better jobs, promotions, higher salaries, and the like), the most potent motivators are internal pressures (the desire for increased job satisfaction, self-esteem, quality of life, and the like). Tough (1979) found in his research that all normal adults are motivated to keep growing and developing, but that this motivation is frequently blocked by such barriers as negative self-concept as a student, inaccessibility of opportunities or resources, time constraints, and programs that violate principles of adult learning.

Putting the Pedagogical and Andragogical Models in Perspective

In the treatment of these two models so far it may appear that I am saying that they are antithetical, that pedagogy is bad and andragogy is good, and that pedagogy is for children and andragogy is for adults. This is pretty much the way I presented the models in the first edition of *The Modern Practice of Adult Education: Pedagogy Versus Andragogy* in 1970. But during the next decade, a number of teachers in elementary and secondary schools and in colleges reported to me that they were experimenting with applying the andragogical model and that children and youths seemed to learn better in many circumstances when some features of the andragogical model were applied. So, in the revised edition of *The Modern Practice of Adult Education* (1980), the subtitle was changed to "From Pedagogy to Andragogy." Also, a number of trainers and teachers of adults described situations to me in which they found that the andragogical model did not work.

So, I would like to put the two models into the perspective in which I now see them. Let me start by making a distinction between an ideology and a system of alternative assumptions. It seems to me that the pedagogical model has taken on many of the characteristics of an ideology, ideology being defined as a systematic body of beliefs that requires loyalty and conformity by its adherents. In most of my previous experience as a student and a teacher I felt pressures from the educational system to adhere to the pedagogical model. For example, the best motivator of performance, I was told, is competition for grades; and, therefore, grades must be on a curve of normal distribution— only so many A's are allowed and there must be some failures. The pedagogical ideology is typically sanctified by the shibboleth "academic standards." (If you give too many A's, you are violating academic standards.)

The andragogical model, as I see it, is *not* an ideology; it is a system of alternative sets of assumptions. And this leads us to the critical difference between the two models. The pedagogical model is an ideological model which excludes the andragogical assumptions. The andragogical model is a system of assumptions which includes the pedagogical assumptions.

What this means in practice is that we educators now have the responsibility to check out which assumptions are realistic in a given situation. If a pedagogical assumption is realistic for a particular learner in regard to a particular learning goal, then a pedagogical strategy is appropriate, at least as a starting point. For example, when learners are indeed dependent (such as when entering into a totally strange content area), when they have in fact had no previous experience with a content area, when they do not understand the relevance of a content area to their life tasks or problems, when they do need to accumulate a given body of subject matter in order to accomplish a required performance, and when they feel no internal need to learn that content, then they need to be taught by the pedagogical model. (If I were to enroll tomorrow in a course in nuclear physics, I would need to have a didactic instructor teach me what the content is, how it is organized, what its special terminology is, and what the resources are for learning about it before I would be able to start taking the initiative in learning more about it.)

But there is one big difference between how an ideological pedagog and an andragog would go from here. The pedagog, perceiving the pedagogical assumptions to be the *only* realistic assumptions, will insist that the learners remain dependent on the teacher; whereas the andragog, perceiving that movement toward the andragogical assumptions is a desirable goal, will do everything possible to help the learners take increasing responsibility for their own learning.

Even dyed-in-the-wool pedagogical teachers have reported to me that their teaching has become more effective when they adapted some of the andragogical concepts to the pedagogical model—for example, by providing a climate in which the learners feel more respected, trusted, unthreatened, and cared about; by exposing them to the need to know before instructing them; by giving them some responsibility in choosing methods and resources; and by involving them in sharing responsibility for evaluating their learning.

Implications for Practice

The implications for applying these assumptions to planning and conducting programs of adult education and human resources development are explored in Chapter 5.

4

Theories of Teaching

Principles of Teaching from Theories of Learning

Theories of learning are of use only to laboratory scientists unless they are applied somehow to the facilitation of learning, a function assigned usually in our society to a person designated as teacher.

> A distinction can be made between theories of learning and theories of teaching. While theories of learning deal with the ways in which an organism learns, theories of teaching deal with the ways in which a person influences an organism to learn. [Gage, 1972, p. 56]

Presumably, the learning theory subscribed to by a teacher will influence his theory of teaching.

> Teaching becomes the process of providing for the learner what a given learning theory regards as essential. For the conditioning theorists, the teacher must provide cues for a given response and reinforcement of that response. For the modeling theorist, the teacher must provide a model to be observed and imitated. For the cognitive theorist, the teacher must provide a cognitive structure or the stimuli that will produce one. [Gage, 1972, p. 19]

Gage apparently didn't recognize humanistic theorists.

Hilgard, resisting this fragmentation of learning theory, has identified twenty principles from three different families of theories—S-

R theory, cognitive theory, and motivation and personality theory—which are potentially useful:

A. *Principles emphasized in S-R theory*
 1. The learner should be *active*, rather than a passive listener or viewer.
 2. *Frequency of repetition* is still important in acquiring skill, and for retention through overlearning.
 3. *Reinforcement* is important; that is, in repetition desirable or correct responses should be rewarded.
 4. *Generalization* and *discrimination* suggest the importance of practice in varied contexts, so that learning will become (or remain) appropriate to a wider (or more restricted) range of stimuli.
 5. *Novelty* in behavior can be enhanced through imitation of models, through cueing, through shaping, and is not inconsistent with a liberalized S-R approach.
 6. *Drive* is important in learning, but all personal-social motives do not conform to the drive-reduction principles based on food-deprivation experiments.
 7. *Conflicts* and *frustrations* arise inevitably in the process of learning difficult discriminations and in social situations in which irrelevant motives may be aroused. Hence we must recognize and provide for their resolution or accommodation.

B. *Principles emphasized in cognitive theory*
 1. *The perceptual features* of the problem given the learner are important conditions of learning—figure-ground relations, directional signs, sequence, organic interrelatedness. Hence a learning problem should be so structured and presented that the essential features are open to the inspection of the learner.
 2. The *organization of knowledge* should be an essential concern of the teacher or educational planner so that the direction from simple to complex is *not* from arbitrary, meaningless parts to meaningful wholes, but instead from *simplified wholes to more complex wholes.*
 3. Learning is *culturally relative,* and both the wider culture and the subculture to which the learner belongs may affect his learning.
 4. *Cognitive feedback* confirms correct knowledge and corrects faulty learning. The learner tries something provisionally and then accepts or rejects what he does on the basis of its consequences. This is, of course, the cognitive equivalent of reinforce-

ment in S-R theory, but cognitive theory tends to place more emphasis upon a kind of hypothesis-testing through feedback.

5. *Goal-setting* by the learner is important as motivation for learning and his successes and failures determine how he sets future goals.

6. *Divergent thinking,* which leads to inventive problem solving or the creation of novel and valued products, is to be nurtured along with *convergent* thinking, which leads to logically correct answers.

C. *Principles from motivation and personality theory*

1. The learner's *abilities* are important, and provisions have to be made for slower and more rapid learners, as well as for those with specialized abilities.

2. *Postnatal development* may be as important as hereditary and congenital determiners of ability and interest. Hence the learner must be understood in terms of the influences that have shaped his development.

3. Learning is *culturally relative,* and both the wider culture and the subculture to which the learner belongs may affect his learning.

4. *Anxiety level* of the individual learner may determine the beneficial or detrimental effects of certain kinds of encouragements to learn.

5. The same objective situation may tap *appropriate motives* for one learner and not for another, as for example, in the contrast between those motivated by affiliation and those motivated by achievement.

6. The *organization of motives* and values within the individual is relevant. Some long-range goals affect short-range activities. Thus college students of equal ability may do better in courses perceived as relevant to their majors than in those perceived as irrelevant.

7. The *group atmosphere* of learning (competition vs cooperation, authoritarianism vs democracy, individual isolation vs group identification) will affect satisfaction in learning as well as the products of learning. [Hilgard and Bower, 1966, pp. 562-564]

One reason for Hilgard's confidence that his twenty principles would be "in large part acceptable to all parties" is that he limits the "parties" with whom he checks them out to control-oriented theorists. In spite of their differences about the internal mechanics of learning, they are fairly close in their conceptualization of the role of the teacher.

Teaching Concepts Derived from Learning Theories of Animals and Children

Let's examine the concepts of a variety of theories about the nature of teaching and the role of the teacher. First, the members of Hilgard's jury.

Thorndike saw teaching essentially as the control of learning by the management of reward. The teacher and learner must know the characteristics of a good performance in order that practice may be appropriately arranged. Errors must be diagnosed so that they will not be repeated. The teacher is not primarily concerned with the internal states of the organism, but instead with structuring the situation so that rewards will operate to strengthen desired responses. The learner should be interested, problem-oriented and attentive. However, the best way to obtain these conditions is to manipulate the learning situation so that the learner accepts the problem posed because of the rewards involved. Attention is maintained and appropriate stimulus-response connections are strengthened through the precise application of rewards toward the goals set by the teacher. A teacher's role is to cause appropriate S-R bonds to be built up in the learner's behavior repertoire. [Hilgard and Bower, 1966, pp. 22-23; Pittenger and Gooding, 1971, pp. 82-83]

Hilgard summarizes Guthrie's suggestions for teaching as follows:

1. If you wish to encourage a particular kind of behavior or discourage another, discover the cues leading to the behavior in question. In the one case, arrange the situation so that the desired behavior occurs when those cues are present; in the other case, arrange it so that the undesired behavior does not occur in the presence of the cues. This is all that is involved in the skillful use of reward and punishment. A student does not learn what was in a lecture or a book. He learns only what the lecture or book caused him to do.
2. Use as many stimulus supports for desired behavior as possible, because any ordinary behavior is a complex of movements to a complex of stimuli. The more stimuli there are associated with the desired behavior, the less likely that distracting stimuli and competing behavior will upset the desirable behavior. [Hilgard and Bower, 1966, pp. 86-87]

From B.F. Skinner's vantage point, "Teaching is simply the arrangement of contingencies of reinforcement." [Skinner, 1968, p.

5] Subsequent statements in *The Technology of Teaching* throw further light on his position:

> Some promising advances have recently been made in the field of learning. Special techniques have been designed to arrange what are called contingencies of reinforcement—the relations which prevail between behavior on the one hand and the consequences of behavior on the other—with the result that a much more effective control of behavior has been achieved. [p. 9]

> Comparable results have been obtained with pigeons, rats, dogs, monkeys, human children and psychotic subjects. In spite of great phylogenic differences, all these organisms show amazingly similar properties of the learning process. It should be emphasized that this has been achieved by analyzing the effects of reinforcement with considerable precision. Only in this way can the behavior of the individual organism be brought under such precise control. [p. 14]

> A teaching machine is simply any device which arranges contingencies of reinforcement. There are as many different kinds of machines as there are different kinds of contingencies. Early experimenters manipulated stimuli and reinforcers and recorded responses by hand, but current research without the help of extensive apparatus is unthinkable. The teacher needs similar instrumental support, for it is impossible to arrange many of the contingencies of reinforcement which expedite learning without it. Adequate apparatus has not eliminated the researcher, and teaching machines will not eliminate the teacher. [p. 65]

> In college and graduate schools the aversive pattern survives in the now almost universal system of "assign and test." The teacher does not teach, he simply holds the student responsible for learning. The student must read books, study tests, perform experiments, and attend lectures, and he is responsible for doing so in the sense that, if he does not correctly report what he has seen, heard, or read, he will suffer aversive consequences .... A test which proves to be too easy is made harder before being given again, ostensibly because an easy test does not discriminate, but more probably because the teacher is afraid of

weakening the threat under which his students are working. A teacher is judged by his employers and colleagues by the severity of the threat he imposes: he is a good teacher if he makes his students work hard, regardless of how he does so or of how much he teaches them by doing so. [pp. 99-100]

The human organism does, of course, learn without being taught. It is a good thing that this is so, and it would no doubt be a good thing if more could be learned in that way . . . But discovery is no solution to the problems of education. A culture is no stronger than its capacity to transmit itself. It must impart an accumulation of skills, knowledge, and social and ethical practices to its new members. The institution of education is designed to serve this purpose . . . It is dangerous to suggest to the student that it is beneath his dignity to learn what others already know, that there is something ignoble (and even destructive of "rational powers") in memorizing facts, codes, formulae, or passages from literary works, and that to be admired he must think in original ways. It is equally dangerous to forego teaching important facts and principles in order to give the student a chance to discover them for himself. [p. 110]

The implications of these concepts of the nature of teaching and the role of the teacher for the specific behavior of the teacher or trainer are described in some detail in Appendix A.

Hull was primarily concerned with the development of a systematic behavior theory that would improve the laboratory study of learning, and so he gave little attention to its implications for teaching. In assessing the significance of his work for education, Kingsley and Garry point out:

Systematic order and arrangement would characterize the class room patterned after Hull's theory. The development of habits and skills would proceed from the simple to the complex with a clear understanding of the stimuli and responses to be associated. The program would have to be dynamic and stimulating in view of the central position that reinforcement holds, inasmuch as aroused drives which can be reduced by satisfying outcomes are an essential condition of learning . . . Practice would be presented for the purpose of building the desired habits and maintaining them, but would not proceed to the point at which the increase in inhibition from repeating the same response would make the child reluctant to respond. [Kingsley and Garry, 1957, pp. 104-105]

Tolman was also principally concerned with the laboratory study of learning, and Kingsley and Garry point out that "the fact that Tolman accepts different forms of learning makes it more difficult to infer how an educational program which followed his theory literally would operate." But the teacher's task would be concerned primarily with "the creating of stimulus-conditions which make it possible for the learner to perceive clearly what leads to what, and to understand the different means by which a given goal can be reached. Emphasis would be placed upon making vivid the relationships between the parts and the whole . . . Because of variations in capacity with age, previous experience, etc., it would be necessary to select learning tasks which can be perceived as wholes." [Kingsley and Garry, 1957, pp. 119-120]

The gestalt psychologists saw the teacher's task as being essentially to help the individual see significant relationships and to manage instruction so that he organizes his experiences into functional patterns. Through verbal explanations, showing pictures, putting words on chalkboards, presenting reading matter, and many other teaching activities, the teacher provides stimulating situations.

> For this reason, careful lesson planning with due regard for suitable arrangement and orderly presentation is essential for good teaching. Practices conducive to the establishment of appropriate relations and organization include starting with the familiar, basing each step on those already taken, putting together facts which belong together, grouping items according to their natural connections, placing sub-topics under the topic to which they belong, using illustrations based on the learner's experience, giving major emphasis to essentials, centering supporting details around the main points, and avoiding irrelevant details. [Kingsley and Garry, 1957, pp. 111-112]

Furthermore, all the divisions and topics of each subject must be integrated, and all the various subjects of a course or program must be related to one another.

Robert Gagne in *The Conditions of Learning* (1965) agrees with these learning theorists that teaching means the arranging of conditions that are external to the learner [p. 26], but he disagrees that learning is a phenomenon which can be explained by simple theories. He believes that there are eight distinct types of learning, each with its own set of required conditions, as follows:

Type 1: *Signal Learning.* The individual learns to make a general, diffuse response to a signal. This is the classical conditioned response of Pavlov.

Type 2: *Stimulus-Response Learning.* The learner acquires a precise response to a discriminated stimulus. What is learned is a connection (Thorndike) or a discriminated operant (Skinner), sometimes called an instrumental response (Kimble).

Type 3: *Chaining.* What is acquired is a chain of two or more stimulus-response connections. The conditions for such learning have been described by Skinner and others.

Type 4: *Verbal Association.* Verbal association is the learning of chains that are verbal. Basically, the conditions resemble those for other (motor) chains. However, the presence of language in the human being makes this a special type because internal links may be selected from the individual's previously learned repertoire of language.

Type 5: *Multiple Discrimination.* The individual learnes to make n different identifying responses to as many different stimuli, which may resemble each other in physical appearance to a greater or lesser degree.

Type 6: *Concept Learning.* The learner acquires a capability of making a common response to a class of stimuli that may differ from each other widely in physical appearance. He is able to make a response that identifies an entire class of objects or events.

Type 7: *Principle Learning.* In simplest terms, a principle is a chain of two or more concepts. It functions to control behavior in the manner suggested by a verbalized rule of the form "If A, then B," which, of course, may also be learned as type 4.

Type 8: *Problem Solving.* Problem solving is a kind of learning that requires the internal events usually called thinking. Two or more previously acquired principles are somehow combined to produce a new capability that can be shown to depend on a "higher-order" principle. [pp. 58-59]

Gagne further believed that the most important class of conditions that distinguishes one form of learning from another is its prerequisites, since the types are in hierarchical order, as follows:

Problem solving (type 8) requires as prerequisites:
Principles (type 7), which require as prerequisites:
Concepts (type 6), which require as prerequisites:
Multiple discriminations (type 5), which require as prerequisites:
Verbal associations (type 4) or other chains (type 3), which require as prerequisites:
Stimulus-response connections (type 2). [p. 60]

Gagne specifies eight component functions of the instructional situation, representing the ways in which the learner's environment acts on him, that must be managed by the teacher:

1. *Presenting the stimulus.* Every type of learning requires a stimulus, and usually these stimuli must be located within the learning environment, outside the learner. If a chain is being learned, an external cue must be provided for each link, even though these may become unnecessary later. If multiple discrimination is to be accomplished, the stimuli to be discriminated must be displayed so that correct connections can become differentiated from incorrect ones. If concepts are being learned, a suitable variety of objects or events representing a class must be displayed. If principles are being acquired, the stimulus objects to which they are expected to apply must somehow be represented to the student. And if problem solving is undertaken, the "problem situation" must similarly be represented in many different ways by objects already in the learner's environment, or by means of pictures, printed books, or oral communication.

2. *Directing attention and other learner activities.* Environmental components also act on the learner by directing his attention to certain stimuli or aspects of stimulus objects and events. In very young children, vivid or suddenly changing stimulation may be used for this purpose. Very soon these can be supplanted by oral commands, and later still by printed directions such as, "Notice the number of electrons in the outer ring," or "Look at the graph in Figure 23." Activities other than attention may also be directed by such instructions, as implied by the statements, "Remember how a line is defined," or "Complete the following sentence." These activities are not themselves learning; they are simply actions that must be taken by the learner in order to create the proper conditions for learning. Verbal directions that have these purposes can be presented either orally or in printed form.

3. *Providing a model for terminal performance.* The importance of the function of informing the learner about the general nature of the performance to be acquired has been emphasized previously on several occasions. There is no single way of doing this, and many different components of the instructional situation may be employed. Most commonly, the "model" of performance to be expected following learning is conveyed by oral or printed communication.

4. *Furnishing external prompts.* In learning chains as well as multiple discriminations, cues may be provided in the instructional situation to establish a proper sequence of connections or to increase the distinctiveness of stimuli. As learning proceeds, these extra cues may be made to "vanish" when they are no longer needed. Stimuli that function as extra cues may take a variety of forms. For example, they may be pictorial, as when a sequence is depicted in a diagram reading from left to right. Or they may be auditory, as in emphasizing the differences in sound of such French words as *rue* and *rouge.* Verbal stimuli are often employed for both these purposes, as well as for the purpose of furnishing distinctive "coding links" in verbal chains. In Gilbert's (1962) example of learning color coding for resistors, the word "penny" is provided as a link between *brown* and *one,* the word "nothingness" as a link between *black* and *zero.*

5. *Guiding the direction of thinking.* When principles are being learned, and particularly when learning takes the form of problem solving, the direction of recalled internal connections (thoughts) may be guided by instructions from the learner's environment. As described previously, such guidance is presumed to have the effect of increasing the efficiency of learning by reducing the occurrence of irrelevant "hypotheses." Generally, instructions having this function of "hinting" and "suggesting" take the form of oral or printed prose statements.

6. *Inducing transfer of knowledge.* Providing for the transfer of learned concepts and principles to novel situations may be accomplished in a number of ways. The conduct of discussion is one of the most convenient. Obviously, this is a special kind of interaction between the learner and his environment, and it is not possible to specify exactly what form will be taken at any given moment by stimulation from the environment. The process is usually initiated, however, by verbally stated questions of the "problem-solving" variety. An important alternative method is to place the individual within a problem situation more or less directly, without the use of words to describe it. A science demonstration may be used to serve this function. Also, motion pictures can be used with considerable

effectiveness to initiate problem-solving discussion by "getting the students into the situation" in a highly realistic manner.

7. *Assessing learning attainments.* The environment of the learner also acts on him to assess the extent to which he has attained a specific learning objective or subobjective. It does this by deliberately placing him in representative problem situations that concretely reflect the capability he is expected to have learned. Most frequently, this is done by asking him questions. Although it is conceivable for the learner to formulate for himself the questions to be asked, this is difficult to do even for the experienced adult learner. Preferably, the questions must come from an independent source, so that they will be uninfluenced by the learner's wishes, but will accurately represent the objective.

8. *Providing feedback.* Closely related to assessment of learning outcomes is the provision for feedback concerning the correctness of the learner's responses. The questions that are asked the learner, followed by his answers, must in turn be followed by information that tells him whether he is right or wrong. Sometimes, the provision for this feedback function of the learner's environment is very simple to arrange: a foreign word pronounced by the student may sound like one he hears on a tape; the color of a chemical solution may indicate the presence of an element he is searching for. At other times it may be considerably more complex, as when the adequacy of a constructed prose paragraph describing an observed event is assessed, and the results fed back to the student.

These eight functions, then, represent the ways in which the learner's environment acts on him. These are the external conditions of learning that, when combined with certain prerequisite capabilities within the learner, bring about the desired change in his performance. Obviously, there are many ways to establish these conditions in the learning environment, and many combinations of objects, devices, and verbal communications may be employed in doing so. Probably the most important consideration for the design of the learning environment, however, is not that several alternative ways of accomplishing the same function are usually available. Rather, the important point is that for a given function, certain means of interacting with the learner are quite ineffective. Accordingly, the characteristics of various *media of instruction* in performing these functions need to be considered carefully in making a choice. [Gagne, 1965, pp. 268-271]

These are the learning theorists who Hilgard believed would agree with his twenty principles (with the exception of the motivation and personality theorists, whom Hilgard didn't identify, so we can't check with them directly). Obviously these theorists are unanimous in seeing teaching as the management of procedures which will assure specified behavioral changes as prescribed learning products. The role of the teacher, therefore, is that of a shaper of behavior. Stated this badly, it smacks of what contemporary critics of education see as a God-playing role. [Bereiter, 1972, p. 25; Illich, 1970, p. 30]

Teaching Concepts Derived from Learning Theories of Adults

These were theories based primarily on studies of animals and children. When we look at the concepts of teaching of those theorists who derived their theories of learning primarily from studies of adults they are very different. Carl Rogers makes one of the sharpest breaks in his lead statement:

Teaching, in my estimation, is a vastly over-rated function. Having made such a statement, I scurry to the dictionary to see if I really mean what I say. Teaching means 'to instruct.' Personally I am not much interested in instructing another in what he should know or think. 'To impart knowledge or skill.' My reaction is, why not be more efficient, using a book or programmed learning? 'To make to know.' Here my hackles rise. I have no wish to *make* anyone know something. 'To show, guide, direct.' As I see it, too many people have been shown, guided, directed. So I come to the conclusion that I *do* mean what I said. Teaching is, for me, a relatively unimportant and vastly overvalued activity. [Rogers, 1969, p. 103]

Rogers goes on to explain that in his view teaching and the imparting of knowledge make sense in an unchanging environment, which is why it has been an unquestioned function for centuries. "But if there is one truth about modern man, it is that he lives in an environment which is *continually changing,*" and therefore the aim of education must be the *facilitation of learning. [Ibid.,* pp. 104-105] He defines the role of the teacher as that of a *facilitator of learning.* The critical element in performing this role is the personal relationship between the facilitator and the learner, which in turn is dependent on the facilitator's possessing three attitudinal qualities:

(1) realness or genuineness, (2) nonpossessive caring, prizing, trust, and respect, and (3) empathic understanding and sensitive and accurate listening. [*Ibid.,* pp. 106-126]

He provides the following guidelines for a facilitator of learning:

1. *The facilitator has much to do with setting the initial mood or climate of the group or class experience.* If his own basic philosophy is one of trust in the group and in the individuals who compose the group, then this point of view will be communicated in many subtle ways.

2. *The facilitator helps to elicit and clarify the purposes of the individuals in the class as well as the more general purposes of the group.* If he is not fearful of accepting contradictory purposes and conflicting aims, if he is able to permit the individuals a sense of freedom in stating what they would like to do, then he is helping to create a climate for learning.

3. *He relies upon the desire of each student to implement those purposes which have meaning for him as the motivational force behind significant learning.* Even if the desire of the student is to be guided and led by someone else, the facilitator can accept such a need and motive and can either serve as a guide when this is desired or can provide some other means, such as a set course of study, for the student whose major desire is to be dependent. And, for the majority of students, he can help to utilize a particular individual's own drives and purposes as the moving force behind his learning.

4. *He endeavors to organize and make easily available the widest possible range of resources for learning.* He endeavors to make available writings, materials, psychological aids, persons, equipment, trips, audio-visual aids—every conceivable resource which his students may wish to use for their own enhancement and for the fulfillment of their own purposes.

5. *He regards himself as a flexible resource to be utilized by the group.* He does not downgrade himself as a resource. He makes himself available as a counselor, lecturer, and advisor, a person with experience in the field. He wishes to be used by individual students, and by

the group, in ways which seem most meaningful to them insofar as
he can be comfortable in operating in the ways they wish.

6. *In responding to expressions in the classroom group, he accepts both
   intellectual content and the emotionalized attitudes, endeavoring to
   give each aspect the approximate degree of emphasis which it has for
   the individual or the group.* Insofar as he can be genuine in doing so,
   he accepts rationalizations and intellectualizing, as well as deep and
   real personal feelings.

7. *As the acceptant classroom climate becomes established, the facilitator is able increasingly to become a participant learner, a member
   of the group, expressing his views as those of one individual only.*

8. *He takes the initiative in sharing himself with the group—his feelings
   as well as his thoughts—in ways which do not demand or impose but
   represent simply the personal sharing which students may take or
   leave.* Thus, he is free to express his own feelings in giving feedback
   to students, in his reaction to them as individuals, and in sharing his
   own satisfactions or disappointments. In such expressions it is his
   "owned" attitudes which are shared, not judgments of evaluations
   of others.

9. *Throughout the classroom experience, he remains alert to the expressions indicative of deep or strong feelings.* These may be feelings of conflict, pain, and the like, which exist primarily within the
   individual. Here he endeavors to understand these from the person's
   point of view and to communicate his empathic understanding. On
   the other hand, the feelings may be those of anger, scorn, affection,
   rivalry, and the like—interpersonal attitudes among members of the
   group. Again he is as alert to these as to the ideas being expressed
   and by his acceptance of such tensions or bonds he helps to bring
   them into the open for constructive understanding and use by the
   group.

10. *In his functioning as a facilitator of learning, the leader endeavors
    to recognize and accept his own limitations.* He realizes that he can
    only grant freedom to his students to the extent that he is comfort-
    able in giving such freedom. He can only be understanding to the
    extent that he actually desires to enter the inner world of his stu-
    dents. He can only share himself to the extent that he is reasonably

comfortable in taking that risk. He can only participate as a member of the group when he actually feels that he and his students have an equality as learners. He can only exhibit trust of the students' desire to learn insofar as he feels that trust. There will be many times when his attitudes are not facilitative of learning. He will find himself being suspicious of his students. He will find it impossible to accept attitudes which differ strongly from his own. He will be unable to understand some of the student feelings which are markedly different from his own. He may find himself feeling strongly judgmental and evaluative. When he is experiencing attitudes which are nonfacilitative, he will endeavor to get close to them, to be clearly aware of them, and to state them just as they are within himself. Once he has expressed these angers, these judgments, these mistrusts, these doubts of others and doubts of himself, as something coming from within himself, not as objective facts in outward reality, he will find the air cleared for a significant interchange between himself and his students. Such an interchange can go a long way toward resolving the very attitudes which he has been experiencing, and thus make it possible for him to be more of a facilitator of learning. [Rogers, 1969, pp. 164-166]

Although Maslow does not spell out his conception of the role of teacher, he no doubt would subscribe to Rogers' guidelines, with perhaps a bit more emphasis on the teacher's responsibility for providing safety. Several followers of both Rogers and Maslow have experimented with translating their theories into classroom behavior. George Brown, for example, describes the development of confluent education ("the term for the integration or flowing together of the affective and cognitive elements in individual and group learning") in the Ford-Esalen Project in Affective Education in California in the late 1960's in his *Human Teaching for Human Learning,* 1971. Elizabeth Drews describes an experiment to test a new program designed to foster self-initiated learning and self-actualization in ninth graders in Michigan, in which the teachers defined their roles as facilitators of learning. [Drews, 1966]

Flowing in the same stream of thought, Goodwin Watson provides the following summary of "what is known about learning"—which is easily read as "guidelines for the facilitation of learning":

1. Behavior which is rewarded—from the learner's point of view—is more likely to recur.
2. Sheer repetition without reward is a poor way to learn.
3. Threat and punishment have variable effects upon learning, but they can and do commonly produce avoidance behavior—in which the reward is the diminution of punishment possibilities.
4. How "ready" we are to learn something new is contingent upon the confluence of diverse—and changing—factors, some of which include:
   a. adequate existing experience to permit the new to be learned (we can learn only in relation to what we already know);
   b. adequate significance and relevance for the learner to engage in learning activity (we learn only what is appropriate to our purposes);
   c. freedom from discouragement, the expectation of failure, or threats to physical, emotional, or intellectual well-being.
5. *Whatever* is to be learned will remain unlearnable if we believe that we cannot learn it or if we perceive it as irrelevant or if the learning situation is perceived as threatening.
6. Novelty (per 4 and 5 above) is generally rewarding.
7. We learn best that which we participate in selecting and planning ourselves.
8. Genuine participation (as compared with feigned participation intended to avoid punishment) intensifies motivation, flexibility, and rate of learning.
9. An autocratic atmosphere (produced by a dominating teacher who controls direction via intricate punishments) produces in learners apathetic conformity, various—and frequently devious—kinds of defiance, scapegoating (venting hostility generated by the repressive atmosphere on colleagues), or escape . . . An autocratic atmosphere also produces increasing dependence upon the authority, with consequent obsequiousness, anxiety, shyness, and acquiescence.
10. "Closed," authoritarian environments (such as are characteristic of most conventional schools and classrooms) condemn most

learners to continuing criticism, sarcasm, discouragement, and failure so that self-confidence, aspiration (for anything but escape), and a healthy self-concept are destroyed.

11. The best time to learn anything is when whatever is to be learned is immediately useful to us.

12. An "open," nonauthoritarian atmosphere can, then, be seen as conducive to learner initiative and creativity, encouraging the learning of attitudes of self-confidence, originality, self-reliance, enterprise, and independence. All of which is equivalent to learning how to learn. [Watson, 1960-1961]

Houle has proposed a "fundamental system" of educational design which rests on seven assumptions:

1. Any episode of learning occurs in a specific situation and is profoundly influenced by that fact.

2. The analysis or planning of educational activities must be based on the realities of human experience and upon their constant change.

3. Education is a practical art (like architecture) which draws on many theoretical disciplines in the humanities, and the social and biological sciences.

4. Education is a cooperative rather than an operative art. ("An operative art is one in which the creation of a product or performance is essentially controlled by the person using the art . . . A cooperative art . . . works in a facilitative way by guiding and directing a natural entity or process. The farmer, physician, and educator are three classic examples of cooperative artists.")

5. The planning or analysis of an educational activity is usually undertaken in terms of some period which the mind abstracts for analytical purposes from the complicated reality.

6. The planning or analysis of an educational activity may be undertaken by an educator, a learner, an independent analyst, or some combination of the three.

7. Any design of education can best be understood as a complex of interacting elements, not as a sequence of events. [Houle, 1972, pp. 32-39]

He then identifies the following components in his fundamental system, which it is the task of the educator to manage:

1. A possible educational activity is identified.
2. A decision is made to proceed.
3. Objectives are identified and refined.
4. A suitable format is designed.
   a. Learning resources are selected.
   b. A leader or group of leaders is chosen.
   c. Methods are selected and used.
   d. A time schedule is made.
   e. A sequence of events is devised.
   f. Social reinforcement of learning is provided.
   g. The nature of each individual learner is taken into account.
   h. Roles and relationships are made clear.
   i. Criteria for evaluating progress are identified.
   j. The design is made clear to all concerned.
5. The format is fitted into larger patterns of life.
   a. Learners are guided into or out of the activity both at the beginning and subsequently.
   b. Life styles are modified to allow time and resources for the new activity.
   c. Financing is arranged.
   d. The activity is interpreted to related publics.
6. The program is carried out.
7. The results of the activity are measured and appraised.
8. The situation is examined in terms of the possibility of a new educational activity. [*Ibid.*, pp. 48-56]

Because Tough's studies have been concerned with the self-initiated learning projects of adults, he has focused on the "helping role" of the teacher or other resource person. His investigations have produced the following "fairly consistent composite picture of the ideal helper":

One cluster of characteristics might be summarized by saying that the ideal helper is warm and loving. He accepts and cares about the learner and about his project or problem, and takes it seriously. He is willing to spend time helping. He is approving, supportive, encouraging, and friendly. He regards the learner as an equal. As a result of these characteristics, the learner feels free to approach this ideal helper, and can talk freely and easily with him in a warm and relaxed atmosphere.

A second cluster of characteristics involves the helper's perceptions of the person's capacity as a self-planner. The ideal helper has confidence in the learner's ability to make appropriate plans and arrangements for this learning. The helper has a high regard for his skill as a self-planner, and does not want to take the decision-making control away from him.

Third, the ideal helper views his interaction with the learner as a dialogue, a true encounter in which he listens as well as talks. His help will be tailored to the needs, goals, and requests of this unique learner. The helper listens, accepts, understands, responds, helps. These perceptions of the interaction are in sharp contrast to those of "helpers" who want to control, command, manipulate, persuade, influence, and change the learner. Such helpers seem to view communication as "an inexhaustible monologue, addressed to everyone and no one in the form of 'mass communication' . . . Such a helper perceives the learner as an object, and expects to do something *to* that object. He is not primarily interested in the other person as a person, and in his needs, wishes, and welfare."

Another cluster of internal characteristics involves the helper's reasons for helping. He may help because of his affection and concern for the learner. Or the helper may, in an open and positive way, expect to gain as much as he gives. Other sorts of motivation, too, are possible—pleasure for knowing he was helpful, satisfaction from seeing progress or from the learner's gratitude . . .

Finally, the ideal helper is probably an open and growing person, not a closed, negative, static, defensive, fearful, or suspicious sort of person. He himself is frequently a learner, and seeks growth and new experiences. He probably tends to be spontaneous and authentic, and to feel free to behave as a unique person rather than in some stereotyped way. [Tough, 1979, pp. 195–197]

These characteristics fit well into my own conception of the role of the andragogical teacher, which I have attempted to make operational as a set of principles as shown in Table 4-1.

Table 4-1.
The Role of the Teacher

Conditions of Learning	Principles of Teaching
The learners feel a need to learn.	1. The teacher exposes students to new possibilities of self-fulfillment. 2. The teacher helps each student clarify his own aspirations for improved behavior. 3. The teacher helps each student diagnose the gap between his aspiration and his present level of performance. 4. The teacher helps the students identify the life problems they experience because of the gaps in their personal equipment.
The learning environment is characterized by physical comfort, mutual trust and respect, mutual helpfulness, freedom of expression, and acceptance of differences:	5. The teacher provides physical conditions that are comfortable (as to seating, smoking, temperature, ventilation, lighting, decoration) and conducive to interaction (preferably, no person sitting behind another person). 6. The teacher accepts each student as a person of worth and respects his feelings and ideas. 7. The teacher seeks to build relationships of mutual trust and helpfulness among the students by encouraging cooperative activities and refraining from inducing competitiveness and judgmentalness.

(continued on next page)

Table 4-1. continued

Conditions of Learning	Principles of Teaching
	8. The teacher exposes his own feelings and contributes his resources as a colearner in the spirit of mutual inquiry.
The learners perceive the goals of a learning experience to be their goals.	9. The teacher involves the students in a mutual process of formulating learning objectives in which the needs of the students, of the institution, of the teacher, of the subject matter, and of the society are taken into account.
The learners accept a share of the responsibility for planning and operating a learning experience, and therefore have a feeling of commitment toward it.	10. The teacher shares his thinking about options available in the designing of learning experiences and the selection of materials and methods and involves the students in deciding among these options jointly.
The learners participate actively in the learning process.	11. The teacher helps the students to organize themselves (project groups, learning-teaching teams, independent study, etc.) to share responsibility in the process of mutual inquiry.
The learning process is related to and makes use of the experience of the learners.	12. The teacher helps the students exploit their own experiences as resources for learning through the use of such techniques as discussion, role playing, case method, etc.
	13. The teacher gears the presentation of his own resources to the levels of experience of his particular students.

Table 4.1. continued

Conditions of Learning	Principles of Teaching
The learners have a sense of progress toward their goals.	14. The teacher helps the students to apply new learning to their experience, and thus to make the learnings more meaningful and integrated. 15. The teacher involves the students in developing mutually acceptable criteria and methods for measuring progress toward the learning objectives. 16. The teacher helps the students develop and apply procedures for self-evaluation according to these criteria.

[Knowles, 1980, pp. 57-58]

Concepts of Teaching Derived from Theories of Teaching

Some teaching theories have evolved directly from learning theories, especially the mechanistic models. Other theories of teaching evolved from analyses of teacher behavior and its consequences and from experimenting with manipulation of the variables in the teaching-learning situation. Since the previous section has presented teaching theories derived from learning theories, let us turn now to concepts derived from theories of teaching.

Dewey's Concepts

Perhaps the most impactful system of ideas about effective teaching was propounded by John Dewey during the first half of this century. Dewey contrasted his basic principles with those of traditional education:

> To imposition from above is opposed expression and cultivation of individuality; to external discipline is opposed free activity; to learning from texts and teacher, learning through experience; to acquisition of isolated skills and techniques by drill, is opposed acquisition of them as means of attaining ends which make direct vital appeal; to preparation for a more or less remote future is opposed making the most of the opportunities of present life; to static aims and materials is opposed acquaintance with a changing world. [Dewey, 1938, pp. 5-6]

Dewey's system is organized around several key concepts. The central concept is *experience:*

> All genuine education comes about through experience. [*Ibid.*, p. 13]

> The central problem of an education based upon experience is to select the kind of present experiences that live fruitfully and creatively in subsequent experiences. [*Ibid.*, pp. 16-17]

A second key concept is *democracy:*

> The question I would raise concerns why we prefer democratic and humane arrangements to those which are autocratic and harsh . . . Can we find any reason that does not ultimately come down to the belief that democratic social arrangements promote a better quality of human experience, one which is more widely accessible and enjoyed, than do non-democratic and anti-democratic forms of social life? [*Ibid.*, pp. 24-25]

Another key concept is *continuity:*

> The principle of continuity of experience means that every experience both takes up something from those which have gone before and modifies in some way the quality of those which come after . . . Growth, or growing and developing, not only physically but intellectually and morally, is one exemplification of the principle of continuity. [*Ibid.*, pp. 27-28]

> It is worth while to say something about the way in which the adult [teacher] can exercise the wisdom his own wider experience gives him without imposing a merely external control. On one side, it is his

business to be on the alert to see what attitudes and habitual tendencies are being created. In this direction he must, if he is an educator, be able to judge what attitudes are actually conducive to continued growth and what are detrimental. He must, in addition, have that sympathetic understanding of individuals as individuals which gives him an idea of what is actually going on in the minds of those who are learning. [*Ibid.*, p. 33]

A primary responsibility of educators is that they not only be aware of the general principle of the shaping of actual experience by environing conditions, but that they also recognize in the concrete what surroundings are conducive to having experiences that lead to growth. Above all, they should know how to utilize the surroundings, physical and social, that exist so as to extract from them all that they have to contribute to building up experiences that are worth while. [*Ibid.*, p. 35]

Another key concept is *interaction:*

The word "interaction" expresses the second chief principle for interpreting an experience in its educational function and force. It assigns equal rights to both factors in experience—objective and internal conditions. Any normal experience is an interplay of these two sets of conditions. Taken together, or in their interaction, they form what we call a *situation.* The trouble with traditional education was not that it emphasized the external conditions that enter into the control of the experiences but that it paid so little attention to the internal factors which also decide what kind of experience is had [the powers and purposes of those taught]. [*Ibid.*, pp. 38-44]

It is not the subject *per se* that is educative or that is conducive to growth. There is no subject that is in and of itself, or without regard to the stage of growth attained by the learner, [an end] such that inherent educational value may be attributed to it. Failure to take into account adaptation to the needs and capacities of individuals was the source of the idea that certain subjects and certain methods are intrinsically cultural or intrinsically good for mental discipline . . . In a certain sense every experience should do something to prepare a person for later experiences of a deeper and more expansive quality. That is the very meaning of growth, continuity, reconstruction of experience. [*Ibid.*, pp. 46-47]

The educator is responsible for a knowledge of individuals and for a knowledge of subject-matter that will enable activities to be selected which lend themselves to social organization, an organization in which all individuals have an opportunity to contribute something, and in which the activities in which all participate are the chief carrier of control. . . . The principle that development of experience comes about through interaction means that education is essentially a social process. . . The teacher loses the position of external boss or dictator but takes on that of leader of group activities. [*Ibid.*, pp. 61-66]

It is possible of course to abuse the office, and to force the activity of the young into channels which express the teacher's purpose rather than that of the pupils. But the way to avoid this danger is not for the adult to withdraw entirely. The way is, first, for the teacher to be intelligently aware of the capacities, needs, and past experiences of those under instruction, and, secondly, to allow the suggestion made to develop into a plan and project by means of the further suggestions contributed and organized into a whole by the members of the group. The plan, in other words, is a cooperative enterprise, not a dictation. [*Ibid.*, p. 85]

Many of Dewey's ideas were distorted, misinterpreted, and exaggerated during the heyday of the progressive school movement a generation ago, which is why I thought it important to quote him directly. In light of contemporary thinking about teaching, though, don't they seem fresh and useful?

Teaching through Inquiry

A second set of concepts about teaching with roots both in Dewey's ideas—especially his formulation of scientific thinking—and in those of the cognitive theorists is variously referred to as the discovery method, the inquiry method, self-directed learning or problem-solving learning.

Jerome Bruner, perhaps the most notable proponent of this approach to teaching, is in the process of constructing a theory of instruction that will meet these four criteria:

1. A theory of instruction should specify the experiences which most effectively implant in the individual a predisposition toward learning.

2. A theory of instruction must specify the ways in which a body of knowledge should be structured so that it can be most readily grasped by the learner.
3. A theory of instruction should specify the most effective sequences in which to present the materials to be learned.
4. A theory of instruction should specify the nature and pacing of rewards and punishments in the process of learning and teaching. [Bruner, 1966, pp. 40-41]

His system is predicated on the existence in all people of the will to learn.

The will to learn is an intrinsic motive, one that finds both its source and its reward in its own exercise. The will to learn becomes a "problem" only under specialized circumstances like those of a school, where a curriculum is set, students confined, and a path fixed. The problem exists not so much in learning itself, but in the fact that what the school imposes often fails to enlist the natural energies that sustain spontaneous learning—curiosity, a desire for competence, aspiration to emulate a model, and a deep-sensed commitment to the web of social reciprocity [the human need to respond to others and to operate jointly with them toward an objective]. [*Ibid.*, pp. 125-127]

Bruner further makes a distinction between teaching in the *expository mode* and teaching in the *hypothetical mode.*

In the former, the decisions concerning the mode and pace and style of exposition are principally determined by the teacher as expositor; the student is the listener. . .In the hypothetical mode, the teacher and the student are in a more cooperative position. . .The student is not a bench-bound listener, but is taking a part in the formulation and at times may play the principal role in it. [Bruner, 1961, p. 126]

The hypothetical mode leads to students' engaging in *acts of discovery,* a process which Bruner sees as having four benefits: (1) increasing intellectual powers, (2) shifting from extrinsic to intrinsic rewards, (3) learning the heuristics of discovering and (4) making material more readily accessible in memory. This mode is more congruent with and more likely to nurture the will to learn.

Bruner conveys the operational aspects of discovery teaching by describing it in action in case studies of actual courses. But Postman and Weingartner provide the following list of behaviors observable in teachers using the inquiry method:

The teacher rarely tells students what he thinks they ought to know. He believes that telling, when used as a basic teaching strategy, deprives students of the excitement of doing their own finding and of the opportunity for increasing their power as learners.

His basic mode of discourse with students is questioning. While he uses both convergent and divergent questions, he regards the latter as the more important tool. He emphatically does not view questions as a means of seducing students into parroting the text or syllabus; rather, he sees questions as instruments to open engaged minds to unsuspected possibilities.

Generally, he does not accept a single statement as an answer to a question. In fact, he has a persisting aversion to anyone, any syllabus, any text that offers The Right Answer. Not because answers and solutions are unwelcome—indeed, he is trying to help students be more efficient problem solvers—but because he knows how often The Right Answer serves only to terminate further thought. He knows the power of pluralizing. He does not ask for the reason, but for the reasons. Not for the cause, but the causes. Never the meaning, the meanings. He knows, too the power of contingent thinking. He is the most "It depends" learner in his class.

He encourages student-student interaction as opposed to student-teacher interaction. And generally he avoids acting as a mediator or judge of the quality of ideas expressed. If each person could have with him at all times a full roster of authorities, perhaps it would not be necessary for individuals to make independent judgments. But so long as this is not possible, the individual must learn to depend on himself as a thinker. The inquiry teacher is interested in students' developing their own criteria or standards for judging the quality, precision, and relevance of ideas. He permits such development to occur by minimizing his role as arbiter of what is acceptable and what is not.

He rarely summarizes the positions taken by students on the learnings that occur. He recognizes that the act of summary of "closure" tends to have the effect of ending further thought. Because he regards learning as a process, not a terminal event, his "summaries" are apt to be stated as hypotheses, tendencies, and directions. He assumes that no one ever learns once and for all how to write, or how to read, or what were the causes of the Civil War. Rather, he assumes that one is always in the process of acquiring skills, assimilating new information, formulating or refining generalizations. Thus, he is always cautious about defining the limits of learning, about saying, "This is what you will learn between now and the Christmas holidays," or even (especially), "This is what you will learn in the ninth grade." The only significant terminal behavior he recognizes is death, and he suspects that those who talk of learning as some kind of "terminal point" are either compulsive travelers or have simply not observed children closely enough. Moreover, he recognizes that learning does not occur with the same intensity in any two people, and he regards verbal attempts to disregard this fact as a semantic fiction. If a student has arrived at a particular conclusion, then little is gained by the teacher's restating it. If the student has not arrived at a conclusion, then it is presumptuous and dishonest for the teacher to contend that he has. (Any teacher who tells you precisely what his students learned during any lesson, unit, or semester quite literally does not know what he is talking about.)

His lessons develop from the responses of students and not from a previously determined "logical" structure. The only kind of lesson plan, or syllabus, that makes sense to him is one that tries to predict, account for, and deal with the authentic responses of learners to a particular problem: the kinds of questions they will ask, the obstacles they will face, their attitudes, the possible solutions they will offer, etc. Thus, he is rarely frustrated or inconvenienced by "wrong answers," false starts, irrelevant directions. These are the stuff of which his best lessons and opportunities are made. In short, the "content" of his lessons are the responses of his students. Since he is concerned with the processes of thought rather than the end results of thought (The Answer!), he does not feel compelled to "cover ground" (There's the traveler again), or to insure that his students embrace a particular doctrine, or to exclude a student's idea because it is not germane. (Not germane to what? Obviously, it is germane to the student's thinking about the problem.) He is engaged in exploring the *way* students think, not what they should think (before the Christmas holidays). That is why he spends more of his time listening to students than talking to or at them.

Generally, each of his lessons poses a problem for students. Almost all of his questions, proposed activities, and assignments are aimed at having his students clarify a problem, make observations relevant to the solution of the problem, and make generalizations based on their observations. His goal is to engage students in those activities which produce knowledge: defining, questioning, observing, classifying, generalizing, verifying, applying. As we have said, *all knowledge is a result of these activities.* Whatever we think we "know" about astronomy, sociology, chemistry, biology, linguistics, etc., was discovered or invented by someone who was more or less an expert in using inductive methods of inquiry. Thus, our inquiry, or "inductive," teacher is largely interested in helping his students to become more proficient as users of these methods.

He measures his success in terms of behavioral changes in students: the frequency with which they ask questions; the increase in the relevance and cogency of their questions; the frequency and conviction of their challenges to assertions made by other students or teachers or textbooks; the relevance and clarity of the standards on which they base their challenges; their willingness to suspend judgments when they have insufficient data; their willingness to modify or otherwise change their position when data warrant such change; the increase in their tolerance for diverse answers; their ability to apply generalizations, attitudes, and information to novel situations.

These behaviors and attitudes amount to a definition of a different *role* for the teacher from that which he has traditionally assumed. The inquiry environment, like any other school environment, is a series of human encounters, the nature of which is largely determined by the "teacher." "Teacher" is here placed in quotation marks to call attention to the fact that most of its conventional meanings are inimical to inquiry methods. It is not uncommon, for example, to hear "teachers" make statements such as, "Oh, I taught them that, but they didn't learn it." There is no utterance made in the Teachers' Room more extraordinary than this. From our point of view, it is on the same level as a salesman's remarking, "I sold it to him, but he didn't buy it"—which is to say, it makes no sense. It seems to mean that "teaching" is what a "teacher" does, which, in turn, may or may not bear any relationship to what those being "taught" do. [Postman and Weingartner, 1969, pp. 34-37]

Suchman has described vividly the success of the Inquiry Training Project at the University of Illinois in developing inquiry skills in elementary school children. As a result of this experience, he feels confident in the feasibility of "an inquiry-centered curriculum."

. . . in which the children would find themselves launched into areas of study by first being confronted by concrete problem-focused episodes for which they would attempt to build explanatory systems. Part of their data gathering might well be in the question-asking mode and certainly along the way time would have to be spent in building inquiry skills through critiques and other such procedures. Yet there would also be room for helping the children enlarge their conceptual systems through more teacher-directed means. [Suchman, 1972, p. 158]

Crutchfield counts four sets of skills involved in *productive thinking,* his synonym for problem-solving or inquiry learning.

(1) skills of problem discovery and formulation
(2) skill in organizing and processing problem information
(3) skill in idea generation, and
(4) skill in the evaluation of ideas. [Crutchfield, 1972, pp. 192-195]

The notion that the development of skills of inquiry should be a primary goal of youth education is the cornerstone of the concept of education as a lifelong process. This makes it especially significant that the Governing Board of the UNESCO Institute for Education in Hamburg, Germany decided in March 1972 to focus on research and experimental projects in an exploratory study, "The Concept of Lifelong Education and Its Implications for School Curriculum." A working paper I prepared for this study is reproduced in Appendix E.

Teaching through Modeling

The most elaborate system of thought on *imitation, identification* or *modeling* as concepts of teaching has been developed by Albert Bandura at Stanford University. He labels the system *social learning.* Bandura regards reinforcement theories of instrumental conditioning, such as Skinner's, as able to account for the control of previously learned matching responses, but unable to account for the way new response patterns are acquired through observation and imitation.

In teaching by modeling, the teacher behaves in ways that he wants the learner to imitate. The teacher's basic technique is *role modeling.* Bandura and Walters (1963) identified three kinds of effects from exposing the learner to a model: (1) a modeling effect, whereby the learner acquires new kinds of response patterns; (2) an inhibitory or disinhibitory effect, whereby the learner decreases or increases the frequency, latency or intensity of previously acquired responses; and (3) an eliciting effect, whereby the learner merely receives from the model a cue for releasing a response that is neither new nor inhibited. For example, the modeling effect occurs when the teacher shows learners how to listen empathically to one another by himself listening empathically to them. The inhibiting or disinhibiting effect occurs when the teacher lets the learners know, through modeling, that it is or is not approved behavior to express their feelings openly, and thus inhibits or disinhibits an old response. The eliciting effect occurs when, through modeling, the teacher teaches the art of giving and receiving feedback by inviting the learners to criticize his own performance helpfully, thus providing a cue eliciting a response neither new nor inhibited.

Gage remarks that "Learning through imitation seems to be especially appropriate for tasks that have little cognitive structure." [Gage, 1972, p. 47] This observation seems to be borne out by the fact that social learning has been applied principally to behavioral modification in therapeutic settings to correct deviant or antisocial behavior, but its application to such positive educational purposes as the development of attitudes, beliefs, and performance skills has also been demonstrated. [Bandura, 1969, pp. 599-624] No doubt every teacher employs modeling as one of his techniques, whether consciously or unconsciously. His potency as a model will be influenced by such characteristics as age, sex, socio-economic status, social power, ethnic background, and intellectual and vocational status. [*Ibid.,* p. 195]

Although social learning has been employed chiefly to achieve behavioral changes through external management of reinforcement contingencies, in recent years there has been a growing interest in self-control processes in which individuals regulate their own behavior by arranging appropriate contingencies for themselves. These self-directed endeavors comprise a variety of strategies, about which Bandura makes these observations.

The *selection of well-defined objectives,* both intermediate and ultimate, is an essential aspect of any self-directed program of change. The goals that individuals choose for themselves must be specified in sufficiently detailed behavioral terms to provide adequate guidance for the actions that must be taken daily to attain desired outcomes.

To further increase goal commitment participants are asked to make *contractual agreements* to practice self-controlling behaviors in their daily activities. Thus, for example, in modifying smoking behavior [Tooley & Pratt, 1967] and obesity [Ferster, Nurnberger, & Levitt, 1962], clients agree to restrict increasingly, in graduated steps, the times and places in which they will engage in the undesired behavior. Under conditions where individuals voluntarily commit themselves to given courses of action, subsequent tendencies to deviate are likely to be counteracted by negative self-evaluations. Through this mechanism, and anticipated social reactions of others, contractual commitments reinforce adherence to corrective practices.

Satisfactions derived from evident changes help to sustain successful endeavors, therefore, utilize *objective records of behavioral changes* as an additional source of reinforcement for their self-controlling behavior. . . .

Since behavior is extensively under external stimulus control, persons can regulate the frequency with which they engage in certain activities by *altering stimulus conditions* under which the behavior customarily occurs. Overeating, for example, will arise more often when appetizing foods are prominently displayed in frequented places in the household than if they are stored out of sight and made less accessible. . . .

Behavior that provides immediate positive reinforcement, such as eating, smoking, and drinking, tends to be performed in diverse situations and at varied times. Therefore, another important aspect of self-managed change involves progressive *narrowing of stimulus control* over behavior. Continuing with the obesity illustration, individuals are encouraged gradually to delimit the circumstances under which they eat until eventually their eating behavior is brought under control of a specific set of stimulus conditions. This outcome is achieved by having the clients commit themselves to a graduated program in which they refrain from eating in non-dining settings, between regular mealtimes, and while engaging in other activities such as watching television, reading, or listening to the radio. . . .

The foregoing procedures are primarily aimed at instituting self-controlling behavior, but unless positive consequences are also arranged the well-intentioned practices are likely to be short-lived . . . Self-control measures usually produce immediate unpleasant effects while the personal benefits are considerably delayed. *Self-*

reinforcing operations are, therefore, employed to provide immediate support for self-controlling behavior until the benefits that eventually accrue take over the reinforcing function.

As a final feature of self-directed change programs, increases in desired behavior and reductions in undesired behavior are attempted gradually. In this way the incidence of experienced discomforts is kept low, and steady progress toward the eventual goal can be achieved. [Bandura, 1969, pp. 254-257]

Change Theory

Another system of thought that has great implications for educational practice has to do with influencing the educative quality of total environments. Concepts and strategies in this system are drawn from field theory, systems theory, organizational development and consultation theories, and ecological psychology.

The systems theorists have provided conceptual frameworks for analyzing organizations of all types as complex social systems with interacting subsystems [Cleland, 1969; Kast and Rosenzweig, 1970; Parsons, 1951; Seiler, 1967; Von Bertalanffy, 1968; Zadeh, 1969]. My own interpretation of some of the applications of their work for human resources development was presented in one of my previous books. [Knowles, 1980, pp. 66-68]

One of the misconceptions in our cultural heritage is the notion that organizations exist purely to get things done. This is only one of their purposes; it is their *work* purpose. But every organization is also a social system that serves as an instrumentality for helping people meet human needs and achieve human goals. In fact, this is the primary purpose for which people take part in organizations—to meet their needs and achieve their goals—and when an organization does not serve this purpose for them they tend to withdraw from it. So organizations also have a human purpose.

Adult education is a means available to organizations for furthering both purposes. Their work purpose is furthered to the extent that they use adult education to develop the competencies of their personnel to do the work required to accomplish the goals of the organizations. Their human purpose is furthered to the extent that they use adult education to help their personnel develop the competencies that will enable them to work up the ladder of Maslow's hierarchy of needs for survival through safety, affection, and esteem to self-actualization.

As if by some law of reciprocity, therefore, organization provides an environment for adult education. In the spirit of Marshall McLuhan's *The Medium Is the Message,* the quality of learning that takes place in an organization is affected by the kind of organization it is. This is to say that an organization is not simply an instrumentality for providing organized learning activities to adults; it also provides an environment that either facilitates or inhibits learning.

For example, if a young executive is being taught in his corporation's management-development program to involve his subordinates in decision-making within his department, but his own superiors never involve him in making decisions, which management practice is he likely to adopt? Or if an adult church member is being taught to "love thy neighbor," but the total church life is characterized by discrimination, jealousy, and intolerance, which value is more likely to be learned? Or if an adult student in a course on "The Meaning of Democratic Behavior" is taught that the clearest point of differentiation between democracy and other forms of government is the citizen's sharing in the process of public policy formulation, but the teacher has never given him a chance to share responsibility for conducting the course and the institution has never asked his advice on what courses should be offered, what is he likely to learn about the meaning of democracy?

No educational institution teaches just through its courses, workshops, and institutes; no corporation teaches just through its in-service education programs; and no voluntary organization teaches just through its meetings and study groups. They all teach by everything they do, and often they teach opposite lessons in their organizational operation from what they teach in their educational program.

This line of reasoning has led modern adult-education theorists to place increasing emphasis on the importance of building an educative environment in all institutions and organizations that undertake to help people learn. What are the characteristics of an educative environment? They are essentially the manifestations of the conditions of learning listed at the end of the last chapter. But they can probably be boiled down to four basic characteristics: 1.) respect for personality; 2.) participation in decision making; 3.) freedom of expression and availability of information; and 4.) mutuality of responsibility in defining goals, planning and conducting activities, and evaluating.

In effect, an educative environment—at least in a democratic culture—is one that exemplifies democratic values, that practices a democratic philosophy.

A democratic philosophy is characterized by a concern for the development of persons, a deep conviction as to the worth of every individual, and faith that people will make the right decisions for themselves if given the necessary information and support. It gives precedence to the growth of *people* over the accomplishment of *things* when these two values are in conflict. It emphasizes the release of human potential over the control of human behavior. In a truly democratic organization there is a spirit of mutual trust, an openness of communications, a general attitude of helpfulness and cooperation, and a willingness to accept responsibility, in contrast to paternalism, regimentation, restriction of information, suspicion, and enforced dependency on authority.

When applied to the organization of adult education, a democratic philosophy means that the learning activities will be based on the real needs and interests of the participants; that the policies will be determined by a group that is representative of all participants; and that there will be a maximum of participation by all members of the organization in sharing responsibility for making and carrying out decisions. The intimate relationship between democratic philosophy and adult education is eloquently expressed in these words of Eduard Lindeman:

One of the chief distinctions between conventional and adult education is to be found in the learning process itself. None but the humble become good teachers of adults. In an adult class the student's experience counts for as much as the teacher's knowledge. Both are exchangeable at par. Indeed, in some of the best adult classes it is sometimes difficult to discover who is learning most, the teacher or the students. This two-way learning is also reflected in the management of adult-education enterprises. Shared learning is duplicated by shared authority. In conventional education the pupils adapt themselves to the curriculum offered, but in adult education the pupils aid in formulating the curricula . . . Under democratic conditions authority is of the group. This is not an easy lesson to learn, but until it is learned democracy cannot succeed. [Gessner, 1956, p. 166]

I have a suspicion that for an organization to foster adult learning to the fullest possible degree it must go even farther than merely practicing a democratic philosophy, that it will really stimulate individual self-renewal to the extent that it consciously engages in continuous self-renewal for itself. Just as a teacher's most potent tool is the example of his own behavior, so I believe an organization's most effective instrument of influence is its own behavior.

This proposition is based on the premise that an organization tends to serve as a role model for those it influences. So if its purpose is to encourage its personnel, members, or constituents to engage in a process of continuous change and growth, it is likely to succeed to the extent that it models the role of organizational change and growth. This proposition suggests, therefore, that an organization must be innovative as well as democratic if it is to provide an environment conducive to learning. Table 4-2 provides some illustrative characteristics that seem to distinguish innovative from static organizations, as I interpret the insights from recent research on this fascinating subject. The right-hand column might well serve as a beginning check list of desirable organizational goals in the dimensions of structure, atmosphere, management philosophy, decision making, and communication.

An expanding group of applicators of systems theory are developing sophisticated procedures and tools for assessing organizational health, diagnosing needs for change, feeding data back into the system for continued renewal and using the data for precision in planning. [Baughart, 1969; Bushnell and Rappaport, 1972; Davis, 1966; Handy and Hussain, 1969; Hare, 1967; Hartley, 1968; Kaufman, 1972; Optner, 1965; Rudwick, 1969; Schuttenberg, 1972]

The change theorists, building largely on the field-theoretical concepts of Kurt Lewin, have been concerned with the planning of change, the choice and use of strategies of change, organizational development, the role of the consultant and change agent, management of conflict, intervention theory, resistance to change, human relations training and the ethics of change agentry. [Argyris, 1962, 1970; Bennis, 1966; Bennis, Benne, and Chin, 1968; Blake and Mouton, 1964; Eiben and Milliren, 1976; Greiner, 1971; Lewin, 1951; Lippitt, 1969; Schein, 1969; Watson, 1967; Zurcher, 1977]

Table 4-2.
Some Characteristics of Static Versus Innovative Organizations

DIMENSIONS	CHARACTERISTICS	
	Static Organizations	Innovative Organizations
Structure	Rigid—much energy given to maintaining permanent departments, committees; reverence for tradition, constitution & by-laws.	Flexible—much use of temporary task forces; easy shifting of departmental lines; readiness to change constitution, depart from tradition.
	Hierarchical—adherence to chain of command.	Multiple linkages based on functional collaboration.
	Roles defined narrowly	Roles defined broadly
	property-bound.	Property-mobile.
Atmosphere	Task-centered, impersonal	People-centered, caring.
	Cold, formal, reserved.	Warm, informal, intimate.
	Suspicious.	Trusting.
Management Philosophy and Attitudes	Function of management is to control personnel through coercive power.	Function of management is to release the energy of personnel; power is used supportively.
	Cautious—low risk-taking.	Experimental—high risk-taking.
	Attitude toward errors: to be avoided.	Attitude toward errors: to be learned from.
	Emphasis on personnel selection.	Emphasis on personnel development.
	Self-sufficiency—closed system regarding sharing resources.	Interdependency—open system regarding sharing resources.
	Emphasis on conserving resources.	Emphasis on developing and using resources.
	Low tolerance for ambiguity.	High tolerance for ambiguity.
Decision-making and Policy-making	High participation at top, low at bottom.	Relevant participation by all those affected.
	Clear distinction between policy-making and policy-execution.	Collaborative policy-making and policy-execution.
	Decision-making by legal mechanisms.	Decision-making by problem-solving.
	Decisions treated as final.	Decisions treated as hypotheses to be tested.
Communication	Restricted flow—constipated.	Open flow—easy access.
	One-way—downward.	Multidirectional—up, down, sideways
	Feelings repressed or hidden.	Feelings expressed.

[Knowles, 1980, p. 69]

A special focus of interest of a number of the researchers and practitioners in this field has been the use of groups as instruments of individual and organizational change. [Bradford, Benne, and Gibb, 1964; Hare, 1962 and 1969; Knowles and Knowles, 1972; Schein and Bennis, 1965; Solomon and Berzon, 1972; Zander, 1982] It is probably a defensible generalization that one of the most pronounced trends in educational practice in schools, universities, industrial and governmental training, and adult educational programs in community and voluntary agencies in the past two decades has been the increasing use of small groups.

The study of group dynamics has begun to produce some generalizations about the factors which affect the value of groups as instruments of change.

1. A group tends to be attractive to an individual and to command his loyalty to the extent that:
   a. It satisfies his needs and helps him achieve goals that are compelling to him.
   b. It provides him with a feeling of acceptance and security.
   c. Its membership is congenial to him.
   d. It is highly valued by outsiders.
2. Each person tends to feel committed to a decision or goal to the extent that he has participated in determining it.
3. A group is an effective instrument for change and growth in individuals to the extent that:
   a. Those who are to be changed and those who are to exert influence for change have a strong sense of belonging to the same group.
   b. The attraction of the group is greater than the discomfort of the change.
   c. The members of the group share the perception that change is needed.
   d. Information relating to the need for change, plans for change, and consequences of change is shared by all relevant people.
   e. The group provides an opportunity for the individual to practice changed behavior without threat or punishment.
   f. The individual is provided a means for measuring progress toward the change goals.

4. Every force tends to induce an equal and opposite counter-force. (Thus, the preferred strategy for change, other things being equal, is the weakening of forces resisting change rather than the addition of new positive forces toward change. For instance, if a group in a factory is resisting a new work procedure, it may be because they don't understand how it will work, in which case a demonstration or trial experience will be superior to exhortation or pressure.)

5. Every group is able to improve its ability to operate as a group to the extent that it consciously examines its processes and their consequences and experiments with improved processes. (In the literature this is referred to as the "feedback mechanism," a concept similar to that used in guided missiles, which correct any deviations from their course while in flight on the basis of data collected by sensitive instruments and fed back into their control mechanism.)

6. The better an individual understands the forces influencing his own behavior and that of a group, the better he will be able to contribute constructively to the group and at the same time to preserve his own integrity against subtle pressures toward conformity and alienation.

7. The strength of pressure to conform is determined by the following factors:
   a. The strength of the attraction a group has for the individual.
   b. The importance to the individual of the issue on which conformity is being requested.
   c. The degree of unanimity of the group toward requiring conformity.

8. The determinants of group effectiveness include:
   a. The extent to which a clear goal is present.
   b. The degree to which the group goal mobilizes energies of group members behind group activities.
   c. The degree to which there is agreement or conflict among members concerning means that the group should use to reach its goal.
   d. The degree to which the activities of different members are coordinated in a manner required by the group's tasks.
   e. The availability to the group of needed resources, whether they be economic, material, legal, intellectual, or other.

f. The degree to which the group is organized appropriately for its task.
g. The degree to which the processes it uses are appropriate to its task and stage of development. [Knowles and Knowles, 1972, pp. 59-61]

Another source of knowledge potentially valuable to educational practice is the emerging field of ecological psychology. Researchers in this field are studying the effects of environmental settings on human behavior and constructing a *theory of behavior settings*. The particular attributes of over- or understaffed settings have been the subject of most of their theoretical work to date. For example, in understaffed settings more people participate in more events and take more responsibility and are less evaluative of one another. Another proposition is that settings in which the participants have a heterogeneity of motives tend to be more stable than those in which there is a homogeneity of motives. [Barker, 1968 and 1963; Barker and Gump, 1964; Ickes and Knowles, 1982; Willems and Raush, 1969]

One of the more or less futile quests of educational researchers over the years has been the identification of the characteristics that distinguish excellent teachers from mediocre teachers. The problem is that the number of variables affecting the teaching-learning situation, (the students' background, genetic equipment, subconscious state, motivation, aspirations) the teacher (the personality, training, educational philosophy, skill) and the environment (social, cultural, physical, administrative forces), are so great, changeable, and hard to measure and control. Stephens (1967), after looking at scores of research reports on the relationship between such variables as teacher characteristics and instructional techniques on the one hand and such measures as test scores and grades on the other, concluded that practically nothing seems to make any difference in the effectiveness of instruction. Similarly, Dubin and Raveggia (1968) examined not only the conclusions but the data of nearly 100 studies made over a forty-year period and concluded that college teaching methods make no difference in student achievement as measured by final examinations. And these are but two of a number of surveys of research that have come to similar conclusions.

The most recent survey, by N.L. Gage in 1972, paints a different picture. Gage questioned the quantitative models and the focus on teacher characteristics in previous research.

> One way to improve these models is to obtain better measures of a large number of the teacher attributes that are significant to the ability of teachers to improve learning. Such measures will come closer to estimating the full effect of teachers, independently of home and school factors. Furthermore, these measures should be aimed at process variables—'those human actions which transform the raw materials of input into opportunities for learning' [Gagne, 1970, p. 170], i.e., teacher activities, rather than teacher characteristics such as amount of education, experience, or verbal ability. [Gage, 1972, p. 34]

Gage examined research using such process measures as the Minnesota Teacher Attitude Inventory and the Flanders' interaction categories and found that "(a) teachers differ reliably from one another on a series of measuring instruments that seem to have a great deal in common. (b) These reliable individual differences among teachers are fairly consistently related to various desirable things about teachers." [*Ibid.*, p. 35]

Among his findings are the following:

> Teachers at the desirable end tend to behave approvingly, acceptantly, and supportively; they tend to speak well of their own students, students in general, and people in general. They tend to like and trust rather than fear other people of all kinds. [*Ibid.*, p. 35]

> Flanders and Simon (1969) concluded from their examination of a dozen studies that *"the percentage of teacher statements that make use of ideas and opinions previously expressed by pupils is directly related to average class scores on attitude scales of teacher attractiveness, liking the class, etc., as well as to average achievement scores adjusted for initial ability"* (p. 1426, italics in original). Ausubel (1963, p. 171) reviewed the experiments on learning by discovery and concluded that the furnishing of completely explicit rules is relatively less effective than some degree of arranging for pupils to discover rules for themselves. It seems safe to say that some use of the guided discovery method, and "indirectness," in teaching is desirable. [*Ibid.*, pp. 36-27]

The third dimension of teacher behavior . . . reflects the teacher's intellectual grasp, or "cognitive organization" of what he is trying to teach. [*Ibid.*, p. 37]

Our last example of a sifting of the literature to identify a desirable kind of teacher behavior is one recently provided by Rosenshine (1970). He reviewed the evidence from a variety of sources on the degree to which the teacher's "enthusiasm" was desirable. Some of the studies reviewed were experiments in which "enthusiasm" was manipulated. In other, correlational, studies, enthusiasm as it occurred "naturally" was rated, counted, or measured with an inventory. In some of the studies, the dependent variable was measured achievement; in others, evaluative ratings of the teacher by his students or other independent observers. The varied evidence seemed remarkably consistent in supporting the desirability of teacher enthusiasm. [*Ibid.*, p. 38]

These four variables—warmth, indirectness, cognitive organization and enthusiasm—merely illustrate the kinds of contributions that research on teaching, in its present early stages, can support. [*Ibid.*, p. 38]

5

Applying Theories of Learning and Teaching to HRD

Coping with the Different Theories

Having explored the jungle of learning and teaching theories, you have a decision to make. What do you do? You have several choices.

Ignore the Theories

For one thing, you can ignore them. You can say they are impractical. They may be all right for the pure psychological scientists and researchers, you can say, but they're too abstract and obtuse to be of much use in planning and operating day-to-day educational programs. The trouble with this choice is that it is unrealistic. The fact is that there are assumptions, concepts, and principles—theories—behind everything you do, whether you are conscious of them or not. If you are planning an educational activity in philosophy, the arts, mathematics, machine operation, orientation of new employees, supervisory training, or management development, you are going to have to make decisions about content, techniques to be used, units of instruction and sequence, time and place, and standards for evaluation. For each decision you will be confronted with a number of options, and your choice will be determined by some idea of what will work best. That is a *theory*.

If you aren't clear about what your theory is—or even whether you have one—the chances are that you will end up with a hodgepodge. You will use different theories in different times or situations, or conflicting theories for different decisions in the same situation. You won't know why you are doing what you are doing. There is a cliche in the applied social sciences—often attributed to Kurt Lewin—that nothing is as practical as a good theory to enable you to make choices confidently and consistently, and to explain or defend why you are making the choices you make.

Pick one Theory

A second choice available is to select one theory and go with it all the way. You can, as does John Murphy in Appendix A, conclude that Skinner's operant conditioning theory makes the most sense to you, provides the clearest guidelines for program design and operation, and assures the most predictable results. Or you can conclude that the *third force* psychologists (Maslow, Rogers et al) are more in touch with human nature as it really is, and make decisions that are congruent with such concepts as self-directed inquiry, positive self-image, and self-actualization. Or you can choose any of the other theories as a workable alternative. But before you take such a big jump, check a few things out.

For example, how does the proposed theory fit your organization's management philosophy? To use Douglas McGregor's (1960) terms, if the management philosophy is Theory X, then Skinner's or any of the other mechanistic theories would fit fine. But if it is Theory Y, one of the organismic theories is indicated. For the assumptions about human nature underlying Theory X management philosophy and the mechanistic learning-teaching models are remarkably similar, as are those underlying Theory Y management philosophy and the organismic learning-teaching models. Table 5-1 presents a comparison of the assumptions about human nature and human behavior by managers subscribing to Theories X and Y as perceived by McGregor (1960, pp. 33-34 and 47-48) with the assumptions implicit in current education and those relevant to significant experiential learning as perceived by Rogers (1972, pp. 272-279).

It seems clear that if a training program based on the assumptions in Rogers' experiential learning model is introduced into an

Table 5-1
A Comparison of the Assumptions About Human Nature and Behavior Underlying Theory X and Theory Y Management Philosophy

Theory X Assumptions about Human Nature (McGregor)	Assumptions Implicit in Current Education (Rogers)
The average human being inherently dislikes work and will avoid it if he can.	The student cannot be trusted to pursue his ow learning.
Because of this characteristically human dislike of work, most people must be coerced, controlled, threatened in the interest of organizational objectives.	Presentation equals learning. The aim of education is to accumulate bric upon brick of factual knowledge.
The average human being prefers to be directed, wishes to avoid responsibility, has relatively little ambition, wants security above all.	The truth is known. Creative citizens develop from passive learner Evaluation is education and education is evalua tion.
Theory Y Assumptions about Human Nature	**Assumptions Relevant to Significant Experiential Learning**
The expenditure of physical and mental effort is as natural as play or rest.	Human beings have a natural potentiality fo learning.
External control and threat of punishment are not the only means for bringing about effort toward organizational objectives. Man will exercise self-direction and self-control in the service of objectives to which he is committed.	Significant learning takes place when the subjec matter is perceived by the student as relevant t his own purposes. Much significant learning is acquired throug doing.
Commitment to objectives is a function of the rewards associated with their achievement.	Learning is facilitated by student's responsibl participation in the learning process.
The average human being learns, under proper conditions, not only to accept but to seek responsibility.	Self-initiated learning involving the whole per son—feelings as well as intellect—is the mos pervasive and lasting.
A high capacity for imagination, ingenuity, and creativity in solving organizational problems is widely, not narrowly distributed in the population.	Creativity in learning is best facilitated whe self-criticism and self-evaluation are primary and evaluation by others is of secondary impor tance.
Under the conditions of modern industrial life, the intellectual potential of the average human being is only partially utilized.	The most socially useful thing to learning i the modern world is the process of learning, continuing openness to experience, an incorpora tion into oneself of the process of change.

organization employing Theory X management philosophy, a dissonance would occur that the organization would not tolerate—unless, of course, the training program is expressly being used to help bring about a change in management philosophy. Equally, if a training program which is based on Rogers' judgment of current education is introduced into an organization employing Theory Y management philosophy, it would be resented and resisted.

Another thing to check before choosing a single theory is its congruence with the organization's long-range developmental goals. If its policy makers see it as a fairly stable, slow-changing organization whose products and processes will remain about the same for ten years, then an HRD program based upon one of the mechanistic models would be appropriate. Educational efforts would be primarily directed at reproducing in new employees the knowledge and skills of the present work force. But if the organization is fast-changing, continuously developing new products and processes, then the HRD program should be based on an organismic model.

Perhaps the fundamental distinction between these two types of organization is in how leadership views the organization as an energy system. Considering the individual as an energy system, Ira Gordon (1968) makes the comparison in Table 5-2 between the Newtonian and the Einsteinian conceptions. [See also, Ingalls, 1976]

The essential difference is that Newtonian physics saw energy as being mechanical, a stable source of power in an absolutely controllable, orderly universe. You get out of a machine what you put into it. This conception of energy is portrayed simplistically in Figure 5-1, in which an input of one erg of energy into a system containing units of matter transforms the energy into one erg of output—less some loss from friction or heat.

In contrast, Einstein's formula $E = mc^2$ presented the idea that atoms of matter contained enormous amounts of energy which could not be released mechanically. But the input of one erg of the right kind (high-speed) of energy into a system containing units of matter would excite these units to release their pent-up energy. Since this energy is uncontrollable it takes lead shields to keep it in bounds and electromagnetic fields to give it direction. This conception of energy is portrayed in Figure 5-2, in which an input of one erg of radiational energy releases (not transforms) hundreds of ergs of energy stored in its units of matter.

Table 5-2 The Individual as an Energy System	
Newtonian Conception	**Einsteinian Conception**
Fixed intelligence	Modifiable intelligence
Development as an orderly unfolding	Development modifiable in rate and sequence
Human potential fixed, though undeterminable at early ages.	Human potential creatable through transaction with the environment
A telephone switchboard brain	A computer brain
Energy output is like that of a steam engine	
Possession of a homeostatic regulator for drive reduction	Possession of an inertial guidance and self-feedback motivational system
Inactivity until the engine is stoked	Continuous activity

If an organization is thought of as an energy system, with the people in it being the units of matter on whom the energy inputs work, Figures 5-1 and 5-2 go a long way toward explaining the differences among organizations I have observed and in which I have worked. In some organizations Newtonian control of the energy of the employees is highly valued and all training is geared to assure that only prescribed behavior is learned. The function of management and supervision is to control the behavior of subordinates. In other organizations Einsteinian release of the energies of the employees is highly valued, and all training is geared to facilitate the development of each individual to his fullest potential.

It is perhaps tempting to make a value judgment about these two kinds of organization, and to proclaim the latter as the only good one. Obviously, both kinds exist and are required. Wherever safety is involved (as in the operating room of a hospital) or absolute precision is necessary (as in an accounting department) the Newtonian model of energy-control is probably appropriate. The important thing is that the learning-teaching theory you choose be one that is congruent with the organization's type of energy system. Appendixes F and G present two examples of the application of the Einsteinian energy system to teaching and human resources development.

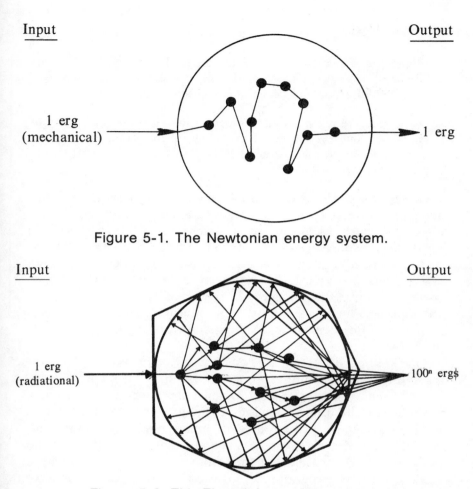

Input   Output

1 erg
(mechanical)   → 1 erg

Figure 5-1. The Newtonian energy system.

Input   Output

1 erg
(radiational)   100^{n} erg$

Figure 5-2. The Einsteinian energy system.

Pick One Theory for Training and One for Education

Nadler, in the foundational book of this series, distinguishes between training and education. Training

is those activities which are designed to improve performance on the job the employee is presently doing or is being hired to do. . .The purpose of training is to either introduce a new behavior or modify the existing behaviors so that a particular and specified kind of behavior results. [Nadler, 1970, pp. 40-41]

Employee education is defined as those HRD activities which are designed to improve the overall competence of the employee in a specified direction and beyond the job now held. [*Ibid.*, p. 60]

In an educational situation, the person likewise brings a variety of behaviors, but it is now hoped that a releasing experience is provided so that he can produce more behaviors than when he entered the situation. [*Ibid.*, p. 41]

Glaser (1962) also distinguishes between education and training and delineates two differences. Training tends to be toward specific objectives, such as operating a machine or following certain regulations, while education tends to be toward broader objectives, such as becoming a cultured gentleman or an effective manager; and training seeks a certain uniformity, a competency that can be counted upon, such as mastery of typing skills that leads to being able to type 60 words a minute, while education seeks to maximize individual differences by discovering and releasing the potential of the individual.

This kind of distinction suggests that different theories of learning and teaching might be appropriate for different kinds of learning. As we have seen previously, Gagne takes the position that there are at least eight different kinds of learning, each requiring different teaching strategies. For purposes of human resources development, Nadler's and Glaser's two-type taxonomy seems more realistic and leads to the proposition that for training, one of the mechanistic models such as programmed instruction or didactic cognitive teaching would be appropriate, while for education an organismic adult educational model such as self-directed learning projects would be more appropriate. Perhaps different types of learning-teaching situations could be put on a continuum, as in Figure 5-3, with two criteria for identifying the appropriate teaching model: complexity of the learning task and level of individual learning ability.

I need to make one thing clear about the meaning of "level of learning ability." Certainly general intelligence is part of it, but I think it also includes previous exposure to the content, readiness to learn, motivation, and perhaps other factors. I have a higher level of ability to learn new things about adult learners (a content area with which I have had previous experience) than to learn new things about nuclear physics (a content area that is totally strange to me).

Let me illustrate how I see this model working in an HRD program. If the operation to be learned is fairly simple (such as operating a simple machine) and the learners' level of learning ability is fairly low, then the behaviorist theories are in touch with that reality, and programmed instruction, linear computer-assisted instruction, behavior modification, or drill are appropriate strategies. If the learning task is moderately complex (such as gaining a knowledge and understanding of the theory behind the operation of the machine), then the cognitive theorists are in touch with that reality, and didactic teaching is appropriate. But if the learning task is highly complex (such as learning to be a more effective manager) and the learners' level of learning ability is high, the humanistic theorists are in touch with that reality, and self-directed learning projects are appropriate. For guidance in selecting the appropriate theorists, I have indicated in Figure 5-3 where I see the major theorists fitting on the continuum.

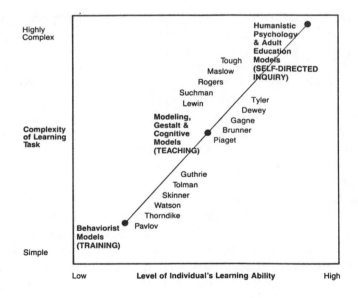

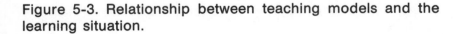

Figure 5-3. Relationship between teaching models and the learning situation.

But if we take seriously the idea of this being a continuum, with self-directed inquiry being the highest form of learning, then we have an obligation to build into our strategies at each level some learning experiences that will help learners move up the continuum. A computer-assisted program could have some branching episodes that help learners upgrade their skills in using teachers and other resource people. Didactic instructors could provide some independent study projects that help learners increase their skill in self-directed inquiry. It has been my experience, in fact, that highly skillful self-directed learners make more effective use of behaviorist programs and didactic teachers than dependent learners do; the more proficient we become as self-directed learners, the better we can make use of all kinds of learning resources. (For case descriptions of self-directed learning programs in a variety of settings, see Boud, 1981.)

Drop the Education of Individuals in Favor of Organization Development

You can take the stand that the training, teaching or self-development of individuals make little long-run difference in the productivity, morale, or effectiveness of the organization, and that therefore the energy of the human resources developer should be directed at changing the organization as a total system. Given this definition of the purpose of human resources development, learning and teaching theories geared to individual development are more or less irrelevant; theories of organizational change are what count. Because Warner Burke has recently made such a strong case for this position (although he makes room for training as part of organization development), I am letting him speak for himself in Appendix K.

I must confess that I have experienced a shift in my role as an adult educator away from managing the logistics of learning activities for collections of individuals and toward educating institutions, influencing the educative quality of whole environments. And I see a similar shift occurring in the professional work of many of my colleagues and former students. But I don't see this as an either-or dilemma; there is need for both the direct facilitation of the development of individuals and the indirect facilitation of their development through improving the educative quality of their environments.

Take the Best from Each Theory

> It is natural that in the early development of the relevant sciences the applied users, the technologists, will tend to be eclectic, picking up a plausible idea here and there, and using it somewhat inventively in the practical situation. [Hilgard and Bower, 1966, p. 265]

Schwab believes that there are "arts of eclectic" which contribute to the teacher's ability "to bring a multiplicity of theoretic stands to bear on the concrete case, thus ensuring a wider view of the hardships and facilitations to be expected in the course of instruction." [Schwab, 1971, p. 506]

The risks of this choice are similar to those of the first choice, ignoring the theories altogether, ending up with a hodgepodge and not knowing why you are doing what you do. Rogers has observed that "the person who attempts to reconcile [different schools of thought] by compromise will find himself left with a superficial eclecticism which does not increase objectivity, and which leads nowhere." [Rogers, 1951, p. 8]

Hilgard again comes to our rescue.

> The option is still open of attempting to guide practical developments by way of one or another of the prevailing theories, or by developing some new model which has more unity than a set of eclectic 'principles.' [Hilgard and Bower, 1966, p. 565]

Here is a skeletal description of my andragogical model of human resources development. It is based on the assumptions about adults as learners presented in Chapter 3 and incorporates features of various prevailing theories that make sense to me.

An Andragogical Model of HRD

Two comprehensive treatments of the andragogical model and its application to the designing and operating of adult educational programs of various sorts are available: *Modern Practice of Adult Education,* and Ingalls and Arceri, *A Trainer's Guide to Andragogy,* 1972. Some moving observations about the application of andragogy to developing countries are contained in Appendix N.

Table 5-3

A Comparison of the Assumptions and Designs of Pedagogy and Andragogy

	Assumptions			Design Elements	
	Pedagogy	Andragogy		Pedagogy	Andragogy
Self-concept	Dependency	Increasing self-directiveness	Climate	Authority-oriented Formal Competitive	Mutuality Respectful Collaborative Informal
Experience	Of little worth	Learners are a rich resource for learning	Planning	By teacher	Mechanism for mutual planning
Readiness	Biological development social pressure	Developmental tasks of social roles	Diagnosis of needs	By teacher	Mutual self-diagnosis
Time perspective	Postponed application	Immediacy of application	Formulation of objectives	By teacher	Mutual nego-tiation
Orientation to learning	Subject centered	Problem centered	Design	Logic of the subject matter ⎯⎯ Content units	Sequenced in terms of readiness ⎯⎯ Problem units
			Activities	Transmittal techniques	Experiential techniques (inquiry)
			Evaluation	By teacher	Mutual re-diagnosis of needs ⎯⎯ Mutual measurement of program

The main purpose here is to demonstrate how a unified model can incorporate principles and technologies from various theories and still maintain its own integrity.

The andragogical model is a *process* model, in contrast to the content models employed by most traditional educators. The difference is this: in traditional education the teacher (or trainer or curriculum committee or somebody) decides in advance what knowledge or skill needs to be transmitted, arranges this body of content into logical units, selects the most efficient means for transmitting this content (lectures, readings, laboratory exercises, films, tapes, etc.), and then develops a plan for presenting these content units in some sort of sequence. This is a *content model* (or design). The andragogical teacher (facilitator, consultant, change agent) prepares in advance a set of procedures for involving the learners (and other relevant parties) in a process involving these elements: (1) establishing a climate conducive to learning; (2) creating a mechanism for mutual planning; (3) diagnosing the needs for learning; (4) formulating program objectives (which is content) that will satisfy these needs; (5) designing a pattern of learning experiences; (6) conducting these learning experiences with suitable techniques and materials; and (7) evaluating the learning outcomes and rediagnosing learning needs. This is a *process model*. The difference is *not* that one deals with content and the other does not; the difference is that the content model is concerned with transmitting information and skills whereas the process model is concerned with providing procedures and resources for helping learners acquire information and skills. A comparison of these two models and their underlying assumptions is presented in Table 5-3 in which the content model is conceived as being pedagogical and the process model as being andragogical.

Establishing a Climate Conducive to Learning

Just as we have witnessed in the past decade a growing concern for the quality of our environment for living, so during the same period there has been increasing concern among educators for the quality of *environments for learning*. From the ecological psychologists we have begun to obtain valuable information about the effects of the physical properties of environment on learning. The social psychologists have taught us much about the effects of the human environment—especially the quality of interpersonal relations. And from the industrial psychologists have come many useful insights about the effects of the organizational environment—the structure, policies, procedures, and spirit of the institution in which learning takes place.

The *physical environment* requires provision for animal comforts (temperature, ventilation, easy access to refreshments and rest rooms, comfortable chairs, adequate light, good acoustics, etc.) to avoid blocks to learning. More subtle physical features may make even more of an impact. Ecological psychologists are finding, for example, that color directly influences mood; bright colors tend to induce cheerful, optimistic moods, and dark or dull colors the opposite.

If you are saying, "But what can I, a mere educator, do about the color of my institution?" let me share an experience I had several years ago. I was meeting with a class of about 50 students in a large classroom in the basement of one of our university buildings. The windows were small and transmitted very little light, so we had to have the yellow ceiling lights on all the time. The walls were painted dusty institutional beige, and two walls were ringed with black chalkboards. During the third meeting of the class, I became conscious of the fact that this class wasn't clicking the way most classes do, and I shared my feeling of discouragement with the students. It took them no time at all to diagnose the problem as being the dolorous environment of our meetings.

One of our learning-teaching teams agreed to experiment with our environment at the next meeting. They went to the dime store and bought brightly colored construction paper and a variety of other materials and objects, the total cost of which was under $5, and made collages for the walls, mobiles for the ceiling and simulated flagstones for the floor. What a happier mood characterized our fourth meeting!

Ecological psychologists also suggest that the size and layout of physical space affects learning quality. In planning the new Kellogg Centers for Continuing Education during the past several decades, great emphasis has been placed on providing small discussion-group-size rooms in close proximity to larger general-session-size rooms. All of them have been provided with round, oval, or hexagon-shaped tables to encourage interaction among the learners. [Alford, 1968;

Knowles, 1980, pp. 163-165] This concern for environmental facilitation of interaction among the learners is supported by the behaviorists' concept of immediacy of feedback, the importance placed on the learner's having an active role by Dewey, and the utilization of the constructive forces in groups by field theorists and humanistic psychologists. [See especially, Bany and Johnson, 1964; Bergevin and McKinley, 1965; Leypoldt, 1967]

Another aspect of the environment which all theorists agree is crucial to effective learning is the richness and accessibility of resources—both material and human. Provision of a basic learning resources center with books, pamphlets, manuals, reprints, journals, films, film strips, slides, tapes and other audio-visual aids and devices is a minimal requirement. In no dimension of education have there been more explosive developments in recent times than in educational media—closed circuit television, videotape and portable videotape machines, cassette audiotapes, technimation, teaching machines, multimedia systems consoles, a variety of information retrieval systems, amplified telephone (for telelectures), learning center systems, language laboratories, computer-assisted instruction and commercially produced simulations and games. [See Rossi and Biddle, 1966]

The important thing is not just that these resources are available but that learners use them proactively rather than reactively—although mechanistic and organismic theorists disagree on this.

Regarding the *human and interpersonal climate* there are useful concepts from many theories. Behaviorists, although not very concerned with psychological climate, would acknowledge that it may reinforce desired behaviors, especially in motivation and transfer or maintenance of learning. An institutional climate in which self-improvement is highly approved (and even better, concretely rewarded), is likely to increase motivation to engage in learning activities. And a climate which approves and rewards new behaviors will encourage the maintenance of these behaviors especially if it allows frequent practice of these new behaviors. This is why supervisors who learn Theory Y behaviors in an outside human relations laboratory so frequently revert to Theory X behaviors after returning to a Theory X environment.

Cognitive theorists stress the importance of a psychological climate of orderliness, clearly defined goals, careful explanation of expectations and opportunities, openness of the system to inspection and questioning, and honest and objective feedback. The cognitive theorists who emphasize learning by discovery also favor a climate that encourages experimentation (hypothesis-testing) and is tolerant of mistakes provided something is learned from them.

Personality theorists, especially those who are clinically oriented, emphasize the importance of a climate in which individual and cultural differences are respected, in which anxiety levels are appropriately controlled (enough to motivate but not so much as to block), in which achievement motivations are encouraged for those who respond to them and affiliation motivations are encouraged for those who respond to them, and in which feelings are considered to be as relevant to learning as ideas and skills. They prescribe a "mentally healthful" climate. [See especially, Waetjen and Leeper, 1966]

Humanistic psychologists suggest that we create psychological climates experienced by the individuals in them as safe, caring, accepting, trusting, respectful, and understanding. The field theorists among them especially emphasize collaboration rather than competitiveness, encouragement of group loyalties, supportive interpersonal relations and a norm of interactive participation.

The andragog would include these characteristics under the heading, An Atmosphere of Adultness, but would give added emphasis to the conditions of mutuality and informality in the climate.

The notion of an *organizational climate* involves several sets of ideas. One set has to do with the policy framework undergirding the HRD program. In some organizations personnel development is relegated to peripheral status in the policy framework (and therefore, there is not much reinforcement of motivation to engage in it). But contemporary organization theorists (Argyris, Bennis, Blake, Drucker, Lippitt, Likert, MacGregor, Odiorne, Schein) assign it a central role in the achievement of organizational goals, and this is the trend among at least the largest organizations. [For examples of policy statements, see Craig and Bittel, 1967, pp. 493-506; and Knowles, 1980, pp. 274-294]

Another set of ideas regarding organizational climate has to do with management philosophy. As discussed earlier in this chapter, a Theory X management philosophy provides an organizational climate that almost dictates mechanistic models of training, and a

Theory Y philosophy requires an organismic (and probably humanistic) model of HRD.

A third aspect of organizational climate, closely related to the second and possibly a part of it, is the structure of the organization. A number of studies have shown that in hierarchically structured organizations there is less motivation for self-improvement and more blocks to learning (such as high anxiety) than in organizations more functionally structured such as by interlinked work groups or by project task forces. [See Marrow, Bowers, and Seashore, 1968; Katz and Kahn, 1966; and Likert, 1961 and 1967] The rapid growth of quality circles in recent years is another manifestation of this trend.

Organizational climate is also affected by financial policies. At the most primary level, the sheer amount of financial resources made available to HRD influences attitudes toward personnel development all the way down the line. When employees see that their organization values HRD highly enough to support it liberally, they are likely to value it—and vice versa. And if in times of austerity, it is the first budget to be reduced, it will come to be seen as a peripheral activity. Perhaps the ultimate signal that an organization has a deep commitment to human resources *development* is when the HRD budget is handled as a *capital investment* (like a new building) rather than as an operating cost. [See Carnevale, 1983]

Finally, a most crucial determinant of climate is the reward system. All learning and teaching theorists would jump on the S-R theorists' bandwagon in acknowledging that those behaviors (including engaging in education) that are rewarded are likely to be maintained. Accordingly, in those organizations in which participation in the HRD program is given obvious weight in wage and salary increases, promotion, and other job emoluments, the climate will certainly be more conducive to learning than in organizations in which the attitude is that learning should be its own reward.

In my own andragogical model, climate setting is probably the most crucial element in the whole process of HRD. If the climate is not really conducive to learning, if it doesn't convey that an organization values human beings as its most valuable asset and their development its most productive investment, then all the other elements in the process are jeopardized. There isn't much likelihood of having a first-rate program of educational activities in an environment that is not supportive of education.

This emphasis on organizational climate has grave implications for the role of the Human Resources Developer. For it implies that of the three roles Nadler assigns to him [Nadler, 1970, pp. 174-246], by far the most critical is the role of *consultant*, within which the most critical subroles are those of advocate, stimulator, and change agent. If the human resources developer sees himself essentially as a teacher and administrator, managing the logistics of learning experiences for collections of individuals, he will have little influence on the quality of the climate of his organization. Only if he defines his client as the total organization, and his mission as the improvement of its quality as an environment for the growth and development of people, will he be able to affect its climate. This means that he must perceive management to be a prime target in his student body, and all the line supervisors as part of his facility. In this conceptualization, training is not a staff function; it is a line function. The job of the Human Resources Developer is to help everybody be a better educator.

The theories most relevant to this set of functions are those of systems analysis [Baughart, 1969; Bushnell and Rappaport, 1972; Davis, 1966; Handy and Hussain, 1969; Hare, 1967; Hartley, 1968; Kaufman, 1972; Optener, 1965; and Schuttenberg, 1972], change theory, consultation, and intervention theory [Argyris, 1962, 1970; Kaufman, 1972; Optener, 1965; and Schuttenberg, 1972], change theory, consultation, and intervention theory. [Arends and Arends, 1977; Argyris, 1962, 1970; Baldridge, 1977; Bennis, 1966; Bennis, Benne, and Chin, 1968; Blake and Mouton, 1964, 1976; Eiben and Milliren, 1976; Goodlad, 1975; Greiner, 1971; Hornstein, 1971; Lippitt, 1969, 1978; Martorana and Kuhns, 1975; Tedeschi, 1972; Tough, 1982; Watson, 1967; Zurcher, 1977]

Creating a Mechanism for Mutual Planning

One aspect of educational practice that most sharply differentiates the pedagogical from the andragogical, the mechanistic from the organismic, and the "teaching" from the "facilitating of learning" schools of thought is the role of the learner in planning. In the first half of each of the above pairs responsibility for planning is assigned almost exclusively to an authority figure (teacher, programmer, trainer). But this practice is so glaringly in conflict with the adult's need to be self-directing that a cardinal principle of andragogy (and, in fact, all humanistic and adult education theory) is that a mechanism must be provided for involving all the parties concerned in the educational enterprise in its planning. One of the basic findings of applied behavioral science research is that people tend to feel committed to a decision or activity in direct proportion to their participation in or influence on its planning and decision-making. The reverse is even more relevant: people tend to feel *uncommitted* to any decision or activity that they feel is being imposed on them without their having a chance to influence it.

It is for this reason that the most potent HRD programs almost always have planning committees (or councils or task forces) for every level of activity: one for organization-wide programs, one for each departmental or other functional group program, and one for each learning experience. There are guidelines for selecting and utilizing these planning groups that will help to assure their being helpful and effective rather than the ineffectual nuisances that stereotypic committees so often are. [See Houle, 1960; Knowles, 1980, pp. 72-78; Shaw, 1969; Trecker, 1970]

Merely having mechanisms for mutual planning will not suffice. They must be treated in good faith, with real delegation of responsibility and real influence in decision making, or they will backfire. Avoid playing the kind of game that Skinner cites (whether with approval or not I can't quite tell) from Rousseau's *Emile*.

Let [the student] believe that he is always in control though it is always you [the teacher] who really controls. There is no subjugation so perfect as that which keeps the appearance of freedom, for in that way one captures volition itself. The poor baby, knowing nothing, able to

do nothing, having learned nothing, is he not at your mercy? Can you not arrange everything in the world which surrounds him? Can you not influence him as you wish? His work, his play, his pleasures, his pains, are not all these in your hands and without his knowing it? Doubtless he ought to do only what he wants; but he ought to want to do only what you want him to do; he ought not to take a step which you have not predicted; he ought not to open his mouth without your knowing what he will say. [Skinner, 1968, p. 260]

Diagnosing the Needs for Learning

Constructing a Model

Constructing a model of desired behavior, performance, or competencies is an effective vehicle for determining learning needs. There are three sources of data for building such a model: the individual, the organization, and the society.

To the cognitive, humanistic, and adult education (andragogical) theorists the individual learner's own perception of what he wants to become, what he wants to be able to achieve, at what level he wants to perform, is the starting point in building a model of competencies; to the behaviorists such subjective data are irrelevant. (And, incidentally, andragogs prefer *competencies*—requisite abilities or qualities—whereas the behaviorists prefer *behavior*—manner of conducting oneself—or performance.) It is not assumed that the learner necessarily starts out contributing his perceptions to the model; he may not know the requisite abilities of a new situation. The human resources developer has some responsibility for exposing him to role models he can observe, or providing him with information from external sources, so that he can begin to develop a realistic model for himself.

Organizational perceptions of desired performance are obtained through systems analyses, performance analyses [Mager, 1972], and analyses of such internal documents as job descriptions, safety reports, productivity records, supervisors' reports, personnel appraisals, and cost/effectiveness studies.

Societal perceptions of desired performance or competencies are obtained from reports by experts in professional and technical journals, research reports, periodical literature, and books and monographs.

The model that is then used in the diagnostic process is ideally one that represents an amalgamation of the perceptions of desired competencies from all these sources, but in case of conflicting perceptions, my practice is to negotiate with the conflicting sources—usually the organization and the individual. I make no bones about the fact that there are "givens" in every situation—such as minimal organizational requirements, and that we have to accept and live with them.

Commercial firms can be contracted with to develop competency models. Among the most experienced in the field are the Competency Development Corporation in Arlington, Massachusetts, McBer Company in Boston, and McGlagan Associates in Minneapolis. A more common (and less expensive) method is through the use of task forces composed of representatives of the individuals, the organization, and society. Westinghouse used task forces to develop the model illustrated in Appendix H. The model presented in Appendix M was developed by a task force of faculty, students, experienced practitioners, and employers. An elaborate model of the competencies for performing the role of human resource developer, developed by a combination of the above strategies, can be obtained from the American Society for Training and Development in Washington, D.C.

In my own experience the excellence of the model is not the most critical factor in the contribution that competency-based education makes to the effectiveness of the learning. The most critical factor is what it does to the mind-set of the learner. When learners understand how the acquisition of certain knowledge or skill will add to their ability to perform better in life, they enter into even didactic instructional situations with a clearer sense of purpose and see what they learn as more personal. It converts course takers and seminar participants into competency developers. [For references on competency-based education, see Berte, 1975, Grant, 1979, Torshen, 1977.]

Assessing Discrepancies

A learning need can be defined as the discrepancy or gap between the competencies specified in the model and their present level of development by the learners.

According to andragogy, the critical element in the assessment of the gaps is the learners' own perception of the discrepancy between where they are now and where they want (and need) to be. So the assessment is essentially a self-assessment, with the human resource developer providing the learners with the tools and procedures for obtaining data and making responsible judgments about their level of development of the competencies. Humanistic psychologists would urge the human resource developer to provide a safe, supportive, nonthreatening atmosphere for what could be an ego-deflating experience. Behaviorists have developed a variety of feedback-yielding tools and procedures that can be adapted to the self-assessment process. See Appendix L for an example of a self-diagnostic tool.

Examples of programs that incorporate the most advanced concepts and technologies of model-building and discrepancy-assessment in industry are the ROCOM Intensive Coronary Multimedia Learning System (ROCOM, 1971), the General Electric Corporation Career Development Program (Storey, 1972, and the Westinghouse Electric Company's Executive Forum (Appendix H). In higher education outstanding examples are Alverno College in Milwaukee, Holland College in Prince Edward Island, the McMaster University Schools of Nursing and Medicine in Hamilton, Ontario, and the University of Georgia School of Social Work. Other sources of information about tools and procedures for diagnosing needs for learning are: Hospital Continuing Education Project, 1970, pp. 7-34; Ingalls and Arceri, 1972, pp. 20-34; Knowles, 1980, pp. 82-119; and Tough, 1979, pp. 64-75.

Formulating Program Objectives

At this point we hit one of the raging controversies among theorists.

Behaviorists insist that objectives are meaningless unless they describe *terminal behaviors* in very precise, measurable, and observable terms. Gagne, for example, defines an objective as . . .

> . . . a verbal statement that communicates reliably to any individual (who knows the words of the statement as concepts) *the set of circumstances that identifies a class of human performances* . . . The kind of statement required appears to be one having the following components:
> 1. A *verb* denoting observable action (draw, identify, recognize, compute, and many others qualify; know, grasp, see, and others do not)
> 2. A description of the *class of stimuli* being responded to [for example, "Given the printed statement $ab + ac = a (b + c)$"]
> 3. A word or phrase denoting *the object used for action* by the performer, unless this is implied by the verb (for example, if the verb is "draw," this phrase might be "with a ruling pen,"; if it is "state," the word might simply be "orally")

4. A description of the *class of correct responses* (for example, "a right triangle," or "the sum," or "the name of the rule." [Gagne, 1965, p. 243]

Mager gives some practical guidelines for defining objectives.

1. A statement of instructional objectives is a collection of words or symbols describing one of your educational *intents*.
2. An objective will communicate your intent to the degree you have described what the learner will be DOING when demonstrating his achievement and how you will know when he is doing it.
3. To describe terminal behavior (what the learner will be DOING):
   a. Identify and name the over-all behavior act.
   b. Define the important conditions under which the behavior is to occur (givens and/or restrictions and limitations).
   c. Define the criterion of acceptable performance.
4. Write a separate statement for each objective; the more statements you have, the better chance you have of making clear your intent.
5. If you give each learner a copy of your objectives, you may not have to do much else. [Mager, 1962, p. 53]

Moving up the scale from the behaviorists, Taba—with a more cognitive orientation—gives "principles to guide the formulation of objectives."

A statement of objectives should describe both the kind of behavior expected and the content or the context to which that behavior applies.

Complex objectives need to be stated analytically and specifically enough so that there is no doubt as to the kind of behavior expected, or what the behavior applies to.

Objectives should also be so formulated that there are clear distinctions among learning experiences required to attain different behaviors.

Objectives are developmental, representing roads to travel rather than terminal points. [Note that at this point she departs sharply from the behaviorists.]

Objectives should be realistic and should include only what can be translated into curriculum and classroom experience.

The scope of objectives should be broad enough to encompass all types of outcomes for which the school [program] is responsible. [Taba, 1962, pp. 200-205]

In elaboration on her last point, Taba develops a classification of objectives by types of behavior.

Knowledge (facts, ideas, concepts)
Reflective thinking (interpretation of data, application of facts and principles, logical reasoning)
Values and attitudes
Sensitivities and feelings
Skills [Taba, 1962, pp. 211-228]

Building on the thinking of Tyler (1950), as did Taba, Houle identifies these attributes of objectives.

An objective is essentially rational, being an attempt to impose a logical pattern on some of the activities of life.
An objective is practical
Objectives lie at the end of actions designed to lead to them.
Objectives are usually pluralistic and require the use of judgment to provide a proper balance in their accomplishment.
Objectives are hierarchical.
Objectives are discriminative.
Objectives change during the learning process. [Houle, 1972, pp. 139-142]

He goes on to give guidelines for stating objectives.

Educational objectives may be stated in terms of the desired accomplishments of the learner.
Educational objectives may also be stated in terms of the principles of action that are likely to achieve desired changes in the learner.
The understanding and acceptance of educational objectives will usually be advanced if they are developed cooperatively.
An objective should be stated clearly enough to indicate to all rational minds exactly what is intended.

In many teaching and learning situations, but particularly in those sponsored by institutions, objectives can be stated not only in terms of the outcomes of education but also in terms of changes in the design components which will presumably make those outcomes better. (facilitative objectives) [Houle, 1972, pp. 147-149]

Theorists who see learning as a process of inquiry expressly (and sometimes rather vehemently) reject the idea that there should be pre-set or prescribed objectives at all. Schwab, for example, takes an unequivocal position.

Educators have long been accustomed to ask at this point in a curricular discussion, "What is the intended outcome?" The question arises from the dogma that curriculums should be devised, controlled, and evaluated in the light of "objectives" taken as the leading principles. Consideration of the practical character of curriculum and instruction convinces me that this dogma is unsound . . . . I do not intend or expect one outcome or one cluster of outcomes but *any one* of several, a plurality. Recognizance of the several stems from consideration not of possible outcomes, but of the materials under treatment: pluralities of theory, their relations to the matter they try in their various ways to subsume, their relations to one another. [Schwab, 1971, p. 540]

Tough (1979), in his analysis of how adults actually engage in independent learning projects, found that goals tended to emerge organically as part of the process of inquiry, with various degrees of clarity and preciseness, and to be continuously changing, subdividing, and spawning offspring.

Maslow, with his conception of self-actualization as the ultimate aim of learning, also sees goal-formation as a highly dynamic process occurring through the interaction of the learner with his experience.

As might be expected, such a position has certain implications for helping us to understand why conventional education in this country falls so far short of its goals. We shall stress only one point here, namely, that education makes little effort to teach the individual to examine reality directly and freshly. Rather it gives him a complete set of prefabricated spectacles with which to look at the world in every aspect, e.g., what to believe, what to like, what to approve of, what to feel guilty about. Rarely is each person's individuality made much of, rarely is he encouraged to be bold enough to see reality in his own style, or to be iconoclastic or different. [Maslow, 1970, p. 223]

Other theorists focus primarily on developing the skills of self-directed inquiry, holding that all other substantive learning objectives flow from the process of accomplishing this one. [Allender, 1972, pp. 230-238; Appendix E]

Perhaps these differences in viewpoint on objectives are partly reconcilable by assigning the more terminal-behavior-oriented procedures to training and the more inquiry-process-oriented procedures to education, much the way we handled teaching models in Figure 5-3. Even then, according to andragogical theory, the learner is likely to resist unless he freely chooses them as being relevant to his self-diagnosed needs. Among the most helpful treatments of the process of formulating objectives in adult education are Hospital Continuing Education Project, 1970, pp. 35-46; Houle, 1972, pp. 136-150 and 200-212; Ingalls and Arceri, 35-42; and Knowles, 1980, pp. 120-126.

Designing a Pattern of Learning Experiences

To the behaviorists program design is essentially a matter of arranging contingencies of reinforcement so as to produce and maintain the prescribed behaviors—as sketched by Murphy in Appendix A. To cognitive and inquiry theorists it is a matter of arranging a sequence of problems that flow according to organic stages of development, and providing appropriate resources for the solving of these problems by the learner. [Bruner, 1966, pp. 71-112: Suchman, 1972, pp. 147-159] To the *third force* psychologists it is a matter of providing supportive environments (usually relatively unstructured groups) in which the participants (learners and trainers together) can help one another grow in existentially determined directions. [Rogers, 1969]

Adult education theorists have tended to build design models into which aspects of all these approaches can be fitted. The three most recent are by Knowles, Tough and Houle (in order of publication). The andragogical design model involves choosing problem areas that have been identified by the learners through self-diagnostic procedures and selecting appropriate formats (individual, group, and mass activities) for learning, designing units of experiential learning utilizing indicated methods and materials, and arranging them in sequence according to the learners' readiness and aesthetic principles. [Ingalls and Arceri, 1972, pp. 43-49; Knowles, 1980, pp. 127-154]

Tough (1979) employs the concept of a *learning project* consisting of a series of related *episodes* as his basic framework for program design. A program would consist of a number of simultaneous individual and group learning projects, each project having been collaboratively planned by learners and selected helpers and carried on at the learners' initiative. The learners could use the whole gamut of human resources (experts, teachers, colleagues, fellow students, people in the community) and material resources (literature, programmed instruction devices and software, and audio-visual media) almost without regard for the theoretical orientation underlying them. Even the most didactic teacher or linear teaching machine program will be used proactively rather than reactively by a self-directed learner.

Houle (1972) has developed a fundamental system of educational design which was described in outline in Chapter 4 and is recapitulated in graphic form in Table 5-4 and Figure 5-4.

Table 5-4
Major Categories of Educational Design Situations

Individual

An individual designs an activity for himself
An individual or a group designs an activity for another individual

Group

A group (with or without a continuing leader) designs an activity for itself
A teacher or group of teachers designs an activity for, and often with, a group of students
A committee designs an activity for a larger group
Two or more groups design an activity which will enhance their combined programs of service

Institution

A new institution is designed
An institution designs an activity in a new format
An institution designs a new activity in an established format
Two or more institutions design an activity which will enhance their combined programs of service

Mass

An individual, group, or institution designs an activity for a mass audience

Source: Cyril O. Houle, *The Design of Education* (San Francisco: Jossey-Bass, 1972), p. 44.

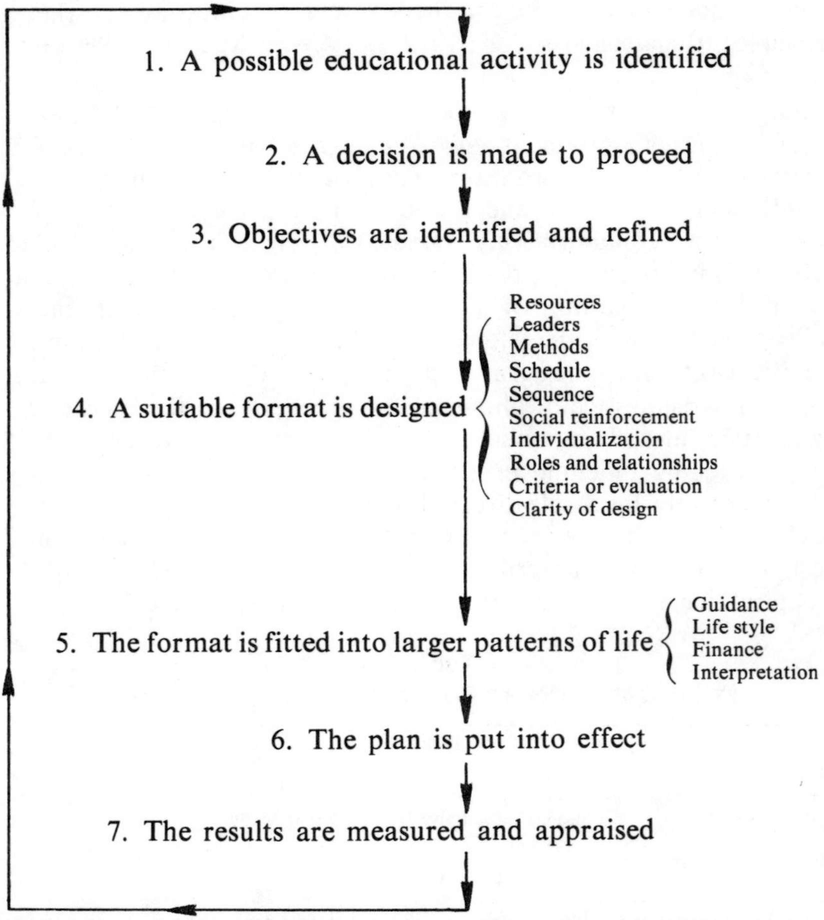

Figure 5-4. Houle's fundamental system: decision points and components of an adult educational framework. (Houle, 1972, p. 47).

One final observation about program design flows from these adult educational models. They assume a high degree of responsibility for learning to be taken by the learner; in the andragogical and learning projects models, especially, the entire systems are built around the concept of self-directed learning. But by and large, the adults we work with have not learned to be self-directing inquirers; they have been conditioned to be dependent on teachers to teach them. And so they often experience a form of culture-shock when first exposed to truly adult educational programs.

For this reason, I am increasingly building into my designs of programs for new entrants a preparatory *learning-how-to-learn* activity. This activity may range from an hour to a day in length, depending upon the length and intensity of the total program, and consists of the following elements:

First, a brief explanation of the difference between proactive and reactive learning, along the lines presented in Appendix I.

Second, a short experience in identifying the resources of the participants (who knows what, or has had experience doing what) and establishing collaborative, I-Thou (rather than It-It) relationships with one another as human beings. For this exercise I use groups of four or five participants.

Third, a miniproject in using the skills of proactive learning described in Appendix G, such as reading a book proactively, or using a supervisor proactively.

It has been my experience that even a brief experiential encounter with the concepts and skills of self-directed learning helps adults to feel more secure in entering into an adult educational program. For a manual on how to help people become self-directed learners, see Knowles, *Self-Directed Learning: A Guide for Learners and Teachers,* 1975.

Operating the Program (Conducting Learning Activities)

This element of the program development process is concerned focally with the human resources developer's role as administrator, and learning-teaching theories have very little to say about this role. Nadler, [1970, pp. 202-231] describes the functions associated with this role, and ideas about how to carry them out andragogically are developed in Ingalls and Arceri, 1972, pp. 54-62 and Knowles, 1980, pp. 155-197.

I see the centrally crucial factor in program operation to be the quality of faculty resources. The current manpower sources for teachers of HRD activities contain people who only know how to teach in the traditional pedagogical fashion, since this is the way they were taught or were taught to teach. You can't rely very much on selection procedures to provide you with good teachers. You have to train them yourself, through both preservice and inservice educational programs. I would say that the single most critical aspect of your role as program administrator is your function as a developer of human resources development personnel. [See Knowles, 1980, pp. 159-162]

Evaluating the Program

Here is the area of greatest controversy and weakest technology in all of education, especially in adult education and training. As Hilgard points out regarding educational technology in general, "*It has been found enormously difficult to apply laboratory-derived principles of learning to the improvement of efficiency in tasks with clear and relatively simple objectives. We may infer that it will be even more difficult to apply laboratory-derived principles of learning to the improvement of efficient learning in tasks with more complex objectives.*" [Hilgard and Bower, 1966, p. 542, italics in original] This observation applies doubly to evaluation, the primary purpose of which is to improve teaching and learning—not, as so often misunderstood, to justify what we are doing. One implication of Hilgard's statement is that difficult as it may be to evaluate training, it is doubly difficult to evaluate education.

Donald Kirkpatrick's [Craig and Bittel, 1976, pp. 18-1 to 18-27; Kirkpatrick, 1971, pp. 88-103] conceptualization of the evaluation process is the most congruent with andragogical principles and the most practical of all the formulations seen to date. He conceives of evaluation as four steps, all of which are required for an effective assessment of a program.

The first step is *reaction evaluation*, getting data about how the participants are responding to a program as it takes place—what they like most and least, what positive and negative feelings they have. These data can be obtained through end-of-meeting reaction forms, interviews or group discussions. It is usually desirable to feed back data from one session at the beginning of the next session, so that indicated program modifications can be negotiated.

The second step is *learning evaluation*, which involves getting data about the principles, facts, and techniques which were acquired by the participants. This step should include both pretests and posttests, so that specific gains resulting from the learning experiences can be measured. Performance tests are indicated (such as operating a machine, interviewing, speaking, listening, reading, writing, etc.) for skill learning. Either standardized or tailor-made information-recall tests or problem-solving exercises can be used to gauge knowledge. Such devices as attitudinal scales, role playing or other simulations, or critical-incident cases may yield helpful progress in attitude-learning.

The third step is *behavior evaluation*, requiring data such as observers' reports about actual changes in what the learner does after the training as compared with what he did before. Sources of this kind of data include productivity or time-and-motion studies, observation scales for use by supervisors, colleagues, and subordinates, self-rating scales, diaries, interview schedules, questionnaires, etc.

The fourth step is *results evaluation*, data for which are usually contained in the routine records of an organization—including effects on turnover, costs, efficiency, frequency of accidents or grievances or tardiness or absences, quality control rejections, etc.

The main difficulty in evaluation, as in research, is in controlling the variables sufficiently to be able to demonstrate that it was the training that was mainly responsible for any changes that occurred. For this reason, Kirkpatrick recommends using control groups whenever possible.

All learning and teaching theorists acknowledge the importance of evaluation. Behaviorists maintain that evaluation is built into their very process—when a learner makes an error in a frame of a teaching machine program it shows up immediately and corrective action is taken and if a program doesn't produce the prescribed behavior, it is modified until it does. They insist that evaluation is intrinsic to their process—not something that happens at a different time from learning. To some degree, Kirkpatrick's *reaction evaluation* employs this principle.

Cognitive theorists stress the importance of the learner's ability to retrieve and apply information to new problems as the key to evaluation, which is what *learning evaluation* is essentially about. Field theorists and humanistic psychologists emphasize the translation of learning into behavior back home or in the field (the humanists, of course, stressing self-actualizing behavior), which is the purpose of *behavior evaluation*. Organization theorists point out that unless desirable results can be demonstrated, management will withhold support from training—which is the essence of *results evaluation*.

I should like to add a fifth dimension which springs directly from the fundamental conception of adult education as continuing education—*rediagnosis of learning needs*. If every learning experience is to lead to further learning, as continuing education implies, then every evaluation process should include some provision for helping the learners re-examine their models of desired competencies and reassess the discrepancies between the model and their newly developed levels of competencies. Thus repetition of the diagnostic phase becomes an integral part of the evaluation phase.

What has been said above describes the state of the art in program evaluation until very recently. But starting around 1977, the leading theorists and practitioners in the field of program evaluation began making almost a 180° turn in their very way of thinking about evaluation. During the preceding 40 years, there had been a growing emphasis on *quantitative* methods of evaluation. The norm was set that if evaluation didn't have numbers and statistics attached to it, it wasn't respectable. In the late 1970's evaluators began having second thoughts about what they were learning from their quantitative evaluations that was making so much difference in what was happening in programs. They began to realize that there is a difference between *measurement* and *evaluation*.

Evaluation, they began to report in the literature, requires getting inside the skulls of the participants—and inside the social systems in which they are performing—and finding out what is happening in their way of thinking, feeling, and doing. This is *qualitative* evaluation. It requires using such methods as participant observation, in-depth interviews, case studies, diaries, and other ways of getting "human" data. By getting the whole picture of "real-life" effects of a program first, they were then able to determine what quantitative data were needed to correlate real outcomes with program operations. So now the state of the art involves *both* quantitative and qualitative data, but with the qualitative coming first. The results have been astounding. So much more useful information is being obtained from this combination. The best current sources of information about this new development are Cronbach, 1980, Guba and Lincoln, 1981, and Patton, 1980, 1981, and 1982. This turn of events becomes even more convincing when one realizes that all of these people made their first reputations as leaders of the quantitative evaluation movement.

Contract Learning—A New Way to Put It All Together

Without question the single most potent tool I have come across in my almost half-century of experience with adult education is contract learning. It has solved more problems that plagued me during my first 40 years than any other invention. It solves the problem of the wide range of backgrounds, education, experience, interests, motivations, and abilities that characterize most adult groups by providing a way for individuals (and subgroups) to tailor-make their own learning plans. It solves the problem of getting the learner to have a sense of ownership of the objectives he or she will pursue. It solves the problem of identifying a wide variety of resources so that different learners can go to different resources for learning the same things. It solves the problem of providing each learner with a visible structure for systemizing his or her learning. Finally, it solves the problem of providing a systematic procedure for involving the learner responsibly in evaluating the learning outcomes.

I now use learning contracts in all of my academic courses and in the in-service education programs in educational institutions, industry, and the professions in which I am a consultant. Learning contracts are being used by a number of continuing professional development programs in medicine, nursing, dentistry, engineering, social work, and the ministry. Appendix H describes how Westinghouse Electric Corporation uses the tool under a different label—"Continuing Personal Development Plan."

Turn to Appendix J to see how it works.

The Evolving Meaning of Human Resources Development

As I see it, Human Resources Development is more than just a higher sounding name for what we have always done. It is *not* just a synonym for training or in-service education or management development or even for manpower development. If it were only this, one or more of the traditional learning theories would serve.

I am beginning to visualize Human Resources Development as something deeper and more comprehensive than any of these concepts, and I hope that this book will stimulate others to sharpen the vision—a vision that includes McGregor's and Likert's (and others') conception of all organizations as human enterprises in their most vital essence. It includes the conception of systems theorists and organization development theorists of an organization as a dynamic complex of interacting subsystems of people, processes, equipment, materials, and ideas. It includes the conception of modern economic theorists that the input of human capital is an even more critical determinant of organizational output than material capital. It also includes the nuclear physicists' conception of an energy system that is infinitely amplifiable through the releasing of energy rather than the control of energy. It envisions the role of the Human Resources Developer as being perhaps more crucial than any other role in determining which organizations will be alive twenty years from now and which will be extinct.

I see a drastically new role evolving for the human resource developer as we begin to conceptualize an organization as a *system of learning resources*. The role of human resource developers then becomes that of manager of these systems—quite a different role from that of the past, as manager of the logistics of operating training programs of courses, workshops, seminars, and other scheduled activities.

In this new role they have to ask a very different set of questions from the questions they have traditionally asked. The first question they have to ask is, "What are *all* of the resources in our system that are potentially available for the growth and development of people?" A typical organization will come up with a list like this:

1. Scheduled instructional activities.
2. All line supervisors and managers.
3. Materials and media, including packaged programs, computer programs, and the like.
4. Content specialists (who often use their content specialty for work, but not for education).
5. Other individuals with special resources, including retired employees.
6. Community resources, including educational institutions and commercial providers.
7. Professional associations.

The second question the human resource developers will then have to ask is, "How can we make more effective use of these resources for the systematic and continuous development of our people?" And some of the answers they might come up with might look like this:

Scheduled instructional activities could be redesigned so as to be more congruent with principles of adult learning. The resource people conducting them could be given special training on how to treat learners as adults.

The line supervisors and managers could be exposed to the idea that their role is not just to supervise work, but to develop their people as well. Substantial blocks of time could be built into the supervisory training and management development programs dealing with the principles of adult learning and the skills of facilitating learning. The human resources developers and their staffs could be available to the line officers as consultants in performing their role as facilitators of learning. An example of how the personnel in an organization can be coached to serve as tutors to others is described in Appendix M.

The materials and media could be selected according to their congruence with the theory of learning appropriate to the situations in which they will be used. They can be made more accessible to all the people in the system than is often the case now.

Information about the remaining resources—content specialists, other individuals, community resources, and professional associations—can be collected and put into a data bank, which can serve as a clearinghouse or educational brokering center. [see Heffernan, Macy, and Vickers, 1976]

Learning contracts—developed as an integral part of the supervisory process—can provide the means for helping individuals make use of all these resources in a systematic program of continuous self-development.

As systems of learning resources evolve, the human resources developers must increasingly radiate a professional confidence. It will no longer suffice to be a good learning specialist, a good administrator, and a good consultant. They will have to know more than learning specialists, administrators, and consultants know. They will have to know a new theory of human resources development and possess a new set of skills in applying that theory to their systems. How much more rewarding this role will be!

The idea of a system of learning resources is spelled out in more detail in Appendix E.

Appendix A

Is It Skinner or Nothing?*

The public response to B.F. Skinner's *Beyond Freedom and Dignity*[1] reveals a good deal more about the public than it does about Skinner or this work; and it reveals a good deal more about management's perceptions of training than you and I can afford to ignore.

The response has been more extensive, more uniformly antagonistic and more intensely stated than that touched off by any other book during 1971. Skinner has been the subject of a *Time* magazine cover story, a *New York Times* interview, editorial and cover book review, a *Newsweek* education column and countless other reviews. He has guest-appeared on Today, Dick Cavett, David Frost, Firing Line, and CBS Morning News. The book was widely circulated as a condensation in *Psychology Today*. The American Psychological Association gave him its annual award. *Time* quoted his colleagues' description as "the most influential psychologist in the country." The book has been number 3 on the best-seller list. But you get the idea.

This would be a remarkable achievement for any semi-technical book, but on top of that:

● The author has been almost entirely out of the public limelight since the early 1960's.

● What image did survive associated ("pigeon-holed?") him with "short step/immediate-feedback," dull rote learning, and the replacement

---

Training and Development Journal, Vol. 26, No. 2 (February, 1972), 2-8. By permission.

of tail-fins by teaching machines as the nation's hardware sex symbol. Who among us has not damned him with the faint praise, "Well, at least we learned to specify behavioral objectives out of that PI thing."

● The targets of the most heated attacks are positions which Skinner presented (and presented more forcibly) years ago.

Any one of these should have given publisher, Alfred Knopf great qualms. But against these odds the spectacular commercial success and critical reaction has occurred, and that suggests that somehow Skinner has struck a sensitive nerve. But this extraordinary emotional reaction has diverted attention away from the only issues that make much practical difference *today*. How much of it is relevant to training? How much of it works? Under what conditions?

To answer that we need to examine:

1. Skinner's fundamental position on *the* cause of behavior (because that will be the acid test of your willingness to implement principles of learning which he derives from it).
2. The most consistent critical reactions (because they are the objections you and I will also encounter) and an imputed Skinnerian rebuttal (because we can't overcome those objections with just our own fancy footwork).
3. The principles of learning which he has developed experimentally and what they tell us about designing training (because if we can't use this technology to increase our reliability in predicting and delivering behavior, we are not about to go very far in the business world).

Skinner on Learning

At a Training Research Forum seminar in 1971, Dr. Skinner brought literally every learning principle he has ever stated back to a six-word premise:

'Behavior is Determined
by Its Consequences'

Period. That's it. Either you buy that or you don't. If you don't, stop reading—there is not much here you can use effectively. If you do, then the other controversial, painful conclusions in *Beyond Freedom and Dignity* follow inescapably from it. Perhaps a lot of the emotionalism about behaviorism springs from discomfort with that unforgiving go/no-go switch. Even if you say, "I believe that *some* behavior is determined by its consequences," the kindly doctor will shoot from the hip with five quick questions and you're dead—shot with your own bullets. "Face it," the man says, "Thursday's behavior is caused by Wednesday's consequences of Tuesday's behavior?"

If behavior is determined by its consequences, then the way to change behavior is to change the consequences and rearrange the "*contingencies* of the reinforcement.*" The question is not only "what *is* the consequence," but "in what way (by what contingency) is the consequence (reinforcement) *related* to the behavior?"

This represents a significant change in emphasis for Skinner, and in fact, much of the current criticism is still aimed at the "stimulus-response" straw-man of the early 1960's. He is concerned by that misperception, because it clouds what he now sees as a more critical concept, the role of *consequences* as the only real shaper of behavior. He now emphasizes that "Learning does not occur because behavior has been primed (stimulated); it occurs because behavior, primed or not, is *reinforced.*"

Critics on Skinner

Unfortunately, the critical response to the book has focused on the academic issue of whether man is inherently autonomous and whether it is ethical to "manipulate" him (just in case it turns out he wasn't autonomous after all). That focus is unfortunate, because the argument leads nowhere and draws attention away from the real issue:

> What evidence is there that behavior is controlled by its consequences, and how can that make us more effective in helping people to learn, and more reliable when we make commitments to develop a specific level of human performance?

Time's definition of behavioral technology may be the most rational summary statement made by the press: "Behavioral technology is a developing science that aims to change the environment rather than people, that seeks to alter actions rather than feelings, and that shifts the customary psychological emphasis on the world inside men to the world outside them."[2]

But from that point on, there is a high content of emotional static because "Skinner's program runs counter to the traditional humanist image of man as an autonymous individual possessed of a measure of freedom and personal dignity."[3] Novelist Arthur Koestler's not-very-helpful response is typical: "(Behavioral technology is) . . . a pseudo-science . . . a monumental triviality that has sent psychology into a modern version of the dark ages."[4] You do have to agree that, if the Koestlers see that much power in behavioral technology as a "trivality," it's certainly understandable that they would not want to recognize it as having any great substance.

The most consistent specific criticisms seem to derive from the autonomy hang-up:

1. "You shouldn't have to bribe or manipulate people with frequent and scheduled bursts of reinforcement." Skinner attributes much of the criticism of his work, and, for that matter, much of the ineffectiveness of our social programs, to the non-scientific concept, "should." John Cline, project director for Project Alpha (one of the performance contracts in public education) expressed his own exasperation with criticism of his use of rewards in the classroom to reinforce learning: "We hear from people that the kid should *want* to succeed. Well, goddamn yeah, he *should*. But he *doesn't*."[5]

2. "People aren't pigeons."
   As far as I know, Skinner has never admitted to an inability to discriminate people from pigeons. What he does say is that "what is common to pigeon and man is a world in which certain contingencies of reinforcement prevail. The schedule of reinforcement which makes a pigeon a pathological gambler is to be found at a racetrack and a roulette table—here it has a comparable effect."[6]

3. "Even if there is some validity to Skinner's position, he makes it impossible to deal with because he insists that his is the only truly scientific way to study behavior and learning."

Well, Skinner argues, what are its alternatives? "Let's evaluate behavioral technology . . . only in comparison with what is done in other ways. What, after all, have we to show for non-scientific good judgment or common sense or the insights gained through experience?" If you believe, with Skinner, that we have here the rudiments of a new science-based technology, then is there any more reason to accept *other* explanations for his experimentally-derived results than the physicist has for agreeing with Aristotle's view that an object falling toward earth increases its velocity because it became more "jubilant" as it neared the ground? Once you have documented the relationship between behavior and its consequences, can you allow for other superstitions and theories which propose undocumented counter positions?

But then, even the critic goes on to say that "the most terrifying thing about Skinner's claim is that he is probably right . . . the behavioral technology capable of eliminating man's inner core of subjectivity is for all practical purposes currently available."[7]

4. "Even though man is autonomous and can't be controlled by others, it's still unethical to do so."

Skinner takes the usually acceptable scientific position that he is merely a systematic observer of what is already going on, the everyday reality which is already much as he describes it. People may be unaware of what they are doing, but conditioning and reconditioning of behavior is going on all the time. "The fundamental mistake" which he attributes to the humanists and inner-man devotees, "is to assume that their methods leave the balance of control to the individual, when in fact they leave it to other conditions."

What's in It for Us Training Types?

Two things:

● We need to get better operational control of Skinner's conclusions about how people learn, because we're not going to become reliably productive in the business world until we do.

● Skinner's critics have done us a service, by verbalizing in a cogent manner the partially-hidden assumptions our top-management people often have about the whole concept of planned behavior change.

Trainers and Unreliability

Seven years have slipped away since Colonel Ofiesh asked, "Can the science of learning be applied to the art of pedagogy? . . . Can the studies of learning be applied to training and education? . . . the effort to apply what we know (?) about learning to the art of teaching has been a colossal failure."[8] And I would argue that we're not much further ahead in 1972.

Let's stop looking at this as a rhetorical question—it isn't. The value of a science is that it permits one to predict outcomes. In the corporation, the success of the marketing or production vice president is based on his ability to predict (budget) and deliver some quantified economic value. The issue of whether he does so on the basis of "science" doesn't come up because he usually predicts tolerably well and seldom is asked to produce a scientific basis for his prediction. If we want to play with the big boys, the name of the game is *predict* (i.e., take accountability for) results and deliver. By and large, we can't do that very well now, and the only light spot on the horizon I see is the opportunity to harness learning theory. If we don't soon command some learning theory and its applications to reliable predictions, we've got about the same chance of getting management to entrust the training department with vital responsibility as has the employees' picnic committee.

Aside from the emotional fluff, what is there in Skinner's work that the trainer can use to increase his reliability and effectiveness? Back to catechism lesson one:

'Behavior is Determined by Its Consequences'

The progression of logic continues as follows:

1. Behavior change (learning) can be achieved only by changing the consequences and their contingent relationship with the behavior in question.
2. The task of teaching thus becomes arranging contingencies of reinforcement.
3. The role of training in an organization can then be defined:

Training is the function in an organization which identifies, develops and maintains those behaviors required for the organization to reach its goals. Where changes in behavior are required, they are achieved by arranging the contingencies of reinforcement under which people learn. This may be accomplished through traditional training programs, or through changes in the operating system if that happens to be where the controlling contingencies are located. This function may be dispersed throughout the organization (to line supervisors, to other staffs, etc.) depending on their natural access to the contingencies involved.[9]

4. Learning manifests itself only when an organism modifies its behavior in response to a given stimulus.
5. Learning proceeds with three kinds of responses:
    a. Discrimination (between classes)
    b. Concept formation (i.e., generalization among classes based on similarity of some characteristic)
    c. Chaining (a series of responses in which the reinforcer of one response becomes the stimulus for the next response).
6. Behavior which has reinforcing consequences (reward) is more likely to occur again.
7. Behavior which has aversive consequences (punishment) is less likely to occur again; but the relative power of punishment in changing behavior is miniscule compared with the power of positive reinforcement.
8. Behavior which goes unreinforced is eventually extinguished.
9. Confirmation to the learner that he has modified his behavior toward a desired outcome is reinforcing to him.
10. The major difference between learners is the rate at which learning occurs, not the way in which it occurs.

11. One of the critical contingencies is the time lapse between behavior and its reinforcement. When the consequences of behavior occur immediately, the chances of that behavior occurring again are greater than if there is a delay of as little as one day. "No one is ever actually reinforced by remote consequences, but rather by mediating reinforcers which have acquired their power through some connection with them." Since most of the reinforcers in the business world are not very immediate (compensation, promotion, formal acclaim), a central task of training is to *meditate the remote reinforcers* (make the ultimate consequences of behavior more immediate).

    For example, the ultimate reinforcer of newly-trained selling behavior is sales closed and other follow on rewards. Usually these occur some days after the behavior is introduced in the sales training session, and are relatively weak reinforcers of behavior occurring in training. A Skinnerian solution would be to simulate reality by paying the salesman off in cash or other tangible values right in the training setting as he exhibits each new approximation to the desired behavior.

    In fact, we could generalize from this to say that Skinner's approach to the problem of transfer would put the highest emphasis on simulating the job situation—its stimuli, its reinforcers, the contingency relationship between response and consequence, and any other important inputs to the individual in that job.

    Communications skills are often "taught" by taking the trainee through an example or a role play. The trainee may indeed engage in the behavior which someone defines as "effective communication," but "if the behavior is entirely under the control of the instructor or role partner, it is probably not being brought under the control of stimuli which will be encountered in similar problems on the job."

12. While the *transfer* of behavior to the job depends on bringing it under the control of stimuli in training that are similar to those on the job, the need to provide for the *maintenance* of that behavior over long periods of time imposes another requirement. Even if the learner's supervisor is supportive of the new behavior, he is not a very reliable reinforcer for two reasons:

    First, he has neither the skills nor the time to discriminate and reinforce the desired behavior on an effective schedule.

    Second, his predictability as a reinforcer is pretty shaky because his own behavior will change in response to the effect his reinforcement has on the learner. The supervisor and learner may start an escalation of mutual reinforcement that is impossible to predict and allow for.[10]

Because of this, Skinner stresses the importance of "making a person dependent on *things* rather than on other people." In other words, build into the environment mechanisms which are triggered when reinforcible behavior occurs. For a salesman, for example, the ideal built-in reinforcer would be a firm order on those calls in which he uses the appropriate behavior. That ideal can in fact be realized if the salesman has been prepared in training to maintain the behavior even if it is reinforced in only a small percent of the occasions in which he uses it.

Where the sales trainer lacks the confidence to rely on that ideal situation, others must be built in. If, for example, the salesman files a written contact report on each call, he might indicate the calls on which he felt he had done a better than usual job of using the particular skill. The sales manager's secretary could be trained to recognize reinforcible reports (a far simpler task than recognizing the degree of the behavior itself). She would flag it for the sales manager who would send it back to the salesman with a short comment recognizing the specific behavior and encouraging him to continue and develop its use.

13. In addition to the accuracy and immediacy of the reinforcement, the other major contingency is the "*schedule* of reinforcement." This concept recognizes that it is impractical (and often undesirable) to reinforce *every* appropriate response, and offers several alternative schedules of the relationship between behavior and reinforcement. Two special situations are worth knowing about:

The Variable-Ratio Schedule

This is the gambler's schedule and the most powerful of all behavior shapers. Reinforcement of the desired behavior occurs randomly. Since the learner does not know which reponse will be reinforced, he will make the response (put the quarter in the slot machine or keep each production unit within specs) many, many times regardless of the infrequency of reinforcement (a jackpot or a satisfactory quality control check). He is "hooked" as they say, and a bare minimum of reinforcement will sustain that behavior for long periods of time.

Stretching the Ratio

This technique ought to be a central objective of any training design. It also deals with the problem of sustaining behavior on the job with the relatively small number of reinforcements available there, as opposed to the 1-1 ratio which is possible in the training situation. Stretching the ratio means that the 1-1 training ratio is gradually stretched to 5-1 or 100-1, or whatever approximation of the job condition can be achieved—*before the learner leaves the training experience.*

14. And this gem: "To *acquire* behavior, the learner must *engage* in behavior." Read that one again.

Applications to Training Design

These learning principles can be used to design and evaluate training by examining the following variables:

1. The stimuli presented on the job.
2. The responses to those stimuli.
3. The consequences of those responses.
4. The contingencies of reinforcement/consequences (their relationship to the response).
5. Items 1—4 in the *training* experience.
6. Items 1—4 in the redesigned job situation.

The questions the behaviorist asks about these variables include:

1. Are the descriptions of each element clear enough to discriminate whether or not it has occurred?
2. Do the elements in the learning situation approximate as closely as possible those of the redesigned job situation?
3. To the extent that the training stimulus and response cannot simulate the work stimulus and response, does the training develop behavior which will enable the worker to adapt to these discrepancies on the job?
4. Have the punishing or interfering consequences of the behavior on the job been minimized?

A Way to Begin

Probably the most successful application of reinforcement theory with dollar payoff has been the work of Ed Feeney, Vice President, Systems Performance, at Emery Air Freight. Feeney's process and spectacular results have been documented elsewhere for ASTD members. For our purpose, a short probing sequence which is the key to his success is a good starting point. Given evidence that some specific performance indicator needs to be improved, Feeney asks:

1. What is the standard of performance?
2. Does the employee know the standard?
3. How well does the employee *think* he is doing?
4. How well does his supervisor think he is doing?
5. What aversive consequences of the desired behavior may be suppressing it?
6. What is reinforcing the undesired behavior?
7. What natural or contrived reinforcers are at hand in the immediate work environment to begin reinforcing the desired behavior?
8. What aversive consequences of the undesired behavior are at hand?
9. What learner responses are already available in embarking on a program of progressive approximation to the desired behavior?
10. What schedule of reinforcement is most efficient for developing and maintaining the desired behavior?
11. What reinforcers are available to reward the worker's supervisor for reinforcing the worker's new behavior?

An important benefit of this approach is that it sidesteps the philosophical issue about autonomous man. It comes across as a straightforward, workmanlike business problem analysis. If the jargon is left out, managers don't feel uncomfortable in proceeding this way, and Emery Air Freight has over $2,000,000 in increased profit, tied directly to this approach, to prove it.

Autonomous Man and Your
Chief Executive Officer

Not all company situations, however, will let you get that far without raising the issue of whether man is or ought to be controlled by things outside himself. If an organization has been infected by the "motivation" virus it will be more difficult to overcome the religious fervor about "building a fire under a man" to get him to "realize his potential," and like that.

I like Tom Gilbert's analysis:

These programs have been sold through articulate and appealing rationales. Mostly, their appeal has been the historical appeal of the "psychology of personality"—theories about the "inner man." They promise to show the executive how to better understand the basic and innermost motives and attitudes of himself and others—and they also seem to promise that such intimate knowledge will lead the executive to being a more effective manager. The appeal of motivational hierarchies, sensitivity training, attitudes that can be plotted on a grid, and the like, has been similar to the appeals of psychoanalysis and religion—these programs really began with Freud and modern theologians who have promised power and peace through inner knowledge. But if the appeal has been as great, the success is equally hard to evaluate . . . We don't get very far by choosing attitudes and inner motives as variables, not because those things don't exist, but because we can't directly manipulate them—and perhaps we have no business trying to. Thus, we look to what we can directly affect: a man's environment . . . his patterns of reinforcement, the feedback of information, those events that interfere with his performance, and the quality of the stimuli to which he is expected to respond . . . This may have the side effects of changing a man's attitudes, his motivation—but these results are in fact side effects, not directly manipulable materials."

At the Training Research Forum Seminar, we asked Skinner to illustrate the difference between his position and those of the various human relations and motivation alchemists. Their problem, he responded, is that "they try to deal with things *in the person.* Our 'knowledge' of people keeps us from looking scientifically at the shaping factors which occurred in their past." Graphically, he sees behavior as the starting point for both himself and motivationalists.

But, they make the mistake of trying to infer from the behavior "what is going on inside" the person that "motivates" him to behave so. "These attempts to explain behavior by recourse to inner-man attributes are no explanation *until someone explains the explanation.*" Skinner has very little patience with the cognitive (or as he calls them, the "mentalism") group. To him, "the important objection to 'mentalism' is that the world of the mind steals the show. Behavior is not recognizable as a subject in its own right." What's more, he says, "those who object most violently to the manipulation of behavior make the most vigorous efforts to manipulate minds."

'The Way I Did It'

The immediate problem which mentalism presents to the training man is that it seems to be widely shared by businessmen generally and by successful (top-level) managers especially. The successful executive likes to attribute his success to his own volition, hard work, perserverance, spirit, etc., and often assumes that people, being autonomous, are responsible for their own development—or lack of it. You really can't change behavior in any fundamental way, except that maybe you can "motivate" people to see the light (definition: "the way I did it.") by appealing to that inner-man potential we all are supposed to have. The consequence of this view for management's confidence in training is clear to us all.

Now the issue has spectacular visibility again because Skinner's critics have convincingly articulated the autonomous man concept and presumably reinforced the belief of our top management people. We need to recognize the intensity of that view and find a strategy for dealing with it, or *we are not going to be given the chance to use behavioral technology* extensively as the basis for improving our reliability and effectiveness.

One response to the humanists/mentalists, on their own terms, has been made by Geary Rummler of Praxis Corporation. He points out that the so-called "humanists" have, in fact, less concern for the human than the behaviorist. Referring to Skinner's diagram of the causes of behavior, Rummler says that the behaviorist "proceeds on the assumption that the employee basically wants to do a good job, and given half a chance and reasonable support will probably do so."[12] (What's that? You didn't know that Skinner was the original theory Y man?) The trainer's task is to construct contingencies of reinforcement which can help him learn the job behavior and others which help him maintain it.

The humanist, on the other hand, sees a performance gap and "instantly jumps right on the *man*. Let's find out what's *wrong with him*. Let's fix him up inside so that he has good values and attitudes." This seems to be not only a less optimistic view of man than the behaviorist approach, but it is what leads us to our irrelevant and ineffective attempts to "motivate" this troublesome person. The focus on the *consequences* of the person's behavior is more effective since the whole point of behavioral research is that *that* is what causes behavior. As Skinner says, "No one directly changes a mind . . . what we change in each case is a *probability of action*."

Or, as an anonymous psychologist put it, "How do I know what I think until I feel what I do?"[13]

We began with three questions, "How much of this is relevant to training? How much of it works? Under what conditions?"

How Relevant?

Skinner's learning theory is relevant to training in direct proportion to your acceptance of our behaviorist definition of training. If you are comfortable with that approach, then this theory of reinforcement is not only relevant, it is probably the only way to carry it off.

How Much of It Works?

If you can accept the proposition that "Behavior is determined by its consequences," then any change in the consequences (and contingencies of reinforcement) of behavior "works" in the sense that it will change behavior. How *well* it works depends on your skill in getting answers to the Skinner and the Feeney analysis questions.

Under What Conditions?

Aye, there's the rub.

The necessary conditions are not scientific or esoteric. They are about the same ones that make or break our present programs:

1. You have to know what you are doing. With reinforcement theory there's no "winging it." Only Dr. Fred can shoot from the hip without shooting himself in the foot. So, learn baby, learn!
2. You need access to the consequences of the present and the desired behavior—wherever they fall in the organization structure.
3. You will want to assure that your management people have some knowledge of what you are doing and your basis for it. Don't try to implement these concepts behind a smoke screen of pretending you're not. That means you will need to deal with the "inner-man motivation" beliefs which are so comfortable to top management.
4. Since the three preceding requirements are tough ones, the fourth is what the humanist will call "courage" and "tenacity," and what B.F. Skinner would call "arranging enough positive reinforcement for yourself to neutralize the aversive consequences of a lot of hard work and high risk."

References

1. Skinner, B.F., *Beyond Freedom and Dignity,* Alfred Knopf, New York, 1971.
2. *Time,* 20 Sep. 1971.
3. Rubenstein, Richard L., (book review) *Psychology Today,* Sep. 1971.
4. *Time, ibid.*
5. Cline, John, "Learning COD—Can the Schools Buy Success?" *Saturday Review,* 18 Sep. 1971.
6. Skinner, B.F., *The Technology of Teaching,* Meredith Corp., 1968.
7. Rubenstein, *ibid.*
8. Ofiesh, Col. Gabriel D., *Programmed Instruction, a Guide to Management,* American Management Assn., New York, 1965.
9. Training Research Forum, Mar. 1971.
10. See Carl Semmelroth, "The Regulation of Behavior by the Behavior of Others," *NSPI Journal,* Vol. IX, No. 8.
11. Gilbert, Thomas S., unpublished paper, 1971.
12. Rummler, Geary, Personal Strategy Clinic No. 1 (Training Research Forum), Jan. 1971.
13. Quoted anonymously by Jerome Bruner, *The Process of Education,* Random House, New York, 1963.

Appendix B

Life Problems of American Adults

**Early Adulthood
(18-30)**

Vocation and Career	Home and Family Living	Personal Development
Exploring career options	Courting	Improving your reading ability
Choosing a career line	Selecting a mate	Improving your writing ability
Getting a job	Preparing for marriage	Improving your speaking ability
Being interviewed	Family planning	Improving your listening ability
Learning job skills	Preparing for children	Continuing your general education
Getting along at work	Raising children	Developing your religious faith
Getting ahead at work	Understanding children	Improving problem-solving skills
Getting job protection	Preparing children for school	Making better decisions
of military service	Helping children in school	Getting along with people
Getting vocational	Solving marital problems	Understanding yourself
counseling	Using family counseling	Finding your self-identity
Changing jobs	Managing a home	Discovering your aptitudes
	Financial planning	Clarifying your values
	Managing money	Understanding other people
	Buying goods and services	Learning to be self-directing
	Making home repairs	Improving personal appearance
	Gardening	Establishing intimate relations
		Dealing with conflict
		Making use of personal counseling

Middle Adulthood
(30-65)

Vocation and Career	Home and Family Living	Personal Development
Learning advanced job skills	Helping teenage children to become adults	Finding new interests
Supervising others	Letting your children go	Keeping out of a rut
Changing careers	Relating to one's spouse as a person	Compensating for physiological chan
Dealing with unemployment	Adjusting to aging parents	Dealing with change
Planning for retirement	Learning to cook for two	Developing emotional flexibility
Making second careers for mothers	Planning for retirement	Learning to cope with crises
		Developing a realistic time perspecti

Later Adulthood
(65 and over)

Vocation and Career	Home and Family Living	Personal Development
Adjusting to retirement	Adjusting to reduced income	Developing compensatory abilities
Finding new ways to be useful	Establishing new living arrangements	Understanding the aging process
Understanding social security, medicare, and welfare	Adjusting to death of spouse	Re-examining your values
	Learning to live alone	Keeping future-oriented
	Relating to grandchildren	Keeping your morale up
	Establishing new intimate relationships	Keeping up to date
	Putting your estate in order	Keeping in touch with young people
		Keeping curious
		Keeping up personal appearance
		Keeping an open mind
		Finding a new self-identity
		Developing a new time perspective
		Preparing for death

Early Adulthood
(18-30)

Enjoyment of Leisure	Health	Community Living
Choosing hobbies	Keeping fit	Relating to school and teachers
Finding new friends	Planning diets	Learning about community resource
Joining organizations	Finding and using health services	Learning how to get help
Planning your time	Preventing accidents	Learning how to exert influence
Buying equipment	Using first aid	Preparing to vote
Planning family recreation		Developing leadership skills

Enjoyment of Leisure	Health	Community Living
Leading recreational activities	Understanding children's diseases	Keeping up with the world
	Understanding how the human body functions	Taking action in the community
	Buying and using drugs and medicines	Organizing community activities for children and youth
	Developing a healthy life style	
	Recognizing the symptoms of physical and mental illness	

Middle Adulthood (30-65)

Enjoyment of Leisure	Health	Community Living
Finding less active hobbies	Adjusting to physiological changes	Taking more social responsibility
Broadening your cultural interests	Changing diets	Taking leadership roles in organizations
Learning new recreational skills	Controlling weight	Working for the welfare of others
Finding new friends	Getting exercise	Engaging in politics
Joining new organizations	Having annual medical exams	Organizing community improvement activities
Planning recreation for two	Compensating for losses in strength	

Later Adulthood (65 and over)

Enjoyment of Leisure	Health	Community Living
Establishing affiliations with the older age group	Adjusting to decreasing strength and health	Working for improved conditions for the elderly
Finding new hobbies	Keeping fit	Giving volunteer services
Learning new recreational skills	Changing your diet	Maintaining organizational ties
Planning a balanced recreational program	Having regular medical exams	
	Getting appropriate exercise	
	Using drugs and medicines wisely	
	Learning to deal with stress	
	Maintaining your reserves	

Appendix C

A Differential Psychology of the Adult Potential*

A differential psychology of the adult years as a unique period in the life span of the individual has long been a period of relative neglect in the productions of the psychological enterprise. But within the last decade or more this situation has begun to improve. That improvement was underway by the late fifties and early sixties came to light in the writer's chapter on 'Psychology and Learning' in the June 1965 Review of Educational Research (14). Since then, additional and cumulative evidence is contained in the appearance of Birren's *Psychology of Aging* (2), Bromley's *Psychology of Human Aging* (5), Botwinick's *Cognitive Processes of Maturity and Old Age* (4), Hurlock's monumental *Developmental Psychology* (10), Neugarten's readings on *Middle Age and Aging* (17), and most recently Bischof's *Adult Psychology* (3).

Bischof is particularly impressive in submitting evidence for the momentum which the study of adult psychology is currently developing. Of the approximately 930 items contained in the 42 and a half pages of bibliography at the end of his book (p255-298), five percent were dated before 1950, nine percent appeared between 1950 and 1960, 20 percent between 1960 and 1965, *while 66 percent were published between 1965 and 1968.*

---

*McClusky, Howard Y. Reprinted by permission from *Adult Learning and Instruction,* edited by Stanley M. Grabowski (Syracuse: ERIC Clearinghouse on Adult Education, 1970), pp. 80-95

But for all this promising development there are as yet few deliberate and systematic attempts to formulate a position from which to develop a differential psychology of the adult years. The following presentation is submitted as a modest effort to move in this direction with particular emphasis on its relevance for an understanding of the adult potential.

To start promptly with our assignment it is proposed that a differential psychology of adults may be derived from an intermingling of selected aspects of the topics of (a) interaction, (b) dynamics, (c) personality change through time, and (d) differentiation. This presentation will deal primarily with the first three. More specifically it will include a variation on the S-O-R formula in developing the theme of interaction, a relatively new concept of MARGIN as an approach to the realm of dynamics, and finally it will draw on developmental and life cycle theory in discussing changes in adult psychology through time.

Learning and the S-O-R Formula

To learn is to change and the scheme most commonly proposed for explaining how learning-change takes place is the S (stimulus), R (response) formula or some variation thereof.

Historically, the S-R formula is essentially a more recent version of antecedent association or connectionist theories of learning. According to this view, learning occurs if we can associate or connect a new stimulus to an earlier response, or a new response to a former stimulus. In either case some change occurs. This focus on relatively objective stimulus-response units of behavior has provided the conceptual framework for bringing the processes of learning out into the open where they could be measured and presumably predicted and controlled. The presumption of the original S-R model was that if we could account for and measure the stimulus, like the impact of a cue on a billiard ball, we could predict the magnitude and direction of the response. Or if we knew enough about the response, we could retroactively reconstruct the characteristics of the stimulus which was originally responsible for its arousal.

The S-R scheme works fairly well as long as learning is confined to simple kinds of learning. But it encounters severe difficulties when learning is more complex and the learner is more mature. Consequently, it is a much better explanation of the quasi-mechanical learning of early childhood than it is of the more complex learning of the adult years. The difficulty lies chiefly in the fact that the raw physical properties of the stimuli are not sufficient to account for individual differences in response. Something more, called the 'intervening variable,' is required. In terms of our formula the intervening variable is the person—O—the one stimulated and the one responding.

At this juncture it is necessary to draw on what we know about perception, for it is the role of perception which constitutes the empirical and theoretical basis for elevating the importance of the O in our formula and thereby stressing the unique importance of the adult condition as a decisive factor in adult behavior.

We return to the point that it requires more than the raw physical properties of the stimulus to account for the individual's response—**R**. We begin with the reality that a person is immersed in an environment of incessant stimulation bombarding in varying degrees the sensory receptors (i.e., eyes, ears, nose, etc.). If unregulated, this all-pervasive bombardment could overwhelm and immobilize the individual. Fortunately, some of this stimulation is blocked out, while some filters through. Insight into the filtering process may be derived from an awareness of the facts and theory of perception.

In the first place, perception is highly selective. That part of stimulation which finally becomes a part of experience is NOT a random sample of what is totally available. There is (a) selective exposure and within the exposure field, (b) selective awareness. That is we do not see, hear, etc. everything and we are not equally aware of everything we see, hear, etc.

In the second place, perception tends to be organized. A person perceives things in patterns that are meaningful to him. For example, note the influence of context (e.g., the Müller-Lyer illusion), figure and ground, grouping and closure. Gestalt psychology has been especially influential in calling attention to the crucial role of perceptual organization.

In the third place, both selection and organization, as well as the interpretation of what is perceived, are clearly influenced by the needs, disposition and set which a person brings to the perceptual experience. Experiments indicate that people are more likely to see an ambiguous picture as containing food objects when they are hungry than when they are satiated. Other research reveals that college students interpret a picture anxiously when hypnotized in an anxious mood, critical in a critical mood, and positively in a positive mood. And in a classic experiment Bruner and Postman demonstrated that in the case of ten-year-old boys the perception of the size of coins was directly related not to the size but the *value* (to the boys) of the coin.

Thus, not the raw physical property of the stimulus but the individual's PERCEPTION of the stimulus is the key factor in determining the response. We cannot then predict—**R**— the response exclusively from our knowledge of the—**S**—stimulus. HENCE, I KNOW WHAT I SAY BUT

I DO NOT KNOW WHAT YOU HEAR; I MAY KNOW WHAT I SHOW BUT I DO NOT KNOW WHAT YOU SEE.

The mistake of the original **S-R** formula has been its reductionist over-simplification of the highly complex nature of the learning process. By overemphasizing both stimulus and response as well as their external character, it has reduced if not ignored the unique importance of the person (the intervening variable, **O**) as the agent receiving and often originating the stimulus as well as the one giving the response. A more valid version requires the insertion of an **O** between the **S** and the **R**, thus reinstating the learner as an indispensible factor in understanding and influencing the learning process. The neglect of the person—**O**—as learner explains why telling—**S**—is not necessarily teaching and why listening—**R**—is not necessarily learning. Both Input—**S**—and Outcome—**R**—must be anchored in the person who is supposed to do the learning. This point is especially relevant in the adult years when experience becomes more and more cumulative and behavior increasingly differentiated.

Learning involves not only elaborate exchanges between stimuli, responses and the learner, but it must be equally dynamic if it is to be effective. As one approach to understanding the dynamics of adult learning, let us turn to an examination of the concept of Margin.

Margin is a function of the relationship of Load to Power. In simplest terms Margin is surplus Power. It is the Power available to a person over and beyond that required to handle his Load.

> By Load we mean the demands made on a person by self and society. By Power we mean the resources, i.e. abilities, possessions, position, allies, etc., which a person can command in coping with Load. Margin may be increased by reducing Load or increasing Power, or it may be decreased by increasing Load and/or reducing Power. We can control both by modifying either Power or Load. When Load continually matches or exceeds Power and if both are fixed and/or out of control, or irreversible, the situation becomes highly vulnerable and susceptible to breakdown. If, however, Load and Power can be controlled, and better yet, if a person is able to lay hold of a reserve (Margin) of Power, he is better equipped to meet unforeseen emergencies, is better positioned to take risks, can engage in exploratory, creative activities, is more likely to learn, etc., i.e. do those things that enable him to live above a plateau of mere self subsistence.

> There is a rough similarity between the ideas of Load and Power and other concepts. For example, Stress may from one viewpoint be considered or regarded as a kind of Load. Load is also quite similar to the idea of Input in communications theory. That is Input is a Load delivered to a system of transmission. If Input is too ambiguous or if its volume and rate become ex-

cessive, a condition of 'overload' arises, resistance sets in, and breakdown may occur.

The idea of Power also has its analogues. For example, Resilience may be regarded as a kind of latent Power. It is the capacity for recovery after expenditure, depletion or exhaustion. Again, Margin is related to the notion of capital in economics. Here, net profit may be considered as a surplus for distribution or reinvestment for expansion, or increased productivity. Also in engineering the factor of safety is a direct application of the idea of Margin. In this case, after estimating the greatest stress to which a building, bridge, airplane, machine, etc. may be subjected, additional units of strength are built into the construction as an assurance that liberal Margins of safety will be available to the client.

But the key to the meaning of Margin lies not only in the subconcepts of Load and Power but even more in the relationship between them. For example, the amount of Power a person possesses will obviously have a strong bearing on the level and range of his performance. But the strategic factor for a person's selfhood is the surplus revealed by the Load Power ratio which he can apply to the achievement of a preferential development (15).[1]

In the light of our theory, therefore, a necessary condition for learning is access to and/or the activation of a Margin of Power that may be available for application to the processes which the learning situation requires.

In the preceding discussion of the **S-R** formula and the theory of Margin, it will be noted that except for a few instances the reader has been left largely on his own to relate these concepts explicitly to the psychology of adults as a special field of inquiry. That they are relatable is quite clear. In the processes of behavioral development the elements of **S, O** and **R** become woven together in complex patterns of acquisitions and as the years advance, as indicated above, the **O** becomes increasingly a uniquely dominant factor in the transactions involved. Likewise in the realm of Margin, the adjustments of Load to Power become matters of overreaching concern as a person accumulates and later relinquishes adult responsibilities and modifies the varying roles which the successive stages of the life cycle require. But a full recital of the relevance of **S-O-R** and Margin requires more attention than this occasion permits.

If we are looking for a subject matter especially germane for adult psychology, we will find it more specifically revealed in the characteristics of changes in the adult years. Added to the concepts of **S-O-R** and Margin

---

[1]The above quotation is taken with permission from the writer's article listed as item 15 in the bibliography.

Change in the Adult Years

Critical Periods

One way to view change in adulthood is to conceive of the 50 plus years following childhood and youth as a procession of critical periods. These may originate in or be terminated by some significant event, but the time prior to, following, or in between events calls for the word 'period' as a more functional designation of the idea we wish to convey. These periods are characteristically productive of experiences decisively important to the persons involved during which marked changes in social role and meaningful relationships may occur. Entry into, advance in, transfer from, or loss of employment would represent one category of such events. Marriage, the birth of a child, or the loss of marriage partner, children, parents, relatives, and other significant associates illustrates another category. The sensitive periods of readjustment leading up to and following these and similiar events often give rise to strategic 'choice points' in life direction and often compel adults to make an 'agonizing reappraisal' of their circumstances and the prospect confronting them in the years ahead. It is in such periods that some of the most meaningful learning may occur, when an older dog may learn some tricks better than younger dogs who have yet to be confronted with some of the critical events of life.

Commitment

In the idea of *commitment* we have another useful way of looking at the changes confronting a person with the passage of the adult years. Our definition of commitment consists of two components: one is an 'intentional attachment' and the other a responsibility unique to adulthood as its object. In general, change would be viewed as incremental and cumulative as well as having varying degrees of intensity and range of involvement.

To illustrate in the family domain, commitment in courtship would be regarded as tentative. Marriage itself would be regarded as the beginning of a major continuing commitment in turn leading to an accumulation of obligations with the coming of children and the widening of the kinship circle. In the occupational field, it would presumably be attached first to the job itself, then to co-workers, the employing institution, and the consumers of the job's services. Similarly, as the years unfold, commitments could be extended to the church, political party, civic associations, special interest groups, the community, and the like, in varying combinations and degrees of priority.

In such a progression commitment could be evaluated typically as follows: in childhood it would be nonexistent or embryonic; in youth, diffuse and provisional; in early adult life, with the arrival of basic job and family obligations, it would become more authentic and binding but still limited in scope; while in the middle and late middle years it would embrace the largest number and variety of concerns including attachments to work, property, civic affairs, and especially the extended family when an obligation to one's aging parents on the one hand begins to compete with one's obligation to one's growing, but still partially dependent children on the other. In later years a shift and reduction in commitments would appear with a selective disengagement in some areas and a deepening of attachment in others.

The preceding sketch constitutes only the bare bones of an approach for mapping the progression of life commitments, but it suggests that in this concept we are not considering a vague, intangible entity, but one which, with appropriate methodological ingenuity, could be counted, scaled, and charted with a degree of operational reliability and validity. But even without measurement we have here an idea with much utility for understanding some of the stubborn aspects of adult learning. For example, it helps explain the binding and 'locked in' character of so much of adult life which may add to the problem of resistance to learning. More specifically it suggests that resistance to learning may not necessarily reflect a reluctance on the part of the adult to learn but simply his unwillingness to dislocate some of the basic commitments around which much of his life is organized. Such an adult would be much more likely to learn if his basic commitments could be eased (e.g., via leaves of absence with pay and allowance for family expenses) so he could be more free to learn.

Time Perception

In the perception of time, we have another fruitful way of looking at the progression of the adult years. It makes a great deal of difference in one's orientation to learning whether life lies ahead as it does at age 21, is about midway as at 40, and is largely in the past in memory or ahead in one's children as at 70. To be behind, on, or ahead of schedule with respect to life expectations, or more important to be aware that one is behind, on, or ahead of schedule, may have a profound effect on life adjustment and consequently one's willingness to undergo a program of systematic instruction.

There is much evidence to show that at about 30 the young adult begins to realize that time is not unlimited and that as time passes his range of options with respect to job, family and other areas of living are becoming correspondingly reduced. A little later he begins to stop measuring his life from the date of birth but instead from the years remaining before death. His thoughts become relatively less concerned with the world of outer activity, and somewhat more absorbed in the inner world of contemplation.

A related feature of time perception is the common experience that time seems to pass more rapidly as one grows older. There may be a partial explanation in the following 'arithmetic of time:' at 16, one year is one 16th of the time a person has lived, at 40 one year is a 40th, and at 70 a 70th of the time lived. Thus with advancing years, a unit of time, e.g., one year, becomes a decreasing fraction of the time experienced and is so perceived. This fact added to the decrease in perception of life expectancy undoubtedly has a profound and pervasive impact on the attitudes of adults as the years unfold—an impact which in turn also affects an adult's perception of his potential as a learner. An unpublished study of the writer's indicates that up to about age 50, middle class adults do not seriously question their ability to take part in activities requiring new learning, but with other factors constant, after 50, doubts about the capacity to learn begin to appear. In the light of our argument, one explanation may be that as one passes beyond age 50 the perception that time is running out may make a great difference in an adult's attitude toward the appropriateness if not legitimacy of resuming a life of systematic inquiry (16).[2]

'Critical Periods,' 'Commitment,' and 'Time Perception' are relatively new topics in the literature of adult psychology. More familiar, however, are the formulations which have come from the field of developmental psychology. In continuing our discussion of 'Change in the Adult Years,' six of these have been brought together in the following Table: 'Comparative Designations of Developmental Stages.'

The items in Table D-1 may be roughly grouped into two categories. One appears under the heading: Biological, Kuhlen and Buhler; the other under the rubrics of: Eriksen, Peck and HYMC. The items in the first category are similar in suggesting an initial stage of consolidation (Stability of Growth, Maintenance, and Culmination) and a final stage of decline (Regressive Growth, Defense Against Loss, and Decline).

In comparison, the second category embodies a somewhat different and more optimistic stance. For example, Peck moves from the issue of Valu-

---

[2]The above quotation is taken with permission from the writer's article listed as item 16 in the bibliography.

Table C-1
Comparative Designations of Development Stages—
Mostly Post Adolescent Through the Life Span

Biological	Kuhlen (12)	Buhler (3)	Eriksen (9)	Peck (20)	HYMC (15)
Progressive Growth (0-25)	Expansion	Preparatory (0-25)	Intimacy vs Isolation		Development of Margin
Stability of Growth (25-45)	Maintenance	Culmination Largest No. Dimensions (25-50)	Generativity vs Stagnation	Valuing Wisdom vs Physical Powers	Expansion of Margin
				Socializing vs Sexualizing	
				Cathectic Flexibility vs Impoverishment	
Regressive Growth (45 plus)	Defense Against Loss	Decline (50 plus)	Ego Integrity vs Despair	Mental Flexibility vs Rigidity	Transvaluation of Margin
				Ego Differentiation vs Work Role Pre-Occupation	
				Body Transcendence vs Body Preoccupation	
				Ego Transcendence vs Ego Preoccupation	

ing Wisdom vs Valuing Physical Powers in early adulthood to Ego Transcendence in the later years and similarly Eriksen moves from the achievement of a Sense of Intimacy to the achievement of a Sense of Ego Integrity, with no suggestion in either case that the direction of change which they imply represents a decline in the adult condition. At the same time this writer (McClusky) holds that by realigning and transvaluing the relationships of Load to Power, the later years may in fact be a period of progressive growth.

The emphasis of the second category of items suggests that there may be a potential for the prolongation of adult development not acknowledged by the conventional view of change in the adult years. We will return to this point in the following section.

Changes in Intelligence (The Ability to Learn) with Age

In general, there have been two kinds of data employed to deal with this issue, one is cross sectional and the other longitudinal in character. The cross sectional kind studies a random number of persons in different groups at successive age levels, while the other studies the same persons over various intervals of time. The first of the cross sectional type was reported by Thorndike in his classic volume on *Adult Learning* (22).

He studied the rate of learning over time, and for his data derived his famous age curve of learning ability with a peak at 22 and a decline of about one percent a year to age 50. A somewhat later investigation by Jones and Conrad of about 1,200 persons ranging from 10 to 60 years of age in several New England villages yielded similar results. They showed a steady rise in intelligence from 10 to 21 followed by a decline in each of the subsequent age groups (11).

Yet again and later, Wechsler in his standardization of the Bellevue Intelligence scale in 1935 showed a high point in performance for his subjects at 22, followed by a gradual decline. Wechsler's data are particularly pertinent since they were derived from the use of an instrument especially designed to measure adult intelligence. Thus, from the cross sectional studies we get a picture of intelligence peaking in the early twenties with performance gradually diminishing thereafter.

But the longitudinal studies, most of which have been conducted since those cited above, have revealed a somewhat different and more optimistic situation. Beginning with studies at mid-adulthood of change in learning ability with age, it is interesting to note the outcome of a follow-up of the famous investigation of gifted children conducted by Terman and Oden—and on another, Oden and Bayley (1) were able to locate and retest a number of the original sample who by the time of the later inquiry were in the middle years of adulthood. In general, the results of both investigations revealed a gain in each of four age groups on tests constituting measures of conceptual thinking (21).

Turning to a study embracing an even wider interval of time, Owens has reported data particularly relevant for our problem. In 1950 when his subjects were about 50, he retested a group of college graduates who had originally taken the same test (Army Alpha) as freshmen at Iowa State College. About 11 years later, when his subjects were 61, he administered the same test a second time. Thus, there were two follow-up administrations of the same test to the same persons—the first after an interval of about 32 years and the second after an additional interval of about 11 years. At 50, the subjects showed a slight gain over their performance as freshmen and at 61, they maintained the level they had attained in general at 50 with a decline only in tests of numerical ability (18, 19).

Support for the Owens picture of the mental ability of adults over 50 is reported by Eisdorfer, who after a three-year interval found little change in the performance of 165 adults on the full scale WAIS (8), and by Duncan and Barrett whose research yielded similar outcomes with 28 men after a ten-year interval (7).

What is the meaning of this apparent discrepancy in the results of cross sectional and longitudinal types of studies?

In attempting to answer this question, Lorge—a student of Thorndike—made a distinction between speed or rate of response on the one hand and power of response on the other. He noted that as persons move through the adult years there is a decline in the speed of their reaction. But he also pointed out that this did not necessarily signify a parallel decline in the power to react. By using tests of power under timed and untimed conditions, he conducted a series of investigations that tended to confirm his theory (13).

Others have objected to the results of the cross sectional studies on the ground that tests of intelligence and learning are biased in favor of youth. Young people have usually had more experience in taking tests than older persons and their contact with the material in the test items is more recent and hence more available.

Finally, perhaps the most serious objection relates to the criterion problem. What is a good criterion with which to correlate measures of adult intelligence? Is it academic achievement, a dimension often used in the validation of intelligence tests? Probably not, but if effective performance in coping with the stress and requirements of the adult years is a criterion and if this could be measured, we might come out with a different view of the structure and growth of adult intelligence. The criterion problem is one of the most difficult to resolve in the entire arena of psychological inquiry. It permits no easy answer, but it raises issues so fundamental that when related to the measurement of adult intelligence, the problem of either its decline or increase must be viewed in a different perspective.

But to this writer the most significant point to be derived from cross sectional investigations stems from two kinds of related data. One is the diminishing scores of successively older groups of adults and the other is that in the 1955 standardization of his scale of adult intelligence, Wechsler reports a five-year advance in peak ability (23).

To elaborate: in the case of the first point, it is well known that older persons have had lesser amounts of formal education than younger persons and that amounts of formal education gradually decline as the age of the study population increases. It appears, therefore, that the peaking of ability in the early twenties revealed by cross sectional investigations and gradual decline thereafter is just as likely to reflect a decline in amounts of formal education achieved by adults as it does a decline in adult ability to learn.

The five-year increase in peak ability reported by Wechsler would tend to support the same point. Because in the 16-year period between 1939 and 1955, the educational level of the general population increased substantially and at the same time advances in availability and usage of the mass media, i.e., radio, TV, and the printed page were equally substantial. Thus, the general environment became more stimulating and educative. This interpretation of the outcomes of cross sectional investigations combined with the results of longitudinal studies showing no decline, give further support to the viewpoint expressed at the conclusion of the preceding section: (1) that the conventional view that changes in the adult years inevitably bring about a decline in intelligence (or the ability to learn) can now be challenged by a growing body of respectable empirical data; and (2) the three-phase model of growth, consolidation, and decline as descriptive of the adult potential must be thoroughly overhauled and restated with a more optimistic stance.

But there are other grounds for believing that the adult potential has been underestimated.

Role and Self Concept Theory

In the prevailing view of society, it is the major task of children and youth to go to school, study, and learn the major task of the adult to get a job and work. In brief, childhood and youth are time for learning and adulthood a time for working. This is beginning to change, but the dominant thrust of society's expectation and equally of his self expectations is that for an adult the learning role is not a major element in his repertoire of living. Thus, both society and the adult view himself as a non-learner. Our theory is that this failure to internalize the learner role as a central feature of the self is a substantial restraint in the adult's realization of his learning potential. Or more positively stated, if and when an adult thinks that studying, learning, and the intellectual adventure is as much a part of life as his occupation and obligation to his family, he will be much more likely to achieve a higher level of intellectual performance. Briefly, it is proposed that the potential is there but it needs self and societal support to bring the potential to fruition.

Sense of Discovery

Similarly it may be argued that another disposition, namely a sense of discovery, tends to be lost in the adult years and if recovered, retained, and cultivated would contribute greatly to intellectual performance.

A brief examination of what happens with the passing years will lend plausibility to this hypothesis.

We are on safe grounds for holding that about 15 months of age, when a child's ego is beginning to take shape, most of an individual's waking hours are devoted to discovering the exciting world about him. Everything is new and everything literally from the ground up must be learned. There are unending mysteries to unravel, new tasks to be mastered, and new frontiers to be explored. But as the strange becomes more familiar, and as skills become habitual, the sense of discovery begins to recede.

This becomes increasingly true as one approaches adulthood and as the skills and activities required for the major responsibilities of living are mastered. Here discovery gradually gives way to repetition, and acquisitions to maintenance. There is nothing essentially reprehensible about this. In fact, a certain amount of habituation is necessary, and in most enterprises effective maintenance is as essential as the original process of building.

It certainly would not be efficient, for example, if we as adults had to devote as much time and attention to learning to tie our shoes, learning to read and write, or even drive a car as children and youth must learn to do. The world of dressing up, of becoming literate, etc. must become as efficient and habitual as possible in order that these skills may be instruments for better things. So a naive belief in the wonders of discovery could easily lead us into a primitive kind of romanticism utterly unrealistic for the exigencies of adult living.

But typically, for most adults the efficient performance of maintenance activities does not release a person to continue the adventure of discovery. Instead, following the Law of Least Effort, he tends to take the convenient road of repetition, gets into a rut and appears gradually to reduce his ability to cope with the intellectual demands of his world. But there is nothing inevitable in the order of things that this should occur. It is the intent of our theory that the loss of the sense of discovery is a reflection of a condition in which an adult allows the requirements for maintenance to override his needs for the pursuit of inquiry, and not a reflection of an absolute decline in ability. More positively, it is also the intent of our theory that a sense of frontiersmanship can be cultivated and restored, that the adventure and wonder of life can be renewed, if not increased. If to his self expectation as a continuing learner, an adult could add a picture of himself as one continuing to discover, he could heighten his ability to learn and inquire, for here the Law of Use would overcome the Law of Disuse, and the thrust of his inquiry would be reinforced by the cumulative satisfactions resulting from his constant probe of the edge of the unknown. What better validation of the preceding hypothesis could there be than the common experience that as one advances in years, and learns more and more about the world about him, the more he realizes how little he really knows and that a vast terrain of the yet-to-be-discovered remains to be explored?

In conclusion, we have attempted to build a case for a differential psychology of the adult years, and in so doing have also proposed a post hoc interpretive hypothesis that the trend of both empirical and theoretical evidence is supportive of the view that adults have a potential for continuing learning and inquiry which historic conventional wisdom has failed to recognize. Ours then is a stance of unrealized potential and not one of *de facto* limitation. It will be interesting to note in years ahead which of these two views the thinking and research of the future will tend to confirm.

Supplementary Bibliography

1. Bayley, Nancy and Oden, Melita H. "The Maintenance of Intellectual Ability in Gifted Adults." in *Journal of Gerontology,* 10 (1) p91-107, January, 1955. 18p.

   A test designed to measure superior intelligence was administered twice, about 12 years apart, to 1,103 adults. Retests give strong evidence that intelligence of a type measured by the Concept Mastery scale continues to increase at least through age 50.

2. Birren, J.E. *The Psychology of Aging.* Englewood Cliffs, New Jersey. Prentice Hall. 1964.

3. Bischof, Ledford J. *Adult Psychology.* Available from Harper & Row Publishers, 49 E. 33rd. St., New York, NY 10016 ($5.00) 1969. 315p.

   This volume comprehensively reviews the research on the psychology of the middle-aged (ages 40-65). Topics include the concept of maturity and maturation models; the measurement and influences of adult self image; marriage and sexual patterns; intergenerational relationships between parents and children; vocations and avocations (work, retirement, play, and the factors influencing them); friendship and religious attitudes and patterns; medical and psychological research on the cases of aging and aging's impact on learning and behavioral patterns, the societal role of the aged in America and other nations, and adult attitudes toward death. A 931-item bibliography is appended.

4. Botwinick, Jack. *Cognitive Processes of Maturity and Old Age*. New York. Springer. 1968.

5. Bromley, D.B. *Psychology of Human Aging*. Baltimore, Maryland. Penguin. 1966.

6. Buhler, C. "The Curve of Life as Studied in Biographies." In *Journal of Applied Psychology*. v19 p405-9.

7. Duncan, D.R. and Barrett, A.M. "A Longitudinal Comparison of Intelligence Involving the Wechsler Bellevue I and the WAIS." in *Journal of Clinical Psychology*. 17 (1961) p318-319.

8. Eisdorfer, C. "The WAIS Performance of the Aged: A Retest Evaluation." In *Journal of Gerontology*. 18 (1963) p169-172.

9. Eriksen, E.H. *Childhood and Society*. New York. W.W. Norton. 1950.

10. Hurlock, E. *Developmental Psychology*. Third Edition. New York. McGraw-Hill. 1968.

11. Jones, H.E. and Conrad, H.S. "The Growth and Decline of Intelligence: A Study of a Homogeneous Group Between the Ages of Ten and Sixty." *Genetic Psychology Monographs*. XIII (1933) p223-298.

12. Kuhen, Raymond G. "Developmental Changes in Motivation During the Adult Years." Chapter 13 in *Relations of Development and Aging*. Edited by James E. Birren; published by Charles C. Thomas, Springfield, Illinois 62703. 1964. 38p.

In many cases, satisfaction of needs or goals results in lack of motivation to seek something similar but more challenging, and the realization that a goal or desire is unattainable results in giving up a desire for it. Status of age, pressures of time and money, physical change and decline, skill deficits, and "locked in" feelings influence motivation by causing one to adapt his goals to those more within his reach. Needs of growth-expansion are less important in later life as feeling of anxiety and threat increase. Later ages have a reduction in ego-involvement with life; an increase in disengagement, in anxiety, and in negative self concepts; and a decrease in happiness. Economic and social class attitudes play roles in determining perception of aging. There is some evidence that old age adjustment depends largely on a person's own self assessment of whether or not he reached fulfillment in his own life.

13. Lorge, Irving. "Capacities of Older Adults." Chapter III in Donahue, Wilma. *Education for Later Maturity*. New York. Whiteside and William Morrow and Company, Inc. 1955.

14. McClusky, H.Y. "Psychology and Learning" in *Review of Educational Research*. vXXV n3 (June, 1965) p191-201.

15. McClusky, H.Y. "A Dynamic Approach to Participation in Community Development. in *Journal of the Community Development Society*. v1 n1 p25-32. Spring 1970.

The writer argues that the person, as a potential or actual participant, is the point of initiation in and entry into community activities and his motivation is the key to the continuation and improvement of participation in community development.

16. McClusky, H.Y. "The Adult as Learner" in the *Management of Urban Crisis*. McNeill and Seashore, editors. New York. The Free Press. 1971. In press.

17. Neugarten, Bernice L., Ed. *Middle Age and Aging; A Reader in Social Psychology*. Available from University of Chicago Press, 5750 Ellis Avenue, Chicago, Illinois 60637. 1968. 606p.

Most of the selections (58) in this anthology discuss the problem of what social and psychological adaptations are required as individuals pass through later life. Major attention is paid to the importance of age status and age-sex roles; psychological changes in the life cycle; social psychological theories of aging; attitudes toward health; changing family roles; work, retirement, and leisure; dimensions of the immediate social environment as friendships, neighboring patterns, and living arrangements; difference in cultural settings; and perspectives of time and death. Empirical studies, and those in which research methods are clearly described, are presented wherever possible, together with theoretical and summary papers and a few investigations that present innovative methods and concepts. Various research methods are illustrated: questionnaires, surveys, interviews, projective tests, participant observation. The four appendixes in particular pose methodological problems in studying longitudinal change. Tables, figures, and an extensive bibliography also appear.

18. Owens, William A. Jr. "Age and Mental Abilities: A Longitudinal Study." *Genetic Psychology Monographs.* 48 (1953) p3-54.

19. Owens, William A. Jr. *Life History Correlates of Age Change in Mental Abilities.* Lafayette, Indiana. Purdue University. 1963.

20. Peck, R.C. "Psychological Development in the Second Half of Life" in *Psychological Aspects of Aging.* Anderson, John E., Ed. Washington, D.C. American Psychological Association. 1956.

21. Terman, L.M. and Oden, M.H. *The Gifted Group at Mid Life.* Stanford, California. Stanford University Press. 1959.

22. Thorndike, E.L., et al. *Adult Learning.* New York. Macmillan Company, 1928.

23. Wechler, D. *The Measurement and Appraisal of Adult Intelligence.* Fourth Edition. Baltimore, Maryland. William and Wilkins Co. 1958.

Appendix D

Memorandum*

To: The personal computer industry
From: Malcolm S. Knowles
Subject: Some suggestions for serving personal
         and professional owners

From my own personal experience, and the experience of scores of other personal and professional users as reported to me in numerous workshops on adult learning around the country—and the world—I can testify that the modern microcomputer industry is facing a serious problem in its attempt to enter into the relatively untapped market of personal and professional computer owners. The problem arises because current software producers and manual writers are basically computer engineers (or have been trained by computer engineers) who understand how the machine works but have no idea about how adults learn. Consequently, their software and manuals are geared to teaching us how a machine works rather than helping us learn how to use the machine to perform the real-life tasks we buy it to perform for us. As a result, we independent users find the instructions we get from the manuals, software, and—I would like to emphasize, local representatives—to be confusing, irrelevant, and frustrating in learning to use a computer for *our* purposes. Unless something is done to correct this situation, I am afraid that the computer industry will suffer a backlash. The word will get around that hundreds of personal and professional users have invested hundreds of thousands of dollars in computers that don't do what they bought them for. Suddenly a

*Training and Development Journal, Vol. 37, No. 5 (May 1983), p. 14. By permission.

crescendo of "computer for sale" ads could appear in the classified ad sections of our newspapers. As an adult educator, I would view this to be a tragedy, since I perceive the computer to be the most potent tool for adult learning to appear in modern history.

In the past decade or so we have learned more about how adults learn—and how different this is from the way we have assumed children learn —than we knew in all previous history. Here are the most important things about adult learners that the people in the computer industry need to know if they are to serve us effectively:

1. Adults have a deep need to know why they need to know something before they are willing to invest the time and energy in learning it. You need to explain to us why we need to know how to format, to move the cursor this way and that, etc., before asking us to memorize the commands.

2. Adults are task-oriented in their learning. We learn those things best which we learn in the context of using them to do what we want to do. So don't ask us to memorize commands—even if you explain why we need to know them. Ask us what we want to use the computer for first—to write letters, to write reports, to keep accounts, to play games, to maintain mailing lists—and then guide us in learning what we have to tell the computer to make it do these things for us. Start with us where we are in our interest, not with the computer where it is in its operation; teach to the person, not to the machine.

3. Adults come into any educational situation with a wide variety of backgrounds of experience. So don't assume that we all are coming to the use of computers with the same experience. Give us choices that will enable us to tie into the use of the computer from different experiential bases. Some of us have had experience using typewriters, others have not; some of us have had some previous experience with computers—at least in game arcades, others have seen their secretaries using word processors, others are complete neophytes. Write your manuals and software programs so that we can enter them from our different experiential bases. Perhaps each manual could be divided into different sections according to different backgrounds of the users.

4. Adults have a deep psychological need to be self-directing; in fact, the psychological definition of "adult" is one who has developed a

self-concept of being responsible for one's own life. We resent being talked down to, having decisions imposed on us, controlled, directed, and otherwise treated like children. So let us figure things out for ourselves—but with caring help. Give us good indexes, using everyday English words, in your manuals so that we can find the instructions we need without reading the manual through several times. We are going to make mistakes; so help us find out why we made them and how to correct them, both in the manuals and in the software programs.

Other things have been discovered about adult learners through research in the last few years, but these are the most critical things you people in the computer industry need to know. In the light of these facts about adult learners, here are the suggestions I would like to make to the computer industry to gear itself up to serving us better:

1. The single most important thing to have happen is for the relevant elements of each computer company's system—particularly the writers of manuals, the producers of software programs, and the local representatives ("salespeople")—to become infused with a knowledge of how adults learn. This could be best accomplished through a series of one-day regional workshops (the design and materials for which I would be glad to provide as a public service). But if this is deemed to be not feasible, then at least these people should be provided with a set of guidelines—which could be an elaboration, with a variety of illustrations, of the information in the first part of this memorandum.
2. The most popular existing software programs should be subjected to a simple field test as follows: Recruit a small sample of several levels of users (two or three beginners, two or three with some experience, and two or three with considerable experience); ask each one to use the computer for a variety of typical purposes, such as to write letters, reports, or articles, to keep accounts and mailing lists, and the like. Have each one be observed by a manual writer to make notes on the mistakes they make and the problems they can't solve. Then have the writers produce supplemental instruction sheets describing precisely how to perform these tasks and solve these problems. These instruction sheets could then be made available to present owners at a price and could automatically be added to the packages to be sold in the future. This procedure should be followed on all new software programs developed.
3. Somewhat along the same lines, an index should be provided for all existing manuals and be made available to present and future

owners. It is important that these indexes contain the words the users employ when they want to look something up, cross-referenced to the computer jargon.

4. All existing and future manuals should be carefully copy edited before being released for sale. I lost my confidence in the *Letter Perfect* manual, for example, when I found so many typographical and editorial errors in it.

5. All software endorsed by Apple or sold by Apple dealers should use a common command language. So far in my Apple career, I have four software programs that I bought from an Apple dealer: Applesoft System Master, Letter Perfect, Apple Writer II, and The Mailroom. Each one has different commands for moving the cursor, formatting, and otherwise operating the programs. I have found it onerously time-consuming to have to learn a new language each time I buy a new program; and I have found that when I have learned a new one, it is most awkward to go back and compose something on a program I had learned previously.

6. Local dealers should be forbidden to sell a new software program until at least one of their local representatives has mastered it. I found it terribly frustrating after I bought my Apple Writer II to ask the salesperson from whom I had bought it how to solve a problem I was having with it only to be told that he didn't know the program (and that nobody else in the shop did, either), and that therefore they couldn't help me.

7. Local dealers should be requested to refer to their Apple experts as "representatives" or "helpers" or "coaches," or something other than "salespeople." Some time ago I called my local Apple dealer and asked to speak to their "Apple expert" about a problem I was having. I was told that "our salespeople are all tied up with customers, but one will call you when he is free." I felt put off, because I had long ago bought my Apple, and so didn't need a salesperson. I needed someone to help me solve a problem.

8. Local dealers should be required to have at least one person in the store at all times who can help owners solve problems. It is frustrating to be in the middle of a report or an article and be stumped by a problem and be told that it will be a day or two before the person who can help me will be back in the store. If this solution is not feasible for a given location, then Apple should have a "HELP" 800 number available.

9. Apple owners should be provided with better linkages to one another, perhaps through a newsletter or lists of local Apple clubs or owners.

Appendix E*

Creating Lifelong Learning Communities

A New Way of Thinking About Education

The Need for a New Way of Thinking

Perceptive observers of modern civilization have been exhorting for some time now that the nineteenth-century model of education, on which our contemporary educational enterprise is based (and seemingly frozen into) is no longer functional in a world of accelerating change. Witness:

> *Alfred North Whitehead* pointed out in 1931 that it was appropriate to define education as a process of transmitting what is known only when the time-span of major cultural change was greater than the life-span of individuals. Under this condition, what people learn in their youth will remain valid and useful for the rest of their lives. But, Whitehead proposed, "We are living in the first period in human history for which this assumption is false . . . today this time-span is considerably shorter than that of human life, and accordingly our training must prepare individuals to face a novelty of conditions." Education must, therefore, now be defined as a lifelong process of continuing inquiry. And so the most important learning of all—for both children and adults—is learning how to learn, acquiring the skills of self-directed inquiry. [Whitehead, 1931, pp. viii-xix]

Donald A. Schon proposed in 1971 in his classic work, *Beyond the Stable State*, that most of our current social institutions, including those of gover-

---

* A working paper prepared for the UNESCO Institute for Education, January 1983, by Malcolm S. Knowles.

nance and education, emerged during the relatively stable state of the last century and therefore are geared to maintaining stability, but that we are now in an era of instability which requires a very different set of assumptions:

1. The loss of the stable state means that our society and all of its institutions are in *continuing* processes of transformation. We cannot expect new stable states that will endure even for our lifetimes.
2. We must learn to understand, guide, influence, and manage these transformations. We must make the capacity for understanding them integral to ourselves and our institutions.
3. We must, in other words, become adept at learning. We must become able not only to transform our institutions, in response to changing situations and requirements; we must invent and develop institutions that are "learning systems," that is to say, systems capable of bringing about their own continuing transformation.
4. The task which the loss of the stable state makes imperative, for the person, for our institutions, for our society as a whole, is to learn about learning. What is the nature of the process by which organizations, institutions, and societies transform themselves? What are the characteristics of effective learning systems? What are the forms and limits of knowledge that can operate within processes of social learning? What demands are made upon a person who engages in this kind of learning? [Schon, 1971, p. 30]

Edgar Faure and his associates on the International Commission on the Development of Education established by UNESCO, observed in 1972 that "for the first time in history, education is now engaged in preparing men for a type of society which does not yet exist." The Commission makes a number of recommendations for the reorganization of our global educational enterprise around the concept of lifelong learning. Its concluding recommendation is as follows:

The concept of education limited in time (to "school age") and confined in space (to school buildings) must be superseded. School education must be regarded not as an end but as the fundamental component of total educational activity, which includes both institutionalized and out-of-school education. A proportion of educational activity should be deformalized and replaced by flexible, diversified models. Excessive prolongation of compulsory schooling, which is beyond certain countries' capacities, must be avoided. The extension of continual training will more than compensate for the shorter average duration of initial studies. Briefly, education must be conceived of as an existential continuum as long as life. [Faure, 1972, p. 233]

Samuel Gould, chairman of the Commission on Nontraditional Study, describes the difficulty the Commission experienced in defining this concept in 1973:

> Despite our lack of a completely suitable definition, we always seemed to sense the areas of education around which our interests centered. This community of concern was a mysterious light in the darkness, yet not at all mysterious in retrospect. Most of us agreed that nontraditional study is more an attitude than a system and thus can never be defined except tangentially. This attitude puts the student first and the institution second, concentrates more on the former's need than the latter's convenience, encourages diversity of individual opportunity rather than uniform prescription, and deemphasizes time, space, and even course requirements in favor of competence and, where applicable, performance. It has concern for the learner of any age and circumstance, for the degree aspirant as well as the person who finds sufficient reward in enriching life through constant, periodic, or occasional study. [Gould, 1973, p. xv]

Botkin, Elmandjra, and Malitza, in the classic report to the Club of Rome, *No Limits to Learning* in 1979, call for a new dimension of learning:

> Serious doubt must be raised as to whether conventional human learning processes are still adequate today. Traditionally, societies and individuals have adopted a pattern of continuous *maintenance learning* interrupted by short periods of innovation stimulated largely by the shock of external events. Maintenance learning is the acquisition of fixed outlooks, methods, and rules for dealing with known and recurring situations. It enhances our problem-solving ability for problems that are given. It is the type of learning designed to maintain an existing system or an established way of life. Maintenance learning is, and will continue to be, indispensable to the functioning and stability of every society.
>
> But for long-term survival, particularly in times of turbulence, change, or discontinuity, another type of learning is even more essential. It is the type of learning that can bring change, renewal, restructuring, and problem reformulation—and which we shall call *innovative learning.* [Botkin, 1979, pp. 9-10]

This list of responsible social analysts who join in the chorus calling for a new way of thinking about education could be added to by the score, with such names as Adiseshiah, Cropley, Dave, Dumazedier, Husen, Jessup, Lengrad, Maheu, Michael, Morphet, Sarason, Shimbori, and Toffler among them. The keynote of this chorus may well have been struck by one of the leading educational historians of our time, Lawrence A. Cremin of Columbia University, when he said at the Fall Conference of the Educators in Non-School Settings in 1981, "We may be living through a revolution in education which may be as fundamental as the original invention of the schools."

The Promise of Systems Theory

Systems theory provides us with the tools for this new way of thinking about education. Ludwig von Bertalanffy (1968), one of the pioneers in the development of systems theory, describes the concept as follows: ". . . systems theory is a broad view which far transcends technological problems and demands, a reorientation that has become necessary in science in general and in a gamut of disciplines from physics and biology to the behavioral and social sciences and to philosophy. (p. vii) . . . In one way or another, we are forced to deal with complexities, with 'wholes' or 'systems,' in all fields of knowledge. This implies a basic re-orientation in scientific thinking." (p. 5)

Hayman (1975) comments that . . . "this is not a theory in the usual scientific sense of a discrete system of assumptions, constructs, and functional relationships which explains and predicts the behavior of some particular phenomena. Systems theory is rather a set of principles, an orientation in thinking, a general body of knowledge applicable in a wide variety of circumstances. It applies in circumstances where 'wholeness' is important, and this is usually the case when dealing with the problems of education." (p. 3)

Capra (1982) makes an even broader and more contemporary case for the application of systems theory to our global situation:

> We find ourselves today in a state of profound, worldwide crisis. We can read about the various aspects of this crisis every day in the newspapers. We have an energy crisis, high inflation and unemployment, pollution and other environmental disasters, the ever-increasing threat of nuclear war, a rising wave of violence and crime, and so on.
>
> All of these threats are actually different facets of one and the same crisis—essentially a crisis of perception. We are trying to apply the concepts of an outdated world view—the mechanistic world view of Cartesian-Newtonian science—to a reality that can no longer be understood in these terms.
>
> We live in a globally interconnected world, in which biological, psychological, social, and environmental phenomena are all interdependent. To describe this world appropriately we need an ecological perspective that the Cartesian world view cannot offer.

What we need, then, is a fundamental change in our thoughts, perceptions, and values. The beginnings of this change are already visible in all fields, and the shift from a mechanistic to a holistic conception of reality is likely to dominate the entire decade. The gravity and global extent of our crisis indicate that the current changes are likely to result in a transformation of unprecedented dimensions, a turning point for our planet as a whole. (p. 19)

Further support of the application of systems theory is given by W. G. Walker in a previous publication of the UNESCO Institute for Education (1980): "Systems theory provides a promising foundation for approaching the question of the administration of lifelong education. The extraordinarily rich and diverse institutional resources which demand co-ordinating and communicating links for their optimum utilization can be seen clearly in their interacting reality through the eyes of this theory. Although it originated in the area of engineering (Griffiths, 1964), its significance in demonstrating relationships among institutions (systems and subsystems) and directions of change is too valuable to ignore. A system is a complex of elements in mutual interaction." (p. 145)

The central thesis of this paper is that any social system (family, neighborhood, organization, agency, community, state, nation, world) can be conceptualized as a system of learning resources, and that when it is so conceptualized, one perceives the organization and delivery of educational services in a different way from the traditional view of education as a mosaic of educational programs conducted by a plethora of largely unconnected institutions. It calls for a new institutional form for education—a lifelong learning resource system or "Learning Community." I shall try to sketch out in broad strokes how I visualize how such a system can be organized and how it will operate in a community in North America.

Assumptions on Which This Model Is Based

This model of a Lifelong Learning Resources System is based on the following assumptions:

1. Learning in a world of accelerating change must be a lifelong process.
2. Learning is a process of active inquiry with the initiative residing in the learner.
3. The purpose of education is to facilitate the development of the competencies required for performance in life situations.

4. Learners are highly diverse in their experiential backgrounds, pace of learning, readiness to learn, and styles of learning; therefore, learning programs need to be highly individualized.
5. Resources for learning abound in every environment; a primary task of a learning system is to identify these resources and link learners with them effectively.
6. People who have been taught in traditional schools have on the whole been conditioned to perceive the proper role of learners as being dependent on teachers to make decisions for them as to what should be learned, how it should be learned, when it should be learned, and if it has been learned; they therefore need to be helped to make the transition to becoming self-directed learners.
7. Learning (even self-directed learning) is enhanced by interaction with other learners.
8. Learning is more efficient if guided by a process structure (e.g., learning plan) than by a content structure (e.g., course outline).

Steps in Creating a Lifelong Learning Resource System

1. Identifying all the learning resources in a community. By using community survey techniques (see Knowles, 1980, pp. 106-118), information can be assembled regarding the wide variety of learning resources available in every community, including the following:
   a. Institutions: educational, religious, health and social service agencies, governmental agencies, libraries, etc.
   b. Voluntary organizations: labor unions, consumer and producer cooperatives, civic and fraternal societies, agricultural organizations, youth organizations, political organizations, professional societies, etc.
   c. Economic enterprises: business and industrial firms, farms, markets, trades, etc.
   d. The media.
   e. Episodic events: fairs, celebrations, exhibits, trips, rituals, etc.
   f. Environmental resources: parks, reserves, zoos, forests, deserts, streams, etc.
   g. People: workers, elders, specialists, families, neighbors, etc.
   h. The inner resources of the individual learner: curiosities, aspirations, past and present experiences, etc.
2. Incorporating information about these resources into a data bank. What is called for here is a new institutional form that is spreading rapidly in North America and is being called an "educational bro-

kering agency." [See Heffernan, et al., 1976] Its function is to assemble information about the learning resources in a community, organize it according to categories, and make it available for individual learners, teachers, and counselors. This information can be stored in card files or, where available, in computers.

3. Establishing a mechanism for policy making and administration. A cardinal principle in systems theory is that all parties that have a stake in a system should be represented in its management. In the case of our Lifelong Learning Resources System, this would include representatives of the participating institutions, organizations, economic enterprises, media, and various categories of learners. The kind of "flat" administration and "adhocracy" proposed by Cropley (1980) and his associates would seem to be most appropriate for a system such as this.

4. Designing a lifelong learning process. As Capra (1982, p. 23) puts it, "Systems thinking is process thinking; form becomes associated with process, interrelation with interaction, and opposites are unified through oscillation . . . The systems view is an ecological view. Like the view of modern physics, it emphasizes the interrelatedness and interdependence of all phenomena and the dynamic nature of living systems. All structure is seen as a manifestation of underlying processes, and living systems are described in terms of patterns of organization." My vision of a *process design* for a Lifelong Learning Resource System is described here.

Process Design for a Lifelong Learning Resource System

This model proposes that the process of lifelong learning consists of individuals engaging in a series (or, perhaps even better, spirals) of learning projects involving these elements: (1) a broadening and deepening of the skills of self-directed inquiry; (2) the diagnosis of learning needs (or, perhaps even better, competency-development needs); (3) translation of these needs into learning objectives; (4) identification of human and material resources, including guided experiences, for accomplishing the objectives; (5) designing of a plan of strategies for using these resources; (6) executing the plan; and (7) evaluating the extent to which the objectives have been accomplished. Let me follow an individual learner through this process:

1. The individual enters one of the centers of the system (and I visualize that there would be a main center with satellite centers within walking distance of every citizen) and is referred to a learning skill assessment

laboratory. Here an assessment would be made of the individual's current level of skill in planning and carrying out a self-directed learning project (see Exhibit E-1). Skill-development exercises would be provided to help the individual move to a higher level of ability in self-directed learning.

2. The individual would then be referred to an educational diagnostician. This person would have access to a set of models of the competencies for performing the various life roles (see Exhibit E-2). The

---

Exhibit E-1
The Skills of Self-Directed Learning

On the assumption that the primary purpose of schooling is to help individuals develop the skills of learning, the ultimate behavioral objective of schooling is: "The individual engages efficiently in collaborative self-directed inquiry in self-actualizing directions." I believe that these skills of learning include at least the following:

1. The ability to develop and be in touch with curiosities. Perhaps another way to describe this skill would be "the ability to engage in divergent thinking."
2. The ability to perceive one's self objectively and accept feedback about one's performance nondefensively.
3. The ability to diagnose one's learning needs in the light of models of competencies required for performing life roles.
4. The ability to formulate learning objectives in terms that describe performance outcomes.
5. The ability to identify human, material, and experiential resources for accomplishing various kinds of learning objectives.
6. The ability to design a plan of strategies for making use of appropriate learning resources effectively.
7. The ability to carry out a learning plan systematically and sequentially. This skill is the beginning of the ability to engage in convergent thinking.
8. The ability to collect evidence of the accomplishment of learning objectives and have it validated through performance.

---

diagnostician and learner would determine which life role, at what level of performance, is appropriate for the learner's next stage of development. The diagnostician would then engage with the learner in a set of performance assessments to determine what knowledge, understandings, skills, attitudes, and values the learner needs to acquire in order to achieve the level of performance specified by the competency model. Much of this process can be accomplished through group activity in conjunction with self-administered assessment modules. Each learner would leave the diagnostician with a profile of diagnosed learning needs.

3. The individual would next be referred to an educational planning consultant. This person would have immediate access to the data bank of learning resources and would work with the individual learner (again, often in groups) in designing a learning plan (currently often called a "learning contract") that would specify: (a) the learning objectives translated from the diagnosed needs; (b) the resources which the learner would utilize in accomplishing each objective; (c) perhaps a time frame for completing each objective; (d) specification of the evidence to be collected to indicate the extent to which each objective has been accomplished; and (e) specification of the means by which the evidence will be validated (preferably through some form of performance assessment rather than information recall).

4. The learner would then go to the resources, wherever they are in the community, alone or with groups, and carry out the learning plan.

5. Upon completion of the learning plan the individual would return to a center of the system for a rediagnosis of learning needs and the development of a next level of learning plan. This is what is meant by "spirals" of learning projects. A three-year-old might start with the simplest competencies of performing the role of "friend," as described in Exhibit E-2 and then move to one of the competencies of the role of "citizen" and then to one of the competencies of the role of "learner." These roles might well be the focus for the next several years, with increasingly complex competencies for each role—particularly those of the role of "learner"—being undertaken. In early adolescence the emphasis would gradually shift to the roles of "unique self," "citizen," and "worker." In the young adult years the emphasis would be on the roles of "worker," "citizen," "family member," and "leisure-time user." In middle-adult years "worker," "family member," and "leisure-time user" might get most attention; and in later years, "leisure-time user."

Notice that there are no "teachers" in this system. There are educational diagnosticians, educational planning consultants, and resource people (and, of course, administrators or coordinators). These are

Exhibit E-2
Competencies for Performing Life Roles

Roles	Competencies
Learner	Reading, writing, computing, perceiving, conceptualizing, imagining, inquiring, aspiring, diagnosing, planning, getting help, evaluating
Being a self (with unique self-identity)	Self-analyzing, sensing, goal-building, objectivizing, value-clarifying, expressing, accepting, being authentic
Friend	Loving, empathizing, listening, collaborating, sharing, helping, giving constructive feedback, supporting
Citizen	Caring, participating, leading, decision-making, acting, "conscientizing," discussing, having perspective (historical and cultural), global citizen
Family member	Maintaining health, planning, managing, helping, sharing, buying, saving loving, taking responsibility
Worker	Career planning, using technical skills, accepting supervision, giving supervision, getting along with people cooperating, planning, delegating managing
Leisure-time user	Knowing resources, appreciating the arts and humanities, performing, playing, relaxing, reflecting, planning, risking.

roles that require a very different set of skills, attitudes, and values from those of the traditional classroom teachers, and so a process of retraining of teachers would be required to put the system into operation. The resource people would function most like teachers, in that they would be the content specialists. But they would be working with proactive rather than reactive learners, and so their content resources would be used differently from those of traditional teachers.

An attempt is made in Exhibit E-3 to portray this model of a Lifelong Learning Resource System graphically.

Exhibit E-3
A Lifelong Learning Resource System
(Learning Community)

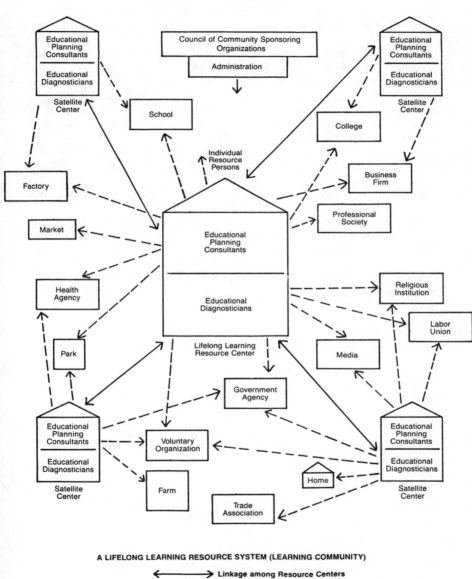

A LIFELONG LEARNING RESOURCE SYSTEM (LEARNING COMMUNITY)

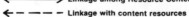

→→ Linkage among Resource Centers

← – – – – Linkage with content resources

Suggested Reading

Botkin, J.W., Elmandjra, M., and Salitza, M. *No Limits to Learning: Bridging the Human Gap.* A Report to the Club of Rome. Oxford: Pergamon Press, 1979.

Capra, F. "The Turning Point: A New Vision of Reality." *The Futurist.* 16 (1982), No. 6, pp. 19–24.

Cropley, J. (ed.) *Towards a System of Lifelong Learning.* Oxford: Pergamon Press; Hamburg: UNESCO Institute for Education, 1980.

Faure, E. and associates. *Learning to Be.* Paris: UNESCO, 1972.

Gould, S. and associates. *Diversity By Design.* San Francisco: Jossey-Bass, 1973.

Hayman, J.L., Jr. "Systems Theory and Human Organization." In Zalatimo, Suleiman D., and Phillip J. Sleeman. *A Systems Approach to Learning Environments.* Roselle, N.J.: MEDED Projects, Inc., 1975.

Heffernan, J.M., Macy, F.L., and Vickers, D. *Educational Brokering: A New Service for Adult Learners.* Washington, D.C.: National Center for Educational Brokering, 1976.

Knowles, S. *The Modern Practice of Education: From Pedagogy to Andragogy.* Chicago: Follett, 1980.

Schon, D.A. *Beyond the Stable State.* New York: W.W. Norton, 1971.

von Bertalanffy, L. *General Systems Theory.* Rev. ed. New York: Braziller, 1968.

Walker, W.G. "Leadership for Lifelong Education: The Role of Educational Administration." In Cropley, A.J. (ed.) *Towards a System of Lifelong Education.* Oxford: Pergamon Press; Hamburg: UNESCO Institute for Education, 1980, pp. 134-161.

Whitehead, A.N. "Introduction." In Donham, Wallace B. *Business Adrift.* New York: McGraw-Hill, 1931.

Appendix F

From Teacher to Facilitator of Learning*

I was brought up to think of a teacher as one who is responsible (accountable is the current jargon) for what students should learn, how, when, and if they have learned. Teachers are supposed to transmit prescribed content, control the way students receive and use it, and then test if they have received it.

That is how all my teachers had performed. It was the only model of teaching I knew. When I was invited to teach at George Williams College in Chicago shortly after World War II, that is how I taught. At first I was pleased and proud concerning my performance. I was a pretty good transmitter. My content was well organized, with a good logical outline. I illustrated abstract concepts or principles with interesting examples. I spoke clearly and dynamically. I brought forth frequent chuckles. I invited interruptions for questions of clarification. I had lively discussions and practice exercises following my lectures. My tests were fair, too—producing a good curve of distribution.

I remember feeling so good when my students did what I told them to do, which was most of the time. Most of the students were preparing for careers as YMCA secretaries, and they were conscientious and well behaved. They took notes, did homework, and were able to feed back on the final exam (most of what I told them), with the A students remembering my very words. I felt psychically rewarded by being such a good transmitter of content and controller of students. I was really a good teacher.

I had started taking courses toward a master's degree in adult education at the University of Chicago a year earlier, and my first courses were with

---

* Malcolm S. Knowles, Follett Publishing Co., Educational Materials Catalog, 1981.

teachers who did just about the same things I was doing in my course. Toward the end of my course at George Williams, I enrolled in a seminar in psychological counseling at the University of Chicago under Professor Arthur Shedlin, an associate of Carl Rogers. I was shocked by what happened at the first meeting. Some 15 students sat around the seminar table for 20 minutes talking small talk. Finally, somebody asked if anyone knew where the teacher was. One of the people responded that his name was Art and that he had been designated by the Psychology Department to meet with us. Somebody else then asked if there was a course outline. Art responded, "You would like a course outline?" Silence for several minutes. Another student broke the silence by saying, "I'd like to know why everybody is here—what did you come to learn?" So we went around the table stating our goals and expectations. When Art's turn came, he said, "I am hoping that you will help me become a better facilitator of learning."

Never Before Worked So Hard

I won't attempt to reconstruct the ensuing events, but I can tell you that during the following week I read all the books Carl Rogers had written, located students who had taken the seminar and asked them what it was all about, and developed a plan for student inquiry teams which I presented at the second meeting (which was adopted, with some modifications). I never read so many books and articles and worked so hard in any course I had ever taken. I had never before experienced taking that degree of responsibility for my own learning, alone and with other students, as I did in that seminar. It was exhilarating. I began to sense what it means to get turned on to learning. I began to think about what it means to be a facilitator of learning rather than a teacher. Fortunately, my next seminar, with Cyril O. Houle, reinforced this line of inquiry.

After my completion of the seminar with Cyril Houle, George Williams College asked me to teach adult education methods again. That was the day I decided to switch from being a teacher to being a facilitator of learning. At the opening session I explained to the students that I wanted to experiment with a different approach to teaching, and described my own experience in being exposed to two role models—Shedlin and Houle—of the role of learning facilitator. I confessed that I was not secure about my ability to bring it off, since I had never done it before, that it would only work if they agreed to take a higher level of responsibility for their own learning and that I wouldn't do it if they felt the risk was too high. They unanimously agreed to experiment with me.

I spent the rest of the first meeting having the students introduce themselves and identify their special interests and resources. I distributed a syllabus that listed the objectives the course was intended to help them accomplish and the content units (I called them "inquiry units"), with references to resource materials, that would lead to the accomplishment of the objectives. I asked them which inquiry units they would take responsibility for during the week. In the second session I had them volunteer for the inquiry units they were especially interested in, and we formed "inquiry teams."

The inquiry teams met, with me as a roving consultant and resource person, for the next four weeks, and then the rest of the semester was spent with the teams putting on "show and tell" sessions. I had never seen such creative presentations and pride of accomplishment. By the end of that semester I was a confirmed facilitator of learning.

Inquiry Units and Teams

When I analyzed what had happened to me, I was able to identify very fundamental changes. My self-concept had changed from teacher to facilitator of learning. I saw my role shifting from content-transmitter to process manager and—only secondarily—content resource.

In the second place, I experienced myself as adopting a different system of psychic rewards. I had replaced getting my rewards from controlling students with getting my rewards from releasing students. And I found the latter rewards much more satisfying.

Finally, I found myself performing a different set of functions that required a different set of skills. Instead of performing the function of content planner and transmitter, which required primarily presentation skills, I was performing the function of process designer and manager, which required relationship building, needs assessment, involvement of students in planning, linking students to learning resources, and encouraging student initiative.

I have never been tempted since then to revert to the role of teacher.

Appendix G

Making Things Happen by Releasing the Energy of Others*

Several years ago I began an intellectual adventure that has paid high dividends in terms of understanding the role of leadership and in selecting more effective leadership strategies. The adventure consisted of seeing what would happen if one conceptualized a social system (family, group, organization, agency, corporation, school, college, community, state, nation, or world) as a system of human energy.

All at once a set of questions very different from those typically asked by leaders started coming to mind: What is the sum total of the human energy available in the system? What proportion of this energy is now being used? Where is the unused energy located? Why is it not being tapped? What kinds of energy (physical, intellectual, psychic, moral, artistic, technical, social) are represented? What might be done to release this energy for accomplishing greater goals for the system and the individuals in it?

By virtue of simply asking these kinds of questions I began to have to think differently about the role of leadership. Having been raised in the era of Frederick Taylor's "scientific management," I had perceived the role of leadership

*Malcolm S. Knowles, *Journal of Management Development,* University of Queensland Business School, Australia, Sept. 1983.

to consist primarily of *controlling* followers or subordinates. Effective leaders, I had been taught, were those who were able to get people to follow their orders. The consequence of this doctrine was, of course, that the output of the system was limited to the vision and ability of the leader, and when I realized this fact I started rethinking the function of leadership. It gradually came to me that the highest function of leadership is *releasing* the energy of the people in the system and managing the processes for giving that energy direction toward mutually beneficial goals.

Perhaps a better way of saying this is that *creative leadership* is that form of leadership which releases the creative energy of the people being led.

In the intervening years since this way of thinking emerged in my mind I have been trying to understand it—and test its validity—in two ways. First, I have been observing leaders of various sorts (teachers, business executives, educational administrators, and organizational and political leaders) through this frame of reference. I have wanted to see if I could identify characteristics that "releasing leaders" possess that "controlling leaders" don't have. Second, I have reexamined the research literature on human behavior, organizational dynamics, and leadership to find out what support it contains for this way of viewing the concept of leadership. I would like to share with you the results of this bifocal inquiry in the form of the following propositions regarding the behavioral characteristics of creative leaders:

1. *Creative leaders make a different set of assumptions (essentially positive) about human nature from the assumptions (essentially negative) made by controlling leaders.* It has been my observation that creative leaders have faith in people, offer them challenging opportunities, and delegate responsibility to them. Two of the clearest presentations of these contrasting assumptions in the literature are reproduced in Exhibit 1: by Douglas McGregor in the case of assumptions by managers and by Carl Rogers in the case of assumptions by educators.

   The validity of the positive set of assumptions is supported by research which indicates that when people perceive the locus of control to reside within themselves, they are more creative and productive (Lefcourt, 1976) and that the more they feel their unique potential is being utilized, the greater their achievement. [Herzberg, 1966; Maslow, 1970]

(text continued on page 196)

Exhibit 1
A Comparison of Assumptions About Human Nature and Behavior by Leaders in Management and Education

Theory X Assumptions about Human Nature (McGregor)* (Controlling)	**Assumptions Implicit in Current Education (Rogers)** (Controlling)**
The average human being inherently dislikes work and will avoid it if he can.	The student cannot be trusted to pursue his own learning.
Because of this characteristically human dislike of work, most people must be coerced, controlled, threatened in the interest of organizational objectives.	Presentation equals learning. The aim of education is to accumulate brick upon brick of factual knowledge.
The average human being prefers to be directed, wishes to avoid responsibility, has relatively little ambition, wants security above all.	The truth is known. Creative citizens develop from passive learners. Evaluation is education and education is evaluation.
Theory Y Assumptions about Human Nature (Releasing)	**Assumptions Relevant to Significant Experiential Learning (Releasing)**
The expenditure of physical and mental effort is as natural as play or rest.	Human beings have a natural potentiality for learning.

External control and threat of punishment are not the only means for bringing about effort toward organizational objectives. Man will exercise self-direction and self-control in the service of objectives to which he is committed.	Significant learning takes place when the subject matter is perceived by the student as relevant to his own purposes.
	Much significant learning is acquired through doing.
Commitment to objectives is a function of the rewards associated with their achievement.	Learning is facilitated by student's responsible participation in the learning process.
The average human being learns, under proper conditions, not only to accept but to seek responsibility.	Self-initiated learning involving the whole person—feelings as well as intellect—is the most pervasive and lasting.
A high capacity for imagination, ingenuity, and creativity in solving organizational problems is widely, not narrowly distributed in the population.	Creativity in learning is best facilitated when self-criticism and self-evaluation are primary, and evaluation by others is of secondary importance.
Under the conditions of modern industrial life, the intellectual potential of the average human being is only partially utilized.	Creativity in learning is best facilitated when self-criticism and self-evaluation are primary, and evaluation by others is of secondary importance. The most socially useful thing to learning in the modern world is the process of learning, a continuing openness to experience, an incorporation into oneself of the process of change.

* Adapted from McGregor (1960), pp. 33–34 and 47–48 in Knowles (1978), p. 102.
** Adapted from Rogers (1972), pp. 272–279 in Knowles (1978), p. 102.

2. *Creative leaders accept as a law of human nature that people feel a commitment to a decision in proportion to the extent that they feel they have participated in making it.* Creative leaders, therefore, involve their clients, workers, or students in every step of the planning process—assessing needs, formulating goals, designing lines of action, carrying out activities, and evaluating results (except, perhaps, in emergencies). The validity of this proposition is supported by locus of control studies [Lefcourt, 1976] and by research on organizational change [Bennis, Benne, and Chin, 1968; Greiner, 1971; Lippitt, 1969; Martorana, 1975], administration [Baldridge, 1978; Dykes, 1968; Getzels, Lipham, and Campbell, 1968; Likert, 1967; McGregor, 1967], decision-making [Marrow, Bowers, and Seashore, 1968; Millett, 1968; Simon, 1961], and organizational dynamics. [Argyris, 1962; Etzioni, 1961; Schein, 1965; Zander, 1977]

3. *Creative leaders believe in and use the power of self-fulfilling prophesy.* They understand that people tend to come up to other people's expectations for them. The creative coach conveys to his team that he knows they are capable of winning; the good supervisor's employees know that he or she has faith that they will do superior work; the good teacher's students are convinced that they are the best students in school. The classic study demonstrating this principle, Rosenthal and Jacobson's *Pygmalion in the Classroom* (1968), showed that the students of teachers who were told that they were superior students *were* superior students whereas the students of teachers who were told that they were inferior students *were* inferior students. And, of course, there was no difference in the natural ability of the two groups of students. The relationship between positive self-concept and superior performance has been demonstrated in studies of students [Chickering, 1976; Felker, 1974; Rogers, 1969; Tough, 1979] and in general life achievement. [Adams-Webber, 1979; Coan, 1974; Gale, 1974; Kelly, 1955; Loevinger, 1976; McLelland, 1975]

4. *Creative leaders highly value individuality.* They sense that people perform at a higher level when they are operating on the basis of their unique strengths, talents, interests, and goals than when they are trying to conform to some imposed stereotype. They are comfortable with a pluralistic culture and tend to be bored with one that is monolithic. As managers, they encourage a team arrangement in which each member works at what he or she does best and enjoys most; as teachers they strive to tailor the learning strategies to fit the individual learning styles, paces, starting points, needs, and interests of all the students. This proposition is widely supported in the research literature. [Combs and Snygg, 1959; Csikzentmihaly, 1975; Erikson,

1974; Goldstein and Blackman, 1978; Gowan, et al., 1967; Kagan, 1967; Maslow, 1971; Messick, et al., 1976; Moustakas, 1974; Tyler, 1978]

I would like to add another dimension to this proposition—more of a philosophical note than a behavioral observation. It is that creative leaders probably have a different sense of the purpose of life from that of the controlling leaders. They see the purpose of all life activities— work, learning, recreation, civic participation, worship—to be to enable each individual to achieve his or her full and unique potential. They seek to help each person become what Maslow (1970) calls a self-actualizing person, whereas the controlling leader's mission is to produce conforming persons.

5. *Creative leaders stimulate and reward creativity.* They understand that in a world of accelerating change, creativity is a basic requirement for the survival of individuals, organizations, and societies. They exemplify creativity in their own behavior and provide an environment that encourages and rewards innovation in others. They make it legitimate for people to experiment, and treat failures as opportunities to learn rather than as acts to be punished. [Barron, 1963; Bennis, 1966; Cross, 1976; Davis and Scott, 1971; Gardner, 1963; Gowan, et al., 1967; Herzberg, 1966; Ingalls, 1976; Kagan, 1967; Schon, 1971; Toffler, 1974; Zahn, 1966]

6. *Creative leaders are committed to a process of continuous change and are skillful in managing change.* They understand the difference between static and innovative organizations (as portrayed in Exhibit 2) and aspire to make their organizations the latter. They are well grounded in the theory of change and skillful in selecting the most effective strategies for bringing about change. [Arends and Arends, 1977; Baldridge and Deal, 1975; Bennis, Benne, and Chin, 1968; Goodlad, 1975; Greiner, 1971; Hefferlin, 1969; Hornstein, et al., 1971; Lippitt, 1973; Mangham, 1978; Martorana and Kuhns, 1975; Schein and Bennis, 1965; Tedeschi, 1972; Zurcher, 1977]

7. *Creative leaders emphasize internal motivators over external motivators.* They understand the distinction revealed in Herzberg's (1959) research between satisfiers (motivators)—such as achievement, recognition, fulfulling work, responsibility, advancement, and growth— and dissatisfiers (hygienic factors), such as organizational policy and administration, supervision, working conditions, interpersonal relations, salary, status, job security, and personal life. They take steps to minimize the dissatisfiers but concentrate their energy on optimizing the satisfiers. This position is strongly supported by subsequent research. [Levinson, Price, et al., 1963; Likert, 1967; Lippitt, 1973]

Exhibit 2
Some Characteristics of Static Vs. Innovative Organizations

DIMENSIONS	CHARACTERISTICS	
	Static Organizations	Innovative Organizations
Structure	Rigid—much energy given to maintaining permanent departments, committees; reverence for tradition, constitution, & by-laws.	Flexible—much use of temporary task forces; easy shifting of departmental lines; readiness to change constitution, depart from tradition.
	Hierarchial—adherence to chain of command.	Multiple linkages based on functional collaboration.
	Roles defined narrowly.	Roles defined broadly.
	Property-bound.	Property-mobile.
Atmosphere	Task-centered, impersonal.	People-centered, caring.
	Cold, formal, reserved.	Warm, informal, intimate.
	Suspicious.	Trusting.

Management Philosophy and Attitudes	Function of management is to control personnel through coercive power. Cautious, low risk-taking. Attitude toward errors: to be avoided. Emphasis on personnel selection. Self-sufficiency—closed system regarding sharing resources. Low tolerance for ambiguity.	Function of management is to release the energy of personnel; power is used supportively. Experimental—high risk-taking. Attitude toward errors: to be learned from. Emphasis on personal development. Interdependency—open system regarding sharing resources. High tolerance for ambiguity.
Decision-making and Policy-making	High participation at top, low at bottom. Clear distinction between policy-making and policy-execution. Decision-making by legal mechanisms. Decisions treated as final.	Relevant participation by all those affected. Collaborative policy-making and policy-execution. Decision-making by problem-solving. Decisions treated as hypotheses to be tested.
Communication	Restricted flow—constipated. One-way—downward. Feelings repressed or hidden.	Open flow—easy access. Multidirectional—up, down, sideways. Feelings expressed.

8. *Creative leaders encourage people to be self-directing.* They sense intuitively what researchers have been telling us for some time—that a universal characteristic of the maturation process is movement from a state of dependency toward states of increasing self-directedness. [Baltes, 1978; Erikson, 1950, 1959, 1964, 1974; Goulet and Baltes, 1970; Gubrium and Buckholdt, 1977; Havighurst, 1970; Kagan and Moss, 1962; Loevinger, 1976; Rogers, 1961] They realize that because of previous conditioning as dependent learners in their school experience, adults need initial help in learning to be self-directing and look to leaders for this kind of help. [Kidd, 1973; Knowles, 1975, 1978, 1980; Tough, 1967, 1979] And, to provide this kind of help, they have developed their skills as facilitators and consultants to a high level [Bell and Nadler, 1979; Blake and Mouton, 1976; Bullmer, 1975; Carkhuff, 1969; Combs, et al, 1978; Lippitt and Lippitt, 1978; Laughary and Ripley, 1979; Pollack, 1976; Schein, 1969; Schlossberg, et al, 1978]

No doubt additional propositions and behavioral characteristics could be identified, but these are the ones that stand out in my observation of creative leaders and review of the literature as being most central. And I have seen wonderful things happen when they have been put into practice. I have seen low-achieving students become high-achieving students when they discovered the excitement of self-directed learning under the influence of a creative teacher. I have seen bench workers in a factory increase their productivity and get a new sense of personal pride and fulfillment under a creative supervisor. I have seen an entire college faculty (at Holland College, Prince Edward Island, Canada) become creative facilitators of learning and content resource consultants through the stimulation of a creative administration. And I have observed several instances in which the line managers of major corporations moved from controlling managers to releasing managers when their management-development programs were geared to these propositions.

Perhaps we're are on the verge of beginning to understand how to optimize the release of the enormous pent-up energy in our human energy systems.

Appendix H

Westinghouse Corporation's Andragogical Executive Forum

One afternoon some time ago, I received a phone call from A.J. (Bud) Murphy in Pittsburgh. Bud was then director of Executive Course Development for Westinghouse Electric Corporation, and he explained that he had received instructions from "upstairs" (the corporate policy committee) to develop a course for new and near-term general managers. He underlined the urgency of the request by sharing with me the fact that top management was concerned about the ratio of general manager replacements due to poor performance and the non-availability of trained general manager candidates. But Bud was feeling special pressure because the committee had specified that the new course must be different from and better than any existing management development models, and that it must be tailored to developing *Westinghouse* managers.

Bud explained that the reason he was calling me was that he had heard me make a presentation on andragogy at the national convention of the American Society for Training and Development a couple of years earlier, and he wanted to explore the possibility of adapting this model to Westinghouse's specifications. We made a date for him and one of his associates to come down to Raleigh for a day. Our discussion on that day led to our setting up a meeting in Pittsburgh with a group of associates from the corporate staff and the policy committee a month later.

We agreed that the starting point would be to ask Westinghouse top management (with the help of their executive vice-presidents and general managers) to develop a list of the essential competencies required to perform the role of Westinghouse general manager. They generated a list of 123 items which were grouped into six traditional areas: marketing, engineering, manufacturing, finance, personnel and general management. Then, six task forces were established, one for each of the functional areas. Each task force was chaired by an experienced and successful senior general manager, and consisted of five general managers, an executive vice-president as adviser, one or more staff specialists as resources, and an assigned writer to record and report task force deliberations. The task forces were to determine *what* and *how much* a general manager needs to know in the specific functional areas.

While the task force meetings continued, I met with Westinghouse management to discuss in greater depth the ramifications of the adult education process and how it might be used in the Westinghouse program. It was recognized that the outputs of the six task forces would be the basic material from which the course would be fashioned.

The following assumptions were developed in keeping with the reality of the Westinghouse situation and congruent with the concepts of adult learning underlying the andragogical model: (1) all participants would be in the course because they had demonstrated they were high achievers, experienced decision-makers, smart operators, and self-starters; (2) each participant had been more exposed to and experienced in certain areas of general management than others; (3) each participant, therefore, would need strengthening in some areas of competence more than in others; and (4) most useful to the participants would be a supportive environment and a set of resources for helping them assess their own needs and plan a program of continuing self-development (rather than a prescribed course of instruction).

It was further agreed that the purpose of a management development program should be to help new general managers and high potential managers develop the competencies required for performing their role in general management, and that the program must be built around the modelling of the required competencies. Another early decision was that such modelling could best be done by successful Westinghouse managers who could share with the participants their managerial experience, know-how, philosophy, attitudes, sense of values, and priorities (their competencies). Thus, by virtue of participation by the general management in the entire process—determining course content, making presentations, and participating in the program—the course was from the beginning recognized within the corporation as one "from general managers, by general managers, for general managers."

Because of the functional orientation of the task forces, their outputs (except for the general management task force) were, for the most part, too detailed and combersome. They tended to describe competencies required of specialists in the respective categories, rather than competencies for general managers. Thus, after the task forces had completed their work the course developers faced the challenge of refining the task force outputs into a model of the functions uniquely involved in performing the role of general manager.

The planning group then organized these required functions into performance-related sets and constructed a "learning unit module" (LUM) for each set. The LUMs served as stepping stones between the functional requirements listed by the task forces and the development of competencies. Examples of learning module units are given at the end of this appendix.

The planning group next designed a three-week residential "course" (later named the "Executive Forum"). Since I was unable to free my teaching schedule for the amount of time this undertaking would require, one of my former students at Boston University, John Ingalls, was recruited to fill in for me. The framework for this course included assumptions about adult learning (see Table H-1 for "Implications of Learning Theory") and assumptions about the management process as involving:

1. Probing the details to accumulate relevant experience and information.
2. Getting the "big picture" and developing strategic plans, goals, and objectives.
3. Pervading the plans down through the organization.
4. Measuring how the business is doing and modifying to correct, if necessary.

It was clearly a results-oriented course, since the manager is measured by the results achieved, not his or her ability to pass multiple-choice tests.

Finally, the LUMs were grouped into four competency-development units: (1) organizational understanding, (2) mission and planning, (3) people management, and (4) operations (including measurement and control). Almost one hundred Westinghouse executives were recruited to serve as resources for these units, and they were assembled for a one-day orientation seminar to make certain that they understood how to perform the role of resources to self-directed learners. Then the basic design of the course was pretested with twenty-four potential general managers. The basic design included these elements:

1. Some pre-course reading assignments in selected management books sent to participants.
2. A pre-assessment exercise engaged in by the participants prior to the course, in which each participant rated each competency on a

(text continued on page 206)

Table H-1

Characteristics and Implications of Adult Learning Theory

There are a number of implications contained in the learning theory utilized in the Executive Course that flow from the identified characteristics of adult learners. These characteristics and their implications have been developed by Malcolm S. Knowles.

Characteristics of Adult Learners	Implications for Adult Learning	Implications For Presentors
Self Concept: The adult learner sees himself as capable of self-direction and desires others to see him the same way. In fact, one definition of maturity is the capacity to be self-directing.	• A climate of openness and respect is helpful in identifying what the learners want and need to learn. • Adults enjoy planning and carrying out their own learning exercises. • Adults need to be involved in evaluating their own progress toward self-chosen goals.	Presentors recognize participants as self-directing . . . and treat them accordingly. The presentor is a learning reference for the participants rather than a traditional instructor; presentors are, therefore, encouraged to "tell it like it is" and stress "how I do it" rather than tell participants what they should do. The presentor avoids "talking down" to participants who are experienced decision-makers and self-starters. The presentor instead tries to meet the participants' needs.
Experience: Adults bring a lifetime of experience to the learning situation. Youths tend to regard experience as something that has happened to them, while to an adult, his experience is him. The adult defines who he is in terms	• Less use is made of transmittal techniques; more of experiential techniques. • Discovery of how to learn from experience is key to self-actualization.	As the adult is his experience, failure to utilize the experience of the adult learner is equivalent to rejecting him as a person.

learning.

Readiness-to-Learn: Adult developmental tasks increasingly move toward social and occupational role competence and away from the more physical developmental tasks of childhood.

- To reject adult experience is to reject the adult.

- Adults need opportunities to identify the competency requirements of their occupational and social roles.

Learning occurs through helping participants with the identification of gaps in the learner's knowledge.

No questions are "stupid"; all questions are "opportunities" for learning.

- Adult readiness-to-learn and teachable moments peak at those points where a learning opportunity is coordinated with a recognition of the need-to-know.

- Adults can best identify their own readiness-to-learn and teachable moments.

A problem-centered time perspective: Youth thinks of education as the accumulation of knowledge for use in the future. Adults tend to think of learning as a way to be more effective in problem solving today.

- Adult education needs to be problem-centered rather than theoretically oriented.

The primary emphasis in the course is on students learning rather than on teachers teaching.

- Formal curriculum development is less valuable than finding out what the learners need to learn.

Involvement in such things as problems to be solved, case histories, and critical incidents generally offer greater learning opportunity for adults than "talking to" them.

- Adults need the opportunity to apply and try out learning quickly.

nine-point scale from "I don't know what I need to know" at one end to "I know all I need to know" at the other end.

3. One day of orientation, including (a) introduction to the assumptions on which the course is based, (b) explanation of the plan of work, (c) organization of work groups of six persons each, and (d) a group-building exercise.

4. Four content units: (a) organizational understanding, 4 days; (b) mission and planning, 3 days; (c) people management, 4 days; and (d) division operations—measurement and control, 4½ days. Each content unit consisted of presentations by corporation executives followed by group discussions, small group exercises, case problems, role playing, business games, and other learning experiences. During each unit participants diagnosed their competency-development needs and ended up with a "Continuing Personal Development Plan" for the competencies in that unit.

5. A half-day closing session which included reviewing and refining the total Continuing Personal Development Plan (see Table H-2 for an example), arranging times and places for geographical cluster-groups to meet for follow-up clinics, and evaluation of the course by work-groups.

6. A post-course assessment asking participants to rate themselves on the same competencies on which they rated themselves pre-course.

7. A follow-up survey of participants in which they were asked to respond to the question, "Since attending the Executive Course, what are the two most significant improvements or changes in your managerial skill and/or knowledge?"

As a result of data obtained from participant evaluations, changes were made in the schedules and activities of subsequent sessions of the Executive Forum, but the basic design has held up, with two exceptions: (1) the pre-assessment and post-course diagnostic exercise have been eliminated and (2) the original workbook statements of competencies has been eliminated in favor of having participants make their own list of needed competencies as a part of their work in the four content units.

The evaluation of the Forum by the participants has been highly positive with such phrases as "outstanding course," "the best course I ever attended," "a unique experience," and "absolutely superior," being repeated consistently in the group reports. But the most convincing evidence of the payoff of this approach comes from the post-evaluation reports of changes in what they are actually doing on the job, of which the following are but a small sample:

I am involving my key management personnel more frequently in those decisions determining the right strategy, not just those decisions involving tac-

Table H-2
Continuing Personal Development Plan

for John Doe

Subject	Sources/Resources	Strategies and Time Frame	Date	Evidence of Attainment
Time Management	Read Peter Drucker's *The Effective Executive* again.	During the month of January, I will maintain a personal log to determine how I allocate my time.		I will review this log, establish priorities and goals, and then one month hence, repeat the sequence and determine my progress.
Financial Statements	Curt Marquard and Jack Simons	To get a better understanding of financial statements, I plan to have extended monthly reviews of specific statements with my staff. We currently review statements, but not to the depth I believe we should. Each member of my staff will improve our team effectiveness. This will be conducted in lieu of one general staff meeting once a month.		Identification of problem areas and the development of strategies for correction. The follow through will determine the attainment.
Market	Nick Beldecos and Bill Hayward	Schedule discussions with Bill Hayward to learn more about the power generation market specifically and in addition, get a better understanding of the international market. Also, discuss my personal development plans in this area with Nick Beldecos and request he give me greater exposure through the vehicle of meetings, trips, etc. in the marketing area.		When I develop a better understanding, my contribution to the business plan will improve.

(table continued on next page)

Table H-2. Continued
Continuing Personal Development Plan

for John Doe

Subject	Sources/Resources	Strategies and Time Frame	Date	Evidence of Attainment
Interunit Business	Al Cleveland, Bob Simmers, John Harrington and Nick Beldecos	Develop an interunit business mission, something we don't have at this time. This will be complete by year-end. In addition, the present organization is sales oriented instead of marketing. I intend to create a marketing manager position that probably will be filled from outside the division.		Increase market share of interunit business on a competitive basis. The corporation would also benefit because this keeps cash within Westinghouse.
Outlying Plants Irwin-Linhart-Copper Mill	Carroll Sinclair, Steve Miketic, and Bud Murphy	Establish a task force to study the viability of these plants. The task force has been formed and is chaired by Rod Peckham. The study will begin with the Irwin plant and a final report will be issued. Linhart and Copper Mill studies will come later.		The study will give direction on the continuance of the business.

tics. . . . It is now becoming much easier to delegate decisions to functional management.

An objective established during the course was to improve communications with employees. Since the course, I have visited all office locations, spending at least one day in each reviewing our business objectives and planning strategy. Believe this will contribute more to team effort.

I employ more participative management and found it to be much more effective. I also found that the class members are a great source of information.

Have been able to focus more intently on major objectives by allocating more time to planning.

I have started a process of contingency planning which has not existed in the operation.

Increased accounting knowledge most helpful, particularly in understanding where my controller has "honey pots" set up and the importance of the balance sheet accounts. Our records in investment amounts has improved considerably.

The course showed me that I was deficient in understanding the controller function. This has prompted me to take a new interest in things financial. I have developed some simple models for financial and other types of forecasting that have improved my visibility and understanding of my business.

I have been somewhat more effective in controlling the use of my own time both on and off the job. However, I still have a long way to go on this effort.

I have become more conscious of effective time utilization . . . using the tools of better scheduling and more effective planning and control of meeting agendas I feel that I am making better use of my time as well as improving the time utilization of my staff.

I find the biggest single factor to be ability to utilize the class as a resource for background, experience, personnel matters, problem solving—in short, a reliable group of consultants on a full spectrum of business matters.

In some ways perhaps the most impactful outcomes of the Executive Forum have come from the fact that more than 100 executives of the corporation have been involved as faculty resource people, thus enabling potential managers to come into personal contact with the company's leadership and building a sense of identity and a spirit of cohesiveness. But there have been several reports, too, of evidence of a better understanding by management of the role and process of training—and increased support of it.

Perhaps the spirit of the Executive Forum can best be summarized by these remarks made by a corporate executive in opening the eighth Forum:

> Welcome to Westinghouse Executive Forum Eight!
>
> This three-week session used to be called the Executive Course, but we think it is more appropriate to call it the Executive Forum.
>
> If you think about what a "forum" is, I think you will agree. A forum is defined as a meeting for open discussion. That's what goes on during these three weeks—open discussions with about 100 Westinghouse managers.
>
> Why are you here? What do you expect to get out of the Forum? Well, that's pretty much up to you.
>
> There's no material to learn. There are no lessons assigned. It's not necessary to take a lot of notes, because the Forum doesn't require you to remember a lot of details. There are no tests. No one is checking up on you to see if you do well. You're on your own!
>
> During the three weeks you will have an opportunity to find out what's going on in Westinhouse and get some ideas on how you might be a more effective manager in Westinghouse.
>
> You will be able to do this because you are exposed to some 100 successful Westinghouse general managers. They will be sharing with you their experience, know-how, their philosophies, their attitudes, their sense of values, their priorities.
>
> These 100 managers are your faculty. But don't expect them to be teachers and lecturers—in the usual sense. Remember, they are primarily successful managers coming out here to share with you what they *do*, to talk with you about how they manage. They are resources.
>
> During the three weeks you will have lots of opportunities to ask questions. In fact, the success of the Forum depends, to a large degree, on your asking questions.
>
> I would encourage you to get involved in exchanging ideas. Talking with the faculty. Asking questions. Exchanging experiences. Remember! The Forum is a meeting for open discussion. The presenters expect interaction.
>
> Because the Forum is designed to improve managerial performance, you are going to find a heavy emphasis on competencies. If you check the dictionary you will find the word "competent" defined as "having requisite ability or qualities . . . qualified or capable . . . able, fit."
>
> During the three weeks you will have an opportunity to check out the abilities and qualifications of a lot of different general managers. Bob Kirby and the members of the management committee, all the executive vice-presidents, the corporate resources vice-presidents, line vice-presidents and business unit managers, division general managers . . . about 100 of them in all.

You will be exposed to their experiences, knowledge, philosophies, management styles, attitudes, values, and priorities. In short, you will be exposed to their competencies.

Throughout the Forum you will be comparing your experience and knowledge, your skills and abilities, your philosophy, your management style, your attitudes, values and priorities with what the faculty shares with you during the three weeks. *You* will be evaluating *your* competencies, in comparison with *their* competencies.

You will be able to pick out some things you need to learn more about . . . or need to learn to do . . . or perhaps some things you need to learn to do better.

The difference between where you are and where somebody on the faculty is might be thought of as a gap . . . a gap that you discover. During the three weeks you will have many opportunities to identify gaps. You will have to decide which gaps you want to close and how you might go about doing it. What kind of priorities are you going to set on whatever you decide you need to do?

The key to keeping the Forum in perspective is to continually ask yourself "What do I need to do to improve my managerial effectiveness . . . based on what I'm exposed to at the Forum?"

When you get back on the job, what are you going to do better? What are you going to do differently? What are you going to try that's new? That's where the payoff comes. In what you do *after* the Forum is over.

During the three weeks you will be working together in small groups . . . seven managers to a group.

In your groups you will be analyzing . . . sharing ideas and experiences . . . discussing what has been talked about during the Forum . . . evaluating what you have heard and seen . . . making some decisions as a group, making some decisions as individuals.

This is where the Forum really becomes a Forum, in the open discussion you have in your groups.

Each small group is a heterogeneous mix . . . of experience . . . of expertise . . . of skills . . . knowledge . . . and learning needs.

You are sitting in your small groups this afternoon. This is your group for the three weeks.

I hope you will look upon this Forum as a great opportunity. There is nothing like this being done by any other company. We are convinced this is the way to help managers be better managers.

You are here because you are self-starters, decision makers, doers, achievers, action oriented. You are self-directing and competent.

You have a three-week opportunity to interact . . . with the faculty . . . among yourselves.

Any evaluation of the success of the Forum will be based on two things: one is how well you take advantage of the Forum to get what you need and want, and the other is your back-home application of what you get out of this Forum and what you do back home to close some of the competency gaps which you might discover during the three weeks.

Module I—General Management Comprehension

Organizational Structures

Question: How are we organized and are we organized effectively for the task we have to accomplish?
Areas for Consideration:

1. Centralization/decentralization
2. Decentralized corporation with central policy control
3. Alternative models of division organization
4. Line and staff (solid and dotted lines)
5. Multi-product and/or multi-plant divisions
6. Matrix models and functional structures
7. Project teams and task forces
8. Jobs—the functional elements of organizational structures

Organizational Roles

Question: What are the roles played by various individuals with whom the general manager comes in contact? What is the general manager's role?
Areas for Consideration: The roles of individuals within Westinghouse.

1. Board members
2. The chairman and vice-chairman
3. Members of the management committee
4. Corporate staff members
5. Group executives and group staff
6. Controllers' organization
7. Functional representatives (marketing, manufacturing, etc.)
8. Line and staff roles

Question: Do various role incumbents hold conflicting expectations with regard to the role of the general manager?
Areas for Consideration:

1. Responsibility for strategic planning
2. Limits of authority/contracts management
3. Personal management style
4. Financial prerogatives/limits
5. Delegating . . . to whom, what and how
6. Responding and/or reacting to crises
7. Clarification of subordinate roles
8. Problem-finding and problem solving
9. Levels of participation in decision making
10. Role clarification with the boss

Organizational Relationships

Question: What are the appropriate relationships for the general manager to develop in order to perform successfully?
Areas for Consideration:

1. With his boss
2. With subordinates and division functional organizations
3. With those at higher organization levels
4. With peers
5. With the controller's organization
6. With members of other organizational components outside the division
7. Competition and collaboration
8. Coaching, counselling, questioning, and communicating

Operating Effectiveness

Question: What is required to ensure effective divisional operation?
Areas for Consideration:

1. Direction, motivation and control
2. Conflict resolution
3. Formulating goals and objectives
4. Coordinating different operating methodologies and management styles
5. Developing subordinates—handling successes and failures

Organizational Dynamics

Question: How do the various segments and organizational components of Westinghouse interact to operate effectively and ensure forward movement and profitability?
Areas for Consideration:

1. Corporate strategy—how formed and by whom
2. The function and purpose of corporate policy
3. Administrative policy "rules of the club" and directive policy, charter limitations on resources, variations of emphasis, etc.
4. Policy constraint on degrees of freedom
5. Relation between business unit strategy and corporate strategy
6. Policy guidelines to "steer" business units
7. Dialogue between corporate management and business unit management—varying breadth of perspective and varying amounts of detailed information
8. Business unit "strategy" and corporate "tactics"
9. Profit planning and strategic planning
10. Forecasting and corporate expectations
11. Review, approval, and early warning on emerging problems

Module II—Manufacturing

Alternative Forms of Manufacturing Organization

Question: How does the general manager assess what kinds of manufacturing organization is most effective to meet the requirements of his business?
Areas of Consideration:

1. The functional management organization
2. The unit management concept
3. The project management organization
4. The relationship between organization structure and (a) management and employee attitudes, (b) past practice work habits and labor history, and (c) cultural norms and relationships in the area

Module III—Personnel Relations

Functional Structure of a Staff Organization

Question: What must a general manager know about the functional areas of personnel administration?
Areas for Consideration:

1. People relations
2. Employment
3. People compensation
4. Employee benefits and services
5. Training and development
6. Labor relations
7. Safety
8. Plant security
9. Communications
10. Community relations

Roles and Responsibilities of Personnel Relations Specialists

Question: How does the general manager assess the role and responsibility of the personnel relations specialists in supporting the line organizations and maintaining consistent corporate personnel policy and practice?
Areas for Consideration:

1. Grievance handling
2. Equity in classification and compensation
3. Implementation of performance appraisal
4. Staff development and training
5. Safety and OSHA
6. Equal employment—affirmative action
7. Community relations and pressure groups

Government Regulations and Enforcement—External Personnel System

Question: What guidance and support does the general manager require from personnel relations specialists to maintain effective compliance with federal and state regulations?
Areas for Consideration:

1. Notifications of noncompliance
2. Budding relationships with enforcement agencies
3. Internal communication and understanding of nature, scope, and impact of regulatory requirements

Module IV—Finance

How the Finance Function Is Organized

Question: Is the financial organization structured to provide the general manager with the financial information he needs when he needs it?
Areas for Consideration:

1. Overview of the finance organization
2. Roles and responsibilities of:
   a. Group controller
   b. Director of financial policies and procedures
   c. Audit group
   d. Legal department
   e. Treasury department
   f. Corporate business planning department
3. The financial aspects of
   a. R&D
   b. Personnel and administration
   c. Strategic and production resources

Integration of Corporate and Divisional Financial Organizations

Question: What does the general manager need to know about the relationship between corporate and divisional financial organizations?
Areas for Consideration:

1. Corporate and divisional responsibilities
2. Formulation of financial plans and objectives
3. Internal and external monitoring of financial performance

Module V—Engineering

Engineering Is a "Black Box"

Question: How must a general manager approach the engineering organization and analyze it in order to (a) discover it's true value and performance and (b) uncover hidden opportunity for increased sales and profits?
Areas for Consideration:

1. The transition from engineering manager to general manager
2. The general manager who is not an engineer
3. Engineering spoken here
4. The hidden solution in the unasked question
5. Internal and external solutions and discoveries

How Engineering "Fits" with Marketing and Manufacturing

Question: What can a general manager do to ensure "goodness of fit" between engineering, manufacturing, and marketing?
Areas for Consideration:

1. Optimization of functions leads to minimization of problems
2. The internal information flow and "backyard fences"
3. Engineering and marketing; a reciprocal relationship
4. Engineering and manufacturing; a supportive, and adoptive relationship
5. Product design "emerges" from the engineering-manufacturing-marketing "conversation"
6. The general manager's role; secret agent or trouble maker

Engineering Research and Development

Question: What can the general manager do to gain optional performance from the R&D efforts?
Areas for Consideration:

1. The R&D role
2. The difficult we do right now; the impossible will take a little while
3. When to call it off
4. Ivory tower and real world
5. How to get help from R&D

Module VI—Marketing

The Marketing and Sales Organization

Question: What does the general manager need to know to understand the marketing and sales organization?
Areas for Consideration:

1. Organizational structure and components
2. The marketing cycle: business planning, market planning, product planning and sales planning
3. Market research and analysis and market forecasting
4. The product planning organizaton
5. The pricing team
6. The sales organization
7. The marketing communications team

Appendix I

Ways of Learning: Reactive Versus Proactive*

For some time now I have been aware of the fact that the products of our educational system don't know how to learn—they only know how to be taught.

Recently, as I was reflecting on this sad state of affairs, it dawned on me that a more accurate way of conceptualizing this phenomenon was reactive versus proactive learning. For traditional pedagogy conditions the student to respond to the teacher's stimuli; the initiative in the transaction is almost wholly in the teacher; the role of the student is to react.

Obviously, some learning results from being taught this way, but it keeps the learner in a dependent role and limits the learning to the boundaries set by the teacher. It is poor preparation for continuing to learn throughout a lifetime, which is what we are about in adult education.

And so in adult education and training, it seems to me, we have an obligation to help our students learn other—proactive—ways of learning. For in adult life, learning will take place for the most part only if the learner takes the initiative; teachers are not as omnipresent.

In Table G-1 on the following page I have made a beginning in identifying the difference in the skills required by the student in engaging in these two ways of learning. I invite the *Journal's* readers to join with me in elaborating on the skills of learning that we ought to be helping our students develop.

---

*Knowles, Malcolm S., *Journal of Continuing Education and Training*, I (May, 1972), 285-287. By permission.

Table I-1
Ways of Learning

Resources for learning	Required conditions	Required skills
Reactive Teacher in traditional course	Willingness to be dependent. Respect for authority. Commitment to learning as means to an end (e.g., degree). Competitive relationship with fellow students. (The way most of us were taught to learn—not recommended)	Ability to listen uncritically. Ability to retain information. Ability to take notes. Ability to predict exam questions.
Proactive Printed materials (and experts)	Intellectual curiosity. Spirit of inquiry. Knowledge of resources available. Healthy skepticism toward authority. Criteria for testing reliability and validity. Commitment to learning as a developmental process.	Ability to formulate questions answerable by data. Ability to identify data available in printed materials (e.g., by Table of Contents, Index, etc.). Ability to scan quickly. Ability to test data against criteria of reliability and validity. Ability to analyze data to produce answers to questions.
Resource people (supervisors, experts)	Institutional commitment to individual growth as capital investment. Definition of role of supervisor as including "resource for learning." Time availability by both supervisor and employee for conferences. Inclusion of both supervisor's and employee's learning accomplishments in reward system. Spirit of mutual assistance in growth and develop-	By Supervisor: Ability to convey respect, caring, and support. Ability to provide data (and feedback) objectively and nonthreateningly. Ability to ask probing questions while keeping locus of responsibility in employee. Ability to use employees as resource for his own learning. Ability to listen empathically.

		By Employee:
		Ability to formulate goals.
		Ability to assess present level of performance.
		Ability to collect and analyze data about performance nondefensively.
		Ability to relate to supervisor as a resource for learning.
		Ability to be open and honest with supervisor.
On-the-job and life experiences	Collaborative relationships with colleagues.	Ability to collect data through:
	Commitment to learning as a developmental process.	(1) own observation,
	Institutional support for learning from mistakes.	(2) feedback from supervisors, peers, and sub-ordinates,
	High valuation of self-direction.	(3) analysis of records.
		Ability to use data for self-diagnosis of needs for self-improvement.
		Ability to accept responsibility for own learning.
		Ability to experiment with new behavior.

Appendix J

Some Guidelines for the Use of Learning Contracts

Why Use Learning Contracts?

One of the most significant findings from research about adult learning (e.g., Allen Tough's *The Adult's Learning Projects,* Ontario Institute for Studies in Education, Toronto, 1979) is that when adults go about learning something naturally (as contrasted with being taught something), they are highly self-directing. Evidence is beginning to accumulate, too, that what adults learn on their own initiative they learn more deeply and permanently than what they learn by being taught.

Those kinds of learning that are engaged in for purely personal development can perhaps be planned and carried out completely by an individual on his own terms and with only a loose structure. But those kinds of learning that have as their purpose improving one's competence to perform in a job or in a profession must take into account the needs and expectations of organizations, professions, and society. Learning contracts provide a means for negotiating a reconciliation between these external needs and expectations and the learner's internal needs and interests.

Furthermore, in traditional education the learning activity is structured by the teacher and the institution. The learner is told what objectives he is to work toward, what resources he is to use and how (and when) he is to use them, and how his accomplishment of the objectives will be evaluated. This imposed structure conflicts with the adult's deep psychological need to be self-directing and may induce resistance, apathy, or withdrawal. Learning contracts provide a vehicle for making the planning of learning experiences a mutual undertaking between a learner and his helper, mentor, teacher, and often, peers. By participating in the process of diagnosing his needs, formulating his objectives, identifying resources, choosing strategies, and evaluating his accomplishments, the learner develops a sense of ownership of (and commitment to) the plan.

Finally, in field-based learning particularly, there is a strong possibility that what is to be learned from the experience will be less clear to both the learner and the field supervisor than what work is to be done. There is a long tradition of field-experience-learners being exploited for the performance of menial tasks. The learning contract is a means for making the *learning objectives* of the field experience clear and explicit for both the learner and the field supervisor.

How Do You Develop a Learning Contract?

Step 1—Diagnose Your Learning Needs

A learning need is the gap between where you are now and where you want to be in regard to a particular set of competencies.

You may already be aware of certain learning needs as a result of a personnel appraisal process or the long accumulation of evidence for yourself of the gaps between where you are now and where you would like to be.

If not (or even so), it might be worth your while to go through this process: First, construct a model of the competencies required to perform excellently the role (e.g., parent, teacher, civic leader, manager, consumer, professional worker, etc.) you are concerned about. There may be a competency model already in existence that you can use as a thought-starter and check-list; many professions are developing such models. If not, you can build your own, with help from friends, colleagues, supervisors, and expert resource people. A competency can be thought of as the ability to do something at some level of proficiency, and is usually composed of some combination of knowledge, understanding, skill, attitude, and values. For example, "ability to ride a bicycle from my home to the store" is a competency that involves some knowledge of how a bicycle operates and the route to the store; an understanding of some of the dangers inherent in riding a bicycle; skill in mounting, pedaling, steering, and stopping a bicycle; an attitude of desire to ride a bicycle; and a valuing of the exercise it will yield. "Ability to ride a bicycle in cross-country race" would be a higher-level competency that would require greater knowledge, understanding, skill, etc. It is useful to produce a competency model even if it is crude and subjective because of the clearer sense of direction it will give you.

Learning Contract for:			
Name_____			
Activity_____			
Learning Objectives	Learning Resources and Strategies	Evidence of Accomplishment of Objectives	Criteria and Means for Validating Evidence

Figure J-1. This is a typical learning contract.

Having constructed a competency model, your next task is to assess the gap between where you are now and where the model says you should be in regard to each competency. You can do this alone or with the help of people who have been observing your performance. The chances are that you will find that you have already developed some competencies to a level of excellence, so that you can concentrate on those you haven't. An example of a model of competencies for the role of adult educator is provided in Appendix J.

Step 2—Specify Your Learning Objectives

You are now ready to start filling out the first column of the learning contract shown in Figure I-1, "Learning Objectives." Each of the learning needs diagnosed in Step 1 should be translated into a learning objective. Be sure that your objectives describe what you will *learn*, not what you will *do*. State them in terms that are most meaningful to you—content acquisition, terminal behaviors, or directions of growth.

Step 3—Specify Learning Resources and Strategies

When you have finished listing your objectives, move over to the second column of the contract in Figure I-1, "Learning Resources and Strategies," and describe how you propose to go about accomplishing *each* objective. Identify the resources (material and human) you plan to use in your field experience and the strategies (techniques, tools) you will employ in making use of them. For example, if in the "Learning Objectives" column you wrote "Improve my ability to organize my work efficiently so that I can accomplish 20 percent more work in a day," you might list the following in the "Learning Resources and Strategies" column:

1. Find books and articles in library on how to organize your work and manage time and read them.
2. Interview three executives on how they organize their work, then observe them for one day each, noting techniques they use.
3. Select the best techniques from each, plan a day's work, and have a colleague observe me for a day, giving me feedback.

Step 4—Specify Evidence of Accomplishment

After completing the second column, move over to the third column, "Evidence of Accomplishment of Objectives," and describe what evidence you will collect to indicate the degree to which you have achieved each objective. Perhaps the following examples of evidence for different types of objectives will stimulate your thinking about what evidence you might accumulate:

Type of Objective	Examples of Evidence
Knowledge	Reports of knowledge acquired, as in essays, examinations, oral presentations, audio-visual presentations, annotated bibliographies.
Understanding	Examples of utilization of knowledge in solving problems, as in action projects, research projects with conclusions and recommendations, plans for curriculum change, etc.

Type of Objective	Examples of Evidence
Skills	Performance exercises, video-taped performances, etc., with ratings by observers.
Attitudes	Attitudinal rating scales; performance in real situations, role playing, simulation games, critical incident cases, etc., with feedback from participants and/or observers.
Values	Value rating scales; performance in value clarification groups, critical incident cases, simulation exercises, etc., with feedback from participants and/or observers.

Step 5—Specify How the Evidence Will Be Validated

After you have specified what evidence you will gather for each objective in column three, move over to column four, "Criteria and Means for Validating Evidence." For each objective, first specify what criteria you propose the evidence will be judged by. The criteria will vary according to the type of objective. For example, appropriate criteria for knowledge objectives might include comprehensiveness, depth, precision, clarity, authentication usefulness, scholarliness, etc. For skill objectives more appropriate criteria may be poise, speed, flexibility, gracefulness, precision, imaginativeness, etc. After you have specified the criteria, indicate the means you propose to use to have the evidence judged according to these criteria. For example, if you produce a paper or report, who will you have read it and what are their qualifications? Will they express their judgments by rating scales, descriptive reports, evaluative reports, or how? One of the actions that helps to differentiate "distinguished" from "adequate" performance in self-directed learning is the wisdom with which a learner selects his or her validators.

Step 6—Review Your Contract with Consultants

After you have completed the first draft of your contract, you will find it useful to review it with two or three friends, supervisors, or other expert resource people to get their reactions and suggestions. Here are some questions you might have them ask about the contract to get optimal benefit from their help:

1. Are the learning objectives clear, understandable, and realistic; and do they describe what you propose to learn?
2. Can they think of other objectives you might consider?
3. Do the learning strategies and resources seem reasonable, appropriate, and efficient?
4. Can they think of other resources and strategies you might consider?
5. Does the evidence seem relevant to the various objectives, and would it convince them?
6. Can they suggest other evidence you might consider?
7. Are the criteria and means for validating the evidence clear, relevant, and convincing?
8. Can they think of other ways to validate the evidence that you might consider?

Step 7—Carry Out the Contract

You now simply do what the contract calls for. But keep in mind that as you work on it you may find that your notions about what you want to learn and how you want to learn it may change. So don't hesitate to revise your contract as you go along.

Step 8—Evaluation of Your Learning

When you have completed your contract you will want to get some assurance that you have in fact learned what you set out to learn. Perhaps the simplest way to do this is to ask the consultants you used in Step 6 to examine your evidence and validation data and give you their judgment about their adequacy.

Appendix K

The Role of Training in Organization Development*

Training of individuals to perform their jobs more effectively seldom has positive impact on the organization. The type of training I[1] have in mind is in the area of behavioral or attitudinal change, not manual skill development. The training I am discussing does include, however, managerial skill development, like learning to communicate more effectively interpersonally. In this paper, I argue that individual training programs which are not integrated within the context of an overall organization improvement effort will have little if any positive impact on the organization.

A Strategy of Change

Training, as the term is employed by most organizations, is generally an *individually oriented* educational strategy which assumes that individual change is the primary mediator of organization change. This leads to the belief that if the person can be changed, for example, made more democratic in his managerial practices, the organization will, as a consequence, operate more effectively.

Approaches to organizational change differ as a function of their underlying themes and strategies. For example, one approach to organizational change involves some modification in the design of the organizational structure—like to move from a centralized form of

*Burke, W. Warner. *Training and Development Journal*, Vol. 26, No. 9 (September, 1972), pp. 30-34. By permission.

management to a decentralized one. Another approach is to alter the technological system, for example, to automate some aspects of production, or to modify the environmental system by redecorating a group's work area.

In each of these cases the change agent has an underlying assumption that individual behavior will change as a direct function of the modifications and, consequently, that the overall organization will be changed such that the results will be higher production and morale. This assumption of individual change has validity, but such changes may also result in negative attitudes on the part of the person affected, particularly if a structural change is imposed without his consent or consideration.

Individual Strategies Ineffective

As Hornstein, Bunker, and Hornstein[2] have succinctly pointed out, individually oriented strategies of change, such as training, are not effective in producing organizational change. This is due to at least three basic problems. The first relates to an age-old issue in training—transfer of learning. The simple fact that most training occurs in a location other than the individual's work space produces the problem of re-creating the training milieu and learning back on the job.

Critical mass is a second problem. How many people must one train to obtain the desired impact on the organization? In a large organization, the answer to this question is difficult to formulate.

A third problem relates to the social psychological principle, identified in Lewin's classic work,[3] that individual behavior in a group context is considerably shaped and regulated by social norms. Individual training often requires individual deviance from accepted norms, e.g., the individual is trained to be more "open" in his interpersonal communication when the norm of his organization is to be diplomatic and to "play things close to the vest" in interpersonal relationships. Since conformity to social "regulators" is a powerful determinant of human behavior, organization members are more likely to conform to patterns of expected behavior than to violate such norms by applying what they learn in a training environment.

Given these problems with training, why do many trainers still rely on individual approaches to organizational change? One reason may be that trainers know skill training (training people to meet immediate needs of production) does have immediate and observable impact on the organization, and therefore implicitly believe that training in behavioral or attitudinal change should have the same degree of observable success even though other dynamics—group norms—are more directly involved.

Influence Lacking

Another reason may be that trainers do not have enough power and influence in the organization to produce an effective process of organization change, so they rely on the one strategy they can command, i.e., training individuals. Of course, as I have implied, still another reason for trainers continuing to rely on an individual strategy is that they do not understand that groups are easier to change than individuals.[4]

If the target for change is a person, there is some evidence that training makes a positive difference. Campbell and Dunnette[5] have shown, for example, that sensitivity training changes individual behavior. They also point out, however, that it has not been demonstrated that changes in individual behavior result in systematic organizational change. The findings of Campbell and Dunnette are corroborated by a number of similar articles.[6] Thus, if the target for change is the organization, then individually oriented training is clearly an inappropriate strategy.

OD More Effective

Organization development (OD) is a more effective strategy for the trainer (a more appropriate term might be consultant or OD specialist) to employ if his target for change is the organization or some significant part of it. As I have discussed previously,[7] OD as contrasted to training is reported in the literature[8] as an effective means for improving organizational performance, including both morale and productivity.

Organizational development is a process for developing an organization climate based on social science principles for diagnosing and coping with inadequacies in interpersonal, group and intergroup behavior in the organization's culture (normative system, structure, work-flow patterns, etc.). The process leads to behavior changes in formal decision making, communication, planning, problem solving, and the exercise of authority and responsibility. OD focuses also on improving and reinforcing existing strengths of the organization.

In addition, as Adams and I have indicated,[9] OD represents a value statement. For example, values held by many OD practitioners stress participation of all relevant persons during the various phases of an OD effort. Individual respect and dignity are emphasized as well. Typically, the OD practitioner sees to it that his personal values are made explicit and public.

With respect to approach, OD follows a two-phase process of diagnosis, *then* intervention. In other words, information about the organization's climate and culture is gathered as a foundation for diagnosis, and then on the basis of this diagnostic data, a plan is developed for organizational improvement.

Low Congruence Shown

Training is frequently criticized, for example, because programs are planned and conducted on the basis of conscience or convention rather than real organizational need. For example, a friend of mine, who is responsible for training managers in a very large organization, recently conducted research which substantiates this criticism. Specifically, he collected data from one item on managers' appraisal forms—what training does the manager say he needs? My friend compared the answers to this question with the kind of training the managers had actually received. He found that the congruence was no greater than 15 percent. I was pleased to learn from him that he is now working to increase this congruence, and he is utilizing OD principles and practices to help him do it.

Organization Development as a strategy for change focuses on examining and often changing social norms and values as a primary mediator of organizational change.[10] The technology of OD has been described in a variety of articles and books,[11] and I will not try to repeat these descriptions here. For the purposes of this paper, it is primarily important to understand that OD encompasses a variety of change methods, most of which are based on the applications of behavioral science knowledge and techniques. Briefly, the social technology of OD involves first, diagnosis and second, a planned intervention which is based on this diagnosis.[12] The OD specialist may employ a variety of interventions to respond to the diagnosed needs for change. Typical interventions are (a) team building,[13] (b) survey feedback,[14] (c) the management of conflict,[15] (d) technostructural changes,[16] and (e) training, but not training in the traditional sense.

As a part of an OD strategy, training can be used as a method for organizational change and improvement *provided* it is planned and conducted as a result of some diagnosed need for it and is based on sound educational principles. In other words, I conceptualize training, particularly training for managers,[17] as only one of several OD interventions. Stated differently, the same principles used to determine the appropriateness of other interventions should be applied for determining the suitability of training. Besides responding to a real need of organizational members, training, as well as any other OD intervention, should also (a) involve the organizational members collaboratively in planning and implementing the intervention, and (b) lead to value examination and normative changes in the organization's culture.[18]

Respond to Need

There is nothing particularly new or innovative about my insisting that any training program should be planned and conducted on the basis of a diagnosed need. But when there is evidence that training does not (1) respond to what managers report they want and need, and (2) lead to organizational change, then something is amiss. Thus, the problem with most training is not inherent in the training programs themselves (although many programs could be greatly improved), but rather in the process of what transfers (or does not transfer) prior to and following the training event. As part of an OD process training is not only responding to a diagnosed need, but it also facilitates achieving some normative change in organizational functioning.

Training in Management by Objectives (MBO), for example, cannot be conducted as a part of an OD effort unless a prior decision is made that the planning process will be greatly decentralized. If this decision has been made, then training in MBO can be quite helpful in reaching such an objective. It is my impression, however, that most organizations use MBO training to try to reach such a decision before it has been made in violation of the fundamental principle that people support decisions they help to make. And then people wonder later why the training did not "take effect." Training provided in this way creates a feeling on organizational members' part that the program was this year's "gift" from the training or personnel department, like the Christmas tie that one never wears.

Training should *facilitate* organizational change, not attempt to *provide* it. The providing of organizational change comes from managers and subordinates collaboratively diagnosing problems, and strengths, planning action steps for improvement, and then implementing solutions on the basis of joint plans. The OD specialist, and therefore the trainer, can facilitate this process when he functions diagnostically and catalytically, i.e., as a consultant and helper rather than as a specialist who is isolated from any of the "real" problems facing the organization.

Both Are Needed

The effective organization needs both training and OD. Training and OD are not only compatible but highly complementary. Suppose that in an OD process we diagnose the following problem: "A decision has been made by management that all supervisory personnel will conduct quarterly appraisal interviews with their subordinates, but a complaint has arisen among supervisors that they do not know how to conduct interviews of this nature." An appropriate intervention in this case would be to call on the training department to develop a training program in appraisal interviewing. During the training program, on the other hand, it became clear that supervisors were not clear about guidelines for evaluation. The OD process would now call for further diagnostic work possibly in the area of job descriptions to see if changes were needed. In other words, individual changes are supported with organizational modifications and vice versa.

In conclusion, I recommend that persons responsible for training learn more about OD in general, and more about organizational diagnosis and consultation, in particular.

References

1. I am indebted to Drs. John D. Adams, Jerry B. Harvey, and Harvey A. Hornstein for their helpful critique of an earlier draft of this paper.
2. Hornstein, H.A., B.A. Bunker, and M.G. Hornstein, "Some Conceptual Issues in Individual and Group-Oriented Strategies of Intervention into Organizations," *Journal of Applied Behavioral Science*, 1971, 7, No. 5, pp. 557-567.
3. Lewin, K., "Group Decision and Social Change," in E.E. Maccoby, T.M. Newcomb, and E.L. Hartley (Eds.), *Readings in Social Psychology*, New York: Holt, 1958, pp. 197-211.
4. For an example see E.J. Hall and W.H. Watson, "The Effects of a Normative Intervention on Group Decision-Making Performance," *Human Relations*, 1970, 23, No. 4, pp. 299-317.
5. Campbell, J.P. and M.D. Dunnette, "Effectiveness of T-Group Experiences in Managerial Training and Development," *Psychological Bulletin*, 1968, 70, pp. 73-104.
6. Other articles include E.A. Fleishman, "Leadership Climate, Human Relations Training, and Supervisory Behavior," *Personnel Psychology*, 1953, 6, pp. 205-222. R.J. House, "T-Group Education and Leadership Effectiveness: A Review of the Empirical Literature and a Critical Evaluation," *Personnel Psychology*, 1967, 20, pp. 1-32.
7. Burke, W.W., "Organization Development: Here to Stay?" Paper presented at the Annual Convention of the Academy of Management, Aug. 17, 1971, Atlanta, Ga.
8. The six-volume series on OD published by Addison-Wesley and authored by Beckhard, Bennis, Blake and Mouton, Lawrence and Lorsch, Schein, and Walton; W.W. Burke and H.A. Hornstein (Eds.), *The Social Technology of Organization Development*, Washington, D.C.: NTL Learning Research Corporation, 1971; R.A. Schmuck and M.B. Miles (Eds.), *Social Technology of Organization Development in Schools*, Palo Alto, Calif.: National Press Books, 1971; R.R. Blake and J.S. Mouton, *Corporate Excellence Through Grid Organization Development*, Houston: Gulf Publishing Co., 1968; J. Fordyce and R. Weil, *Managing with People*, Reading, Mass.: Addison-Wesley, 1971.
9. Adams, J.D., *The Intentional Development of Organisations*, London, England—Organisation Research and Development Ltd. (in press); W.W.

Burke, "A Comparison of Management Development and Organization Development," *Journal of Applied Behavorial Science*, 1971, 7, pp. 569-579.

10. Hornstein, H.A., B.A. Bunker, W.W. Burke, M. Gindes and R.J. Lewicki, *Social Intervention: A Behavioral Science Approach*, New York: Free Press, 1971, pp. 343-360.

11. See reference No. 8.

12. For an illustration of this two-phase process, as well as an interesting theoretical approach, see the two recent articles by J.B. Harvey and D.R. Albertson: "Neurotic Organizations: Causes and Symptoms," *Personnel Journal*, 1971, 50, No. 9, pp. 649-699; and "Neurotic Organizations: Treatment," *Personnel Journal*, 1971, 50, No. 10, pp. 770-776-783.

13. Crockett, W.S., "Team Building—One Approach to Organizational Development," *Journal of Applied Behavioral Science*, 1970, 6, No. 3, pp. 291-306. R. Beckhard, "Optimizing Team Building Efforts," *Journal of Contemporary Business*. In press. S.A. Davis, "Building more effective teams," *Innovation*, 1970, No. 15; S.A. Davis, "Laboratory training and team building" In A.L. Hite (Ed.), *Organizational Development: The State of the Art*, Ann Arbor, Mich.: Foundation for Research on Human Behavior, 1971, pp. 71-79.

14. Mann, F.C., "Studying and Creating Change: A Means to Understanding Social Organization" in C.M. Arensberg et al. (Eds.), *Research in Industrial Human Relations*. New York: Harper & Row, 1957.

15. Blake, R.R., H.A. Shepard and J.S. Mouton, *Managing Intergroup Conflict in Industry*, Houston: Gulf Publishing Co., 1964. R.E. Walton, *Interpersonal Peacemaking, Confrontation and Third Party Consultation*. Reading, Mass.: Addison-Wesley, 1969.

16. Hornstein, H.A., B.A. Bunker, W.W. Burke, M. Gindes and R.J. Lewicki, *op. cit.*, pp. 143-254.

17. Burke, W.W. and W.H. Schmidt, "Management and Organization Development: What is the target of change?" *Personnel Administration*, 1971, 34, No. 2, pp. 44-56.

18. For a brief statement of these change objectives see "What is OD?" NTL Institute, *News and Reports*, 1968, Vol. 2, No. 3, June.

Appendix L

Core Competency Diagnostic and Planning Guide

SELF-DIAGNOSTIC RATING SCALE
COMPETENCIES FOR THE ROLE OF ADULT
EDUCATOR/TRAINER

Name _____

Program _____

Indicate on the six-point scale below the level of each competency required for performing the particular role you plan to engage in by placing an "R" at the appropriate point. Then indicate your present level of development of each competency by placing a "P" at the appropriate point. For example, if you plan to make your career in teaching, you might rate required competencies as a learning facilitator as high and as a program developer and administrator as low or moderate; whereas if you plan a career as a college administrator, you might rate the competencies as a learning facilitator as moderate and as a program developer and administrator as high. (Blanks have been provided at the end of each section for the learners to add competencies of their own.)

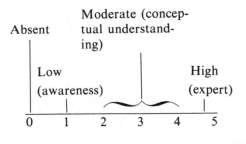

Essential Competencies   **Competency Scale**

As a Learning Facilitator

A. Regarding the conceptual and theoretical framework of adult learning:

   1. Ability to describe and apply modern concepts and research findings regarding the needs, interests, motivations, capacities, and developmental characteristics of adults as learners.

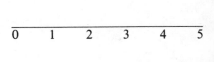

Essential Competencies   **Competency Scale**

2. Ability to describe the differences in assumptions about youths and adults as learners and the implications of these differences for teaching.

0   1   2   3   4   5

3. Ability to assess the effects of forces impinging on learners from the larger environment (groups, organizations, cultures) and manipulate them constructively.

0   1   2   3   4   5

4. Ability to describe the various theories of learning and assess their relevance to particular adult learning situations.

0   1   2   3   4   5

5. Ability to conceptualize and explain the role of teacher as a facilitator and resource person for self-directed learners.

0   1   2   3   4   5

6.

0   1   2   3   4   5

B. Regarding the designing and implementing of learning experiences:

1. Ability to describe the difference between a content plan and a process design.

0   1   2   3   4   5

2. Ability to design learning experiences for accomplishing a variety of purposes that take into account individual differences among learners.

0   1   2   3   4   5

3. Ability to engineer a physical and psychological climate of mutual respect, trust, openness, supportiveness, and safety.

0   1   2   3   4   5

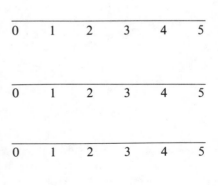

Essential Competencies	Competency Scale

4. Ability to establish a warm, empathic, facilitative relationship with learners of all sorts.

    0   1   2   3   4   5

5. Ability to engage learners responsibly in self-diagnosis of needs for learning.

    0   1   2   3   4   5

6. Ability to engage learners in formulating objectives that are meaningful to them.

    0   1   2   3   4   5

7. Ability to involve learners in the planning, conducting, and evaluating of learning activities appropriately.

    0   1   2   3   4   5

C. Regarding helping learners become self-directing:

1. Ability to explain the conceptual difference between didactic instruction and self-directed learning.

    0   1   2   3   4   5

2. Ability to design and conduct one-hour, three-hour, one-day, and three-day learning experiences to develop the skills of self-directed learning.

    0   1   2   3   4   5

3. Ability to model the role of self-directed learning in your own behavior.

    0   1   2   3   4   5

4.

    0   1   2   3   4   5

D. Regarding the selection of methods, techniques, and materials:

1. Ability to describe the range of methods or formats for organizing learning experiences.

    0   1   2   3   4   5

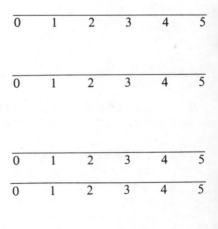

Essential Competencies   **Competency Scale**

2. Ability to describe the range of
   techniques available for facili-   0   1   2   3   4   5
   tating learning.

3. Ability to identify the range of
   materials available as re-   0   1   2   3   4   5
   sources for learning.

4. Ability to provide a rationale
   for selecting a particular
   method, technique, or material   0   1   2   3   4   5
   for achieving particular educa-
   tional objectives.

5. Ability to evaluate various
   methods, techniques, and ma-
   terials as to their effectiveness 0   1   2   3   4   5
   in achieving particular educa-
   tional outcomes.

6. Ability to develop and manage
   procedures for the construction   0   1   2   3   4   5
   of models of competency.

7. Ability to construct and use
   tools and procedures for   0   1   2   3   4   5
   assessing competency-develop-
   ment needs.

8. Ability to use a wide variety of
   presentation methods effec-   0   1   2   3   4   5
   tively.

9. Ability to use a wide variety of
   experiential and simulation   0   1   2   3   4   5
   methods effectively.

10. Ability to use audience-partici- 0   1   2   3   4   5
    pation methods effectively.

11. Ability to use group dynamics
    and small-group discussion   0   1   2   3   4   5
    techniques effectively.

12. Ability to invent new tech-   0   1   2   3   4   5
    niques to fit new situations.

13. Ability to evaluate learning
    outcomes and processes and se-   0   1   2   3   4   5
    lect or construct appropriate
    instruments and procedures for
    this purpose.

Essential Competencies   **Competency Scale**

14. Ability to confront new situations with confidence and a high tolerance for ambiguity.

   0   1   2   3   4   5

15.

   0   1   2   3   4   5

As a Program Developer

A. Regarding the planning process:

1. Ability to describe and implement the basic steps (e.g., climate setting, needs assessment, formulation of program objectives, program design, program execution, and evaluation) that undergird the planning process in adult education.

   0   1   2   3   4   5

2. Ability to involve representatives of client systems appropriately in the planning process.

   0   1   2   3   4   5

3. Ability to develop and use instruments and procedures for assessing the needs of individuals, organizations, and subpopulations in social systems.

   0   1   2   3   4   5

4. Ability to use systems-analysis strategies in program planning.

   0   1   2   3   4   5

5.

   0   1   2   3   4   5

B. Regarding the designing and operating of programs:

1. Ability to construct a wide variety of program designs to meet the needs of various situations (basic skills training, develop-

   0   1   2   3   4   5

Essential Competencies   **Competency Scale**

mental education, supervisory
and management development,
organizational development,
etc.).

2. Ability to design programs with
   a creative variety of formats, ac-   0   1   2   3   4   5
   tivities, schedules, resources,
   and evaluative procedures.

3. Ability to use needs assessments, census data, organiza-
   tional records, surveys, etc., in   0   1   2   3   4   5
   adapting programs to specific
   needs and clienteles.

4. Ability to use planning mecha-
   nisms, such as advisory coun-   0   1   2   3   4   5
   cils, committees, task forces,
   etc., effectively.

5. Ability to develop and carry out
   a plan for program evaluation
   that will satisfy the requirements   0   1   2   3   4   5
   of institutional accountability
   and provide for program improvement.

6.   0   1   2   3   4   5

As an Administrator

A. Regarding organizational development and maintenance:

   1. Ability to describe and apply
      theories and research findings   0   1   2   3   4   5
      about organizational behavior,
      management, and renewal.

   2. Ability to formulate a personal
      philosophy of administration   0   1   2   3   4   5
      and adapt it to various organi-
      zational situations.

Essential Competencies   **Competency Scale**

3. Ability to formulate policies that clearly convey the definition of mission, social philosophy, educational commitment, etc., of an organization.

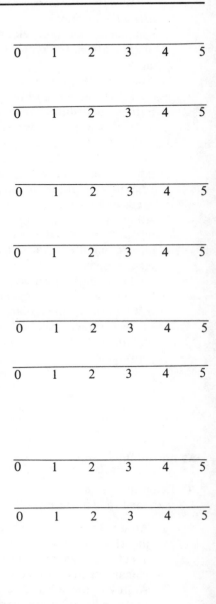

4. Ability to evaluate organizational effectiveness and guide its continuous self-renewal processes.

5. Ability to plan effectively with and through others, sharing responsibilities and decision-making with them as appropriate.

6. Ability to select, supervise, and provide for inservice education of personnel.

7. Ability to evaluate staff performance.

8. Ability to analyze and interpret legislation affecting adult education.

9. Ability to describe financial policies and practices in the field of adult education and to use them as guidelines for setting your own policies and practices.

10. Ability to perform the role of change agent vis-à-vis organizations and communities utilizing educational processes.

11.

B. Regarding program administration:

1. Ability to design and operate programs within the framework of a limited budget.

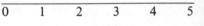

Essential Competencies   **Competency Scale**

2. Ability to make and monitor financial plans and procedures.

   0   1   2   3   4   5

3. Ability to interpret modern approaches to adult education and training to policy-makers convincingly.

   0   1   2   3   4   5

4. Ability to design and use promotion, publicity, and public relations strategies appropriately and effectively.

   0   1   2   3   4   5

5. Ability to prepare grant proposals and identify potential funding sources for them.

   0   1   2   3   4   5

6. Ability to make use of consultants appropriately.

   0   1   2   3   4   5

7. Ability and willingness to experiment with programmatic innovations and assess their results objectively.

   0   1   2   3   4   5

8.

   0   1   2   3   4   5

9.

   0   1   2   3   4   5

10.

   0   1   2   3   4   5

Permission to reproduce and use this rating scale is granted without limitation. Reports of results would be appreciated.

Malcolm S. Knowles
1506 Delmont Drive
Raleigh, N.C. 27606

Revised January 1981

Appendix M

Becoming a Tutor*

One of the more innovative applications of the andragogical model that I have come across is the Tutor Development Program of the Australian Department of Aviation. The program involves the use of tutors selected from all levels of the staffs of the various units of the Department. The selection excerpted here is in the introductory section of the manual, "Tutoring: Staff Development Techniques" which is distributed internally by the Department.

The program is the product of a "Program Design Group" of six staff members, several of whom participated in a workshop I did in Australia in 1978.

Introduction

The aim of this program is to increase your skill in staff development on the job. Your role in developing staff is identified by the word *Tutor* for good reasons, apart from the fact that this approach is a new concept being introduced throughout the Department of Aviation. As a tutor, you are a key person in your work area in the development of skills, knowledge, and attitudes. You will be promoting the development of others by providing a supportive framework for the trainees' self-development.

---

* This selection is from the manual, "Tutoring," published by the Tutor Development Program of the Australian Department of Aviation (Canberra: Australian Government Publishing Service, 1983), pp. 1-5.

There are many reasons for adopting the Tutor system:

1. The financial and staffing limitations in a dynamic organization such as the Department of Aviation mean that we must aim for maximum job satisfaction as well as maximum productivity with available resources.
2. To achieve projected goals, you need to use the most effective methods of staff development.
3. A variety of on-the-job training techniques currently in use are ineffective in terms of cost and time taken.
4. In recent years major advances have been made in the field of adult learning: adults want to be self-directed in their learning, but they often need a specialist such as a Tutor to help their growth.

The Benefits of Being a Tutor

The Department of Aviation needs trained Tutors at all levels because staff development is essential to the effective functioning of the organization.

Tutors will become increasingly important for many reasons. But there are also reasons why you will gain immediate and long-term benefits as a Tutor:

1. Staff development skills are being specified more often in selection criteria.
2. Immediate benefits to your work group include:

   a. Productivity increases.
   b. Greater job satisfaction for your staff.
   c. Development is easily adapted to fit in with normal work schedules.
   d. Reduced time away from the job.
   e. Building of good work relationships.

3. You are seen to be effective if your work group is effective.

Why Use These Staff Development Techniques?

The most common technique used for on-the-job training is that of telling or showing someone a new task or procedure. Not only is this technique inefficient and time-consuming, but the learners become dependent on trainers to solve their future problems. Learners are often treated in the same way as children and are only given instructions on what to do, rather than learning by experience to solve their own problems. Tutors need to be skilled in the field of adult learning.

The Tutor program will give you experience in various aspects of this field. The reasons for developing the techniques used in this program are:

1. Finance is not available to train staff at central locations.
2. On-the-job development must be introduced but using only proven techniques.
3. On-the-job learning covers the real problems faced at work rather than contrived case studies designed for classroom training.
4. Learning must be seen to be a normal part of work life, not something that occurs occasionally in a classroom.

Most adults have a mature and natural interest in self-directed learning:

1. When faced with a problem, they seek solutions.
2. They want to work out ways to learn which are appropriate to their past experience.
3. They prefer active rather than passive learning.
4. They want to work with someone like a Tutor who is genuinely interested in their development but does not act in the role of a conventional teacher.

An effective Tutor will need to develop skills and attitudes which facilitate learning. The learners can expect the Tutor to assist in aspects such as:

1. Identifying the needs for learning.
2. Designing learning objectives.
3. Creating a positive environment where learning is seen to be worthwhile.
4. Designing experiences and projects which are interesting and appropriate.

The attitude you display as a Tutor will be seen as positive by the learner if you:

1. Tolerate errors so long as learning occurs.
2. Acknowledge achievement, even though the learner usually knows what his achievements have been.
3. Give expert support when needed.
4. Are a good listener.

Description of the Program

The program is divided into three phases. All officers nominated by their branches will undertake the first phase of the program and, on completion, proceed to the third stage of on-the-job experiential learning.

Phase 1: Reading and Research

This book provides basic information about the role of a tutor. During this phase you should examine your own development needs as a Tutor so that you are fully prepared for the third phase, experiential learning on the job. Contact the Staff Development Officers in the Regional Office if you want additional information or assistance; further information is available in any of the areas covered in this book.

Phase 2: Group Activity for Tutor Coordinators

Branches will be asked to nominate senior officers who will become Tutor coordinators. A more detailed description of their role is given in Part III. These officers will, in addition to completing Phase 1, undertake further development in the skills required for organizational analysis which will help them in their role as coordinators.

This phase includes:

1. Setting your own learning objectives.
2. Getting experience in the various aspects of the process of adult learning.
3. Analyzing whether you have achieved your objectives and what additional development you intend to undertake.
4. Preparations for introducing programs in your own work area.

Phase 3: On the Job

You will introduce a program under observation and be informed of your progress. This is the point at which your skills will be progressively improved, provided you adopt a positive attitude. You should also look for opportunities to develop other tutors to support you, because we need to have the Tutor system operating successfully at all levels in the department. You will be kept informed of relevant staff development news after you return to the job so that both you and your staff know about information affecting career development.

Later on, you will find a more detailed explanation of adult learning techniques. At this stage I will merely give you an idea of the abilities you should aim to develop:

Preparation for Learning

Being able to identify the type of physical environment which will assist learning (lighting, equipment, and accommodation). Knowing what factors will assist or hinder learning, such as your attitudes or those of your work group, and being able to maintain a positive "climate." Knowing how to work out, with the learner, what needs to be learned and what benefits will result.

Developing a Program

Being able to clarify objectives jointly with the learner in terms which enable him to know whether those objectives have been achieved and whether further learning is needed. In conjunction with the learner, designing experiences aimed at reaching the objectives. Being able to identify resources which assist learning, such as procedure manuals, equipment, books and brochures, and other internal or external staff development opportunities.

Conducting a Program

Assisting the learner to reach the objectives through your active support. Providing guidance through any difficulties. Knowing where to find additional assistance, such as training techniques, rotation opportunities, or whatever also is needed.

Evaluation of Outcomes

Knowing how to assess the results of learning against the objectives set earlier. Being able to clarify, with the learner, what further learning is important. The skill in encouraging further self-development through such techniques as delegation, visits to other groups, projects, or job rotation.

Starting the Program

Now that you have a general idea of the way the Tutor Department program is intended to operate, you should be aware of some reactions to this approach to adult learning:

1. While it is an effective method, it is new to most people who are used to classroom-style learning. You need to help the learners to make the changes as comfortably as possible. They need to see it as aiding mature, self-directed people more effectively than the traditional teacher-student approach.

2. Most of our past education or learning has involved being told what to learn, when to learn it, and how to learn it. For this reason, some people find it difficult to actively plan their own learning. This also involves planning the time for learning to occur. A surprising number of people need assistance in planning a schedule so that they do tasks according to their relative importance. You will experience this need for planning and scheduling your own time when completing the work in Phase 1 of this program. Remember that you will not be able to proceed to Phases 2 and 3 unless you are fully conversant with the material in this Phase 1 workbook.

3. Make sure you locate a place where you can complete your work for Phase 1. You will need to find about 20-30 hours, depending on your past experience.

Appendix N

Andragogy in Developing Countries*

Charles Kabuga

Author's note: This is one of the most impassioned statements I have
seen for the organization of all of education around the andragogical
model in developing countries, particularly in Africa. It is not in itself
a case example of an application, but a plea for the application of the
andragogical model.

It can be illustrated that education in any society—whether African, European, or any other, which employs the techniques of pedagogy—is oppressive, silencing, and domesticating, among many other ills. For example,
there is no doubt in my own mind that because traditional African education
was one-way traffic, glorifying the teacher whose wisdom could not be questioned, it oppressed, silenced, and domesticated the learner. Such an education might have produced men with great memories, but not so many men
with developed thinking faculties. It appears to me that people who remember
most may not necessarily be the ones who think more. While remembering is
a backward-looking activity, thinking is a future-looking one, and it is my

---

* From *Adult Education and Development* (half-yearly Journal for Adult Education in Africa, Asia, and Latin America), September 1977. It was titled,
"Why Andragogy?"

conviction that any dynamic society needs more of such future-looking citizens. It is because pedagogy does nothing other than develop the memory of the learner that it is outmoded, either as a tool for the education of children or of adults.

There is no doubt in my mind too that Western education is oppressive, domesticating, and silencing not for any other reason than that it employs the techniques of pedagogy. It is no wonder therefore that white educators themselves have expressed their distrust in this education. Ivan Ilich's *Deschooling Society* (1970) is a typical example of a violent attack on Western education which we are anxious to modify rather than throw overboard. In this book the author advocates that there should be no schools in society, that whoever has a skill to sell should advertise it, and those who wish to learn it should apply.

Whether such pedagogically conceived education is locally consumed or is exported to other countries as it was to Africa, it still retains its oppressive characteristics. However, it is worse when it is exported than when it stays in its natural habitat.

Oppression at the Level of Content and Techniques

It is worse abroad because it oppresses at two levels: (1) *the level of content* and, like all pedagogically conceived education, at (2) *the level of techniques.* Consider the white man's content of education in Africa, for example. The white man stressed the empire where the sun never set but not the Great Sudanic Kingdoms. The white man taught the greatness of the Duke of Wellington and the barbarism of Shaka the Zulu. Such irrelevant, ethnocentric information devalued and demoralized the knowledge of the old men with their accumulated relevant experiences. The white man's irrelevant and alien information violated a basic educational principle—that of learning from the known to the unknown. We started with the unknown and we have remained in the unknown. The violation of this principle therefore meant that we were turned into human tape recorders or meaningless and static pieces of knowledge.

Meaningless as it was, the converted young African teachers reaped large economic and social benefits from teaching the content of the white man's education. To learn, or rather to cram, the white man's content of education became such a profitable industry that all the Africans hankered after it. In turn, this devalued the content of traditional African education. Even today, many of us seem to be happy that our children speak English better than they speak the mother tongue.

In Africa, therefore, we should be unhappy about this education not only at the level of content but also at the level of techniques. Unfortunately, because the content of our education is alien, we seem to have concentrated more on its modification than on the modification of techniques. For example, we have been very anxious to include in our curriculum subjects like agriculture as though it is possible to turn out farmers from school gardens. If we wish to rid our education of its crippling characteristics, we must show equal concern for both the content and the techniques. As far as I am concerned, Africanizing the syllabus does not liberate the learner as long as the techniques used carry with them oppressive, domesticating, and silencing characteristics. Thus, any content transmitted pedagogically is incapable of being useful or functioning or liberating. It is incapable because such content of education merely gets stored in the heads of learners and awaits recollection at an appropriate moment. Such content may be likened to undigested food. Just as food builds our bodies when we have digested it and made it a part of us, the educational content we acquire becomes useful when it helps us solve the problems we meet through our processes of growth and development. Pedagogy, with its techniques of narrating, receiving, memorizing, and repeating, prevents the digestion of the content, particularly the alien content, so that it is not used. We need new techniques.

Before thinking about such new techniques, we have to be absolutely clear about what we want out of education. It will be only then that we shall look for techniques which will give us what we want. We can, however, straightaway say that unlike the case of pedagogy, the new techniques have to be premised both on the dynamic nature of society and that of the students and teachers—all of whom are in a constant process of maturation. These techniques must lead the learner to the realization of the most important thing education can give.

In my view, the most important thing education can give to anyone is "how to learn." This concept is beautifully illustrated by the words of a great Chinese poet by the name of Kuan Tzu who once said:

> If you give a man a fish, he will have a single meal.
> If you teach him how to fish, he will eat all his life.

Life is such an endless research problem that no student can ever come out of any educational institution with ready-made solutions to it. The best that a student can hope to come out with are the techniques of learning and thinking about any problem life might present. With such techniques, the student will have been prepared to manage life on his own and discover new knowledge for himself. Then, it will be easy for him with such techniques to see the relationship of things and facts which were otherwise isolated and meaningless. These techniques will be his master-key both to the doors of life and the rooms of ignorance where the light of knowledge must shine.

Why Andragogy?

Unlike pedagogy, which is premised on a static culture, andragogy is premised on a dynamic culture. This is so because of the dynamic learner characteristics on which andragogy is built. Of the adult learner characteristics, I wish to address myself to only three, the instructional implications of which appear more difficult to apply to the education of children. The first one of these is that of *self-concept.*

Simply put, self-concept is the image each one of us has of himself. As each person grows, his self-concept moves from being a dependent personality to a self-directing one. Increasingly, we become autonomous individuals capable of taking decisions and facing their consequences. We resent being treated as if we were children. Because of such self-concepts, Knowles [1970, 1973] observes that no adult learner will ever learn under conditions incongruent with his self-concept.

In such a situation, andragogy recommends that the learner be allowed to participate in diagnosing his educational needs, planning his experiences, and developing a suitable learning climate.

It might be argued that these andragogical techniques cannot be employed in the education of children who, after all, are dependent personalities—at least physically and emotionally. These techniques may further be considered unsuitable on the grounds that children cannot be involved in the diagnosis of their needs and the planning of their educational experiences because they are too young to know their needs and their experiences are limited.

In my view, the school strikes, riots, rebellions, and all the abundant discipline problems in classrooms together with the cry for involvement in the university decision-making processes by students largely stem from lack of recognition of the self-concept of students. It is my submission that because it recognizes this learner characteristic, andragogy becomes a relevant and meaningful tool in education at all levels.

Unfortunately, we have shied away from it with regard to youth education and as a consequence done irreparable harm to the creativity of our children that comes with the development of the self-concept. In spite of their rebellions and strikes, children have failed to liberate themselves from the horrors of pedagogy simply because we have tamed them with either the stick or the carrot of a desired career. Because self-concept is so closely linked with intrinsic motivation, techniques which do not exploit it, at any level, are ineffective educational tools. As I see it, the techniques of andragogy are capable of adequately exploiting the learner's self-concept. This being so, these techniques should be employed at all levels of education because children see themselves as self-directing fairly early in life.

Experience is the second characteristic of the adult learner that I propose to discuss. It is argued that because the adult has lived longer than the child he has a variety of experiences which make him a rich resource in the class. In order to exploit this educational resource, andragogy requires techniques like work conferences, group discussions, seminars, field projects, and consultative supervision. In this way, the learners and teachers share experience to the advantage of all.

Such techniques may appear inapplicable to the education of children because it is difficult to imagine seminars and conferences for children. However, let it be said that children, like adults, have experiences, and each child is definitely a rich resource. Where pedagogy went wrong was to require children to learn adult experiences which children never appreciated because they did not understand these experiences. What needs to be pointed out is that just as adults may benefit from the experiences of their fellow adults, children will also benefit from the experiences of their fellow children. As a matter of fact, children learn more (at least horizontally) from their peers than they learn from adults. By using the techniques of andragogy, peer learning will be greatly enhanced and made more meaningful and rewarding. And these techniques can be used in the education of children because andragogy does not over-emphasize the student contributions. Rather, it invites a dialogue between the teacher and the learner and between learner and learner with the teacher serving as a guide, a resource person, and a manipulator of the environment in order for the learner to be afforded experiences appropriate to his needs and potentialities.

In youth education, just like in the education of adults, the teacher has to discover the language of the learner in order for him to pitch what he wants to teach at the level of the experiences of the learner. Without first discovering the language of their experiences, the teacher will merely be turning the learner—child or adult—into a receptacle of the meaningless words of the teacher. Learners will inevitably be tongue-tied, for the words in the experience of the teacher are alien to them. By way of an illustration, it was only after Paolo Freire [1970] had discovered that he should go to the people in order to discover the words in their universe which he used to write ABC primers for them that he was able to teach them how to read and write in 45 days. Otherwise, the other primers written in words from Freire's universe were meaningless to the learners. Discovering the universe of adults, therefore, is just as important, necessary and possible as discovering the universe of children if our teaching is to be liberating.

The third learner characteristic I wish to discuss is that of *time perspective*. Because most adults learn in order to be equipped to overcome problems which current-life situations present, they wish to put to immediate use what they learn. They are mostly motivated to learn because they are seeking solutions to the problems they encounter in their roles as parents, workers, citizens, and so on.

In this regard, andragogy recommends that teachers of adults be people-centered rather than being subject-matter-centered and, as such, the subject matter concept of curricula should give way to one which is problem-centered. Andragogy further recommends that the starting point for every learning situation ought to be the problems which the learners have on their minds.

It might be argued that since the problems of children are taken care of by their parents, children are not so much motivated to learn in order to overcome problems of current-life situations. As such, children are considered to have a perspective of postponed application of what they learn. Consequently, it may be argued that in their case we can afford a curriculum of seven or eight subjects rather than a curriculum of problem areas.

Further, it might be argued that since their problems are taken care of by the adult world, children have no problems with which teachers can start as in the education of adults.

Let it be emphasized that if this learner characteristic holds true for adults, it also holds true for children. One may ask: Are we sure that the children do not wish to apply immediately what they learn? Are we adults not the ones who have decided that children should be stores of information in the hope that it will be useful to them at some future date? And what is wrong with children applying what they have learned immediately? What is wrong with using problem-centered ways in teaching children? If the aim of education is to develop the children to think, must we not systematically and consciously teach for transfer through formulating trial problems for children to solve? Are we not aware that such problem-solving activities for young children lead to new learning?

Conclusions

In my estimation the few inventors Africa has had are not necessarily a creation of the white man's education. They invented even though education did not use the techniques of andragogy. The pedagogical methods of postponed application killed our interests to be creative. That is why we must go barefoot when we export our hides and skins. We must either wear nylon or dress shoddily because we export our excellent cotton. We must import glue because we throw away the hoofs of the animals we butcher. We must import buttons because we cannot make them. We must import barley for beer brewing because we do not see the value of sorghum. We must import plastic toys because we cannot see how rich our environment is. We must borrow colors to name our things as though our vegetation does not have all these colors. We are poor because the products of our education have no respect for local things. We are consumers rather than producers because we are parrots rather than thinkers.

It is a fact that all of us have been disillusioned by this Western-type education. We have attempted to modify it to serve our needs. Unfortunately, by trying to adapt it to our habitat, we have made it impossible to think afresh about an education that will save and serve us.

As I see it, true education may be found in andragogy. Accordingly, I invite all serious-minded educators to examine it and give it the appraisal it deserves. For me, the advantages of andragogy are many. First, it is a double-barreled gun with tremendous potential for liberating both youths and adults to believe in themselves, to think and to create. Second, by inviting a dialogue between the teacher and the taught, it puts an end to the long-standing problem of teacher-student contradiction where, in the words of Freire, "the teacher teaches and the students are taught; the teacher knows everything and the students know nothing; the teacher thinks and the students are thought about . . . [1970, p. 59]. Andragogy, therefore, shatters the myth that knowledge is the private property of teachers. Because it rightly assumes that no teacher can really teach in the sense of make a person learn, andragogy believes that one person merely helps another person learn.

The third advantage of andragogy is that is does not divide education into compartments of adult and youth education. It means helping human beings learn. With it, education is a meaningful whole seeking to exploit the best in a human being at whatever age he is. It seeks to utilize all sources of information and rejects the myth that the written word is the only source of information. With andragogy, therefore, it is possible to educate without necessarily making people literate for immediate social and economic development. It is only after we have weaned ourselves from falsely equating knowledge and learning with schools and have acquired skills of how to learn that we shall become self-directed learners making use of any resources available to turn ourselves into fully functioning, liberated human beings.

Bibliography

Adams-Webber, J. R. *Personal Construct Theory: Concepts and Application.* New York: Wiley-Interscience, 1979.

Adult Education Association. *Adult Learning.* Washington, D.C.: Adult Education Association, 1965.

_____. *Processes of Adult Education.* Washington, D.C.: Adult Education Association, 1965.

_____. *Psychology of Adults.* Washington, D.C.: Adult Education Association, 1963.

Alford, H. J. *Continuing Education in Action: Residential Centers for Lifelong Learning.* New York: Wiley, 1968.

Allender, J. S. "New Conceptions of the Role of the Teacher." *The Psychology of Open Teaching and Learning.* Edited by M. L. Silberman, et al. Boston: Little, Brown, 1972.

Allport, Gordon. *Becoming.* New Haven: Yale University Press. 1955.

_____. *Pattern and Growth in Personality.* New York: Holt, Rinehart, and Winston, 1961.

_____. *Personality and Social Encounter.* Boston: Beacon, 1960.

Anderson, Scarvia, et al. *Encyclopedia of Educational Evaluation.* San Francisco: Jossey-Bass, 1974.

Arends, R. I., and Arends, J. H. *System Change Strategies in Educational Settings.* New York: Human Sciences Press, 1977.

Argyris, Chris. *Integrating the Individual and the Organization.* New York: John Wiley and Sons, 1964.

———. *Increasing Leadership Effectiveness.* New York: Wiley Interscience, 1976.

———. *Interpersonal Competence and Organizational Effectiveness.* Homewood, Ill.: Dorsey, 1962.

———. *Intervention Theory and Method: A Behavioral Science View.* Reading, Mass.: Addison-Wesley, 1970.

Ashton-Warner, Sylvia. *Teacher.* New York: Simon and Shuster, 1963.

Ausubel, D. P. *The Psychology of Meaningful Verbal Learning: An Introduction to School Learning.* New York: Grime and Stratton, 1963.

Axford, R. W. *Adult Education: The Open Door.* Scranton, Penn.: International Textbook Co., 1969.

Baldridge, J. V., et al. *Policy Making and Effective Leadership: A National Study of Academic Management.* San Francisco: Jossey-Bass, 1978.

———, and Deal, T. S. *Managing Change in Educational Organizations.* Berkeley: McCutchan Publishing Corp., 1975.

Baltes, Paul D. *Life-Span Development and Behavior* Vol. I. New York: Academic Press, 1978.

Bandura, Albert. *Principles of Behavior Modification.* New York: Holt, Rinehart and Winston, 1969.

———, and Walters, R. H. *Social Learning and Personality Development.* New York: Holt, Rinehart and Winston, 1963.

Bany, M. A., and Johnson, L. V. *Classroom Group Behavior.* New York: Macmillan, 1964.

Barker, Roger G. *Ecological Psychology: Concepts and Methods for Studying the Environment of Human Behavior.* Stanford, Cal.: Stanford University Press, 1968.

——— (ed.). *The Stream of Behavior.* New York: Appleton-Century-Crofts, 1963.

———, and Gump, P. V. *Big School, Small School: High School Size and Student Behavior.* Stanford, Cal.: Stanford University Press, 1964.

Barrett, James H. *Gerontological Psychology.* Springfield, Ill.: Charles C. Thomas, 1972.

Barron, F. *Creativity and Psychological Health.* Princeton: Van Nostrand, 1963.

Baughart, F. W. *Educational Systems Analysis.* New York: Macmillan, 1969.

Becker, J. (ed.). *Architecture for Adult Education.* Washington, D.C.: Adult Education Association, 1956.

Beckhard, R. *Organization Development: Strategies and Models.* Reading, Mass.: Addison-Wesley, 1969.

Bell, C. R., and Nadler, L. *The Client-Consultant Handbook.* Houston: Gulf Publishing Co., 1979.

Bengston, V. L. *The Social Psychology of Aging.* Indianapolis: Bobbs-Merrill, 1973.

Bennis, W. G. *Changing Organizations.* New York: McGraw-Hill, 1966.

_____. *Organization Development: Its Nature, Origins, and Prospects.* Reading, Mass.: Addison-Wesley, 1969.

_____, Benne, K. D., and Chin, R. *The Planning of Change.* New York: Holt, Rinehart and Winston, 1968.

_____, and Slater, P. E. *The Temporary Society.* New York: Harper and Row, 1968.

Bereiter, C. "Moral Alternatives to Education." *Interchange,* III (1972), 25-41.

Bergevin, P., and McKinley, J. *Participation Training for Adult Education.* St. Louis: Bethany Press, 1965.

Berte, N. R. *Individualizing Education by Learning Contracts.* New Directions for Higher Education, No. 10. San Francisco: Jossey-Bass, 1975.

Birren, James E. *The Psychology of Aging.* Englewood Cliffs, N.J.: Prentice-Hall, 1964.

Bischoff, L. J. *Adult Psychology.* New York: Harper and Row, 1969.

Blake, R. R., and J. S. Mouton. *Consultation.* Reading, Mass.: Addison-Wesley, 1976.

Blake, R. R., and Mouton, J. S. *The Managerial Grid.* Houston: Gulf Publishing Co., 1964.

Block, J. H. *Mastery Learning: Theory and Practice.* New York: Holt, Rinehart and Winston, 1971.

Bloom, B. S., et al. *Handbook of Formative and Summative Evaluation of Student Learning.* New York: McGraw-Hill, 1973.

_____, et al. *Taxonomy of Educational Objectives*. Handbook I: Cognitive Domain. New York: McKay, 1956.

Boone, Edgar, and Associates. *Serving Personal and Community Needs Through Adult Education*. San Francisco: Jossey-Bass, 1980.

Borich, Gary D. (ed.). *Evaluating Educational Programs and Products*. Englewood Cliffs, N.J.: Educational Technology Publications, 1974.

Botkin, J. W., Elmandjra, M., and Salitza, M. *No Limits to Learning*. A Report to the Club of Rome. New York: Pergamon Press, 1979.

Botwinick, J. *Cognitive Processes in Maturity and Old Age*. New York: Springer, 1967.

Boud, David. *Developing Student Autonomy in Learning*. New York: Nichols Publishing Co., 1981.

Bower, E. M., and Hollister, W. G. (eds.). *Behavioral Science Frontiers in Education*. New York: Wiley, 1967.

Boyd, R. D., Apps, J. W., and Associates. *Redefining the Discipline of Adult Education*. San Francisco: Jossey-Bass, 1980.

Bradford, L. P., Benne, K. D., and Gibb, J. R. *T-Group Theory and Laboratory Method*. New York: Wiley, 1964.

Brady, H. G. *Research Needs in Adult Education*. Tampa: University of South Florida, 1982.

Britton, Joseph H., and Britton, Jean O. *Personality Changes in Aging*. New York: Springer Publishing Co., 1972.

Bromley, D. B. *The Psychology of Human Aging*. Baltimore: Penguin, 1966.

Brown, G. *Human Teaching for Human Learning*. New York: Viking, 1971.

Bruner, J. S. "The Act of Discovery." *Harvard Educational Review*, XXXI (1961), 21–32.

_____. *The Process of Education*. Cambridge, Mass.: Harvard University Press, 1961.

_____. *Toward a Theory of Instruction*. Cambridge, Mass.: Harvard University Press, 1966.

Brunner, E. deS. *An Overview of Adult Education Research*. Washington, D.C.: Adult Education Association, 1959.

Buber, Martin. *I and Thou*. 2nd ed. New York: Scribner's, 1958.

Bullmer, K. *The Art of Empathy*. New York: Human Sciences Press, 1975.

Burton, W. H. "Basic Principles in a Good Teaching-Learning Situation." *Readings in Human Learning.* Edited by L. D. and Alice Crow. New York: McKay, 1963, pp. 7-19.

Bushnell, D., and Rappaport, D. (eds.). *Planned Change in Education: A Systems Approach.* New York: Harcourt, Brace, Jovanovich, 1972.

Carkhuff, Robert R. *Helping and Human Relations: A Primer for Lay and Professional Helpers.* 2 vols. New York: Holt, Rinehart and Winston, 1969.

Carnevale, A. P. *Human Capital: A High Yield Corporate Investment.* Washington, D.C.: American Society for Training and Development, 1983.

Chalofsky, N., and Lincoln, C. I. *Up the HRD Ladder: A Guide for Professional Growth.* Reading, Mass.: Addison-Wesley, 1983.

Charters, A. N., and Associates. *Comparing Adult Education Worldwide.* San Francisco: Jossey-Bass, 1981.

Chickering, A. W. *Education and Identity.* San Francisco: Jossey-Bass, 1976.

_____. *An Introduction to Experiential Learning.* New Rochelle, N.Y.: Change Magazine Press, 1977.

_____, and Associates. *The Modern American College.* San Francisco: Jossey-Bass, 1981.

Claxton, C. S., and Ralston, Y. *Learning Styles: Their Impact on Teaching and Administration.* Washington, D.C.: American Association of Higher Education.

Cleland, D. (ed.) *Systems, Organization Analysis, Management.* New York: McGraw-Hill, 1969.

Coan, A. W., et al. *The Optimal Personality.* New York: Columbia University Press, 1974.

Collins, Z. W. *Museums, Adults and the Humanities.* Washington, D.C.: American Association of Museums, 1981.

Combs, Arthur W., et al. *Helping Relationships: Basic Concepts for the Helping Professions.* Boston: Allyn and Bacon, 1971.

_____, and Snygg, Donald. *Individual Behavior.* Rev. ed. New York: Harper, 1959.

Craig, R. L., and Bittel, L. R. *Training and Development Handbook.* New York: McGraw-Hill, 1967, 1976.

Cronbach, L. J. *Educational Psychology.* 2nd ed. New York: Harcourt, Brace and World, 1963.

_____. *Toward Reform of Program Evaluation.* San Francisco: Jossey-Bass, 1980.

Cropley, A. J. *Towards a System of Lifelong Education.* Hamburg, Germany: UNESCO Institute for Education, 1980.

Cross, K. P. *Accent on Learning.* San Francisco: Jossey-Bass, 1976.

_____. *Adults As Learners.* San Francisco: Jossey-Bass, 1981.

Crow, L. D., and Crow, A. (eds.). *Readings in Human Learning.* New York: McKay, 1963.

_____. "Meaning and Scope of Learning." *Readings in Human Learning.* New York: McKay, 1963, pp. 1-3.

Crutchfield, R. S. "Nurturing Cognitive Skills of Productive Thinking." Silberman, M. L., Allender, J. S., and Yanoff, J. M. *The Psychology of Open Teaching and Learning.* Boston: Little, Brown, 1972, pp. 189-196.

Crystal, J. C., and Bolles, R. N. *Where Do I Go From Here With My Life.* New York: Seabury Press, 1974.

Csikszentmihalyi, M. *Beyond Boredom and Anxiety.* San Francisco: Jossey-Bass, 1975.

Darkenwald, G. G., and S. B. Merriam. *Adult Education: Foundations of Practice.* New York: Harper & Row, 1982.

Dave, R. H. *Lifelong Education and School Curriculum.* Monograph No. 1. Hamburg, Germany: UNESCO Institute for Education, 1973.

_____ (ed.). *Reflections on Lifelong Education and the School.* Monograph No. 3. Hamburg, Germany: UNESCO Institute for Education, 1975.

David, Thomas G., and Wright B. D. (eds). *Learning Environments.* Chicago: University of Chicago Press, 1975.

Davis, G. A., and J. A. Scott. *Training Creative Thinking.* New York: Holt, Rinehart, and Winston, 1971.

Davis, R. C. *Planning Human Resource Development.* Chicago: Rand-McNally, 1966.

Dentwhistle, N. *Styles of Learning and Teaching.* New York: John Wiley & Sons, 1982.

Dewey, John. *Experience and Education.* New York: Macmillan, 1938.

Dobbs, R. C. *Adult Education in America: An Anthological Approach.* Cassville, Mo.: Litho Printers, 1970.

Donahue, Wilma, and Tibbitts, Clark. *The New Frontiers of Aging.* Ann Arbor: University of Michigan Press, 1957.

Dressel, Paul L. *Handbook of Academic Evaluation.* San Francisco: Jossey-Bass, 1976.

Drews, E. M. "Self-Actualization. A New Focus for Education." *Learning and Mental Health in School.* Edited by W. B. Waetjen and R. R. Leeper. Washington, D.C. Association for Supervision and Curriculum Development, N.E.A., 1966, pp. 99-124.

Drucker, P. F. *The Effective Executive.* New York: Harper and Row, 1967.

Dubin, R., and Raveggia, T. C. *The Teaching-Learning Paradox: A Comparative Analysis of College Teaching Methods.* Eugene, Ore. Center for the Advanced Study of Educational Administration, University of Oregon, 1968.

Dykes, A. R. *Faculty Participation in Academic Decision Making.* Washington, D.C.: American Council on Education, 1968.

Eble, Kenneth E. *The Craft of Teaching.* San Francisco: Jossey-Bass, 1976.

Eiben, R., and Milliren, A. (eds.). *Educational Change: A Humanistic Approach.* La Jolla, CA: University Associates, 1976.

Erikson, E. H. *Childhood and Society.* New York: W. W. Norton, 1950.

_____. *Identity and the Life Cycle.* New York: International Universities Press, 1959.

_____. *Insight and Responsibility.* New York: Norton, 1964.

Estes, W. J. "The Statistical Approach to Learning Theory." *Psychology: A Study of a Science.* Edited by S. Koch. Vol. II. New York: McGraw-Hill, 1959.

Etzioni, Amatai. *Complex Organizations.* New York: The Free Press, 1961.

_____. *A Sociological Reader on Complex Organizations.* New York: Holt, Rinehart and Winston, 1969.

Faure, Edgar, et al. *Learning to Be: The World of Education Today and Tomorrow.* Paris: UNESCO, 1972.

Felker, D. W. *Building Positive Self-Concepts.* Minneapolis: Burgess Publishing Co., 1974.

Flanders, N. A., and Simon, A. *Teacher Influence, Pupil Attitudes, and Achievement.* U.S. Department of Health, Education and Welfare, Office of Education. Cooperative Research Monograph No.

12 (OE-25040). Washington, D.C., Government Printing Office, 1965.

Flavell, J. H. "Cognitive Changes in Adulthood." Goulet, L. R., and Baltes, P. B. *Life-Span Development Psychology.* New York: Academic Press, 1970, pp. 247-253.

Friere, Paulo. *Pedagogy of the Oppressed.* New York: Herder and Herder, 1970.

Froland, C., et al. *Helping Networks and Human Services.* Beverly Hills, CA: Sage Publications, 1981.

Gage, N. L. *Teacher Effectiveness and Teacher Education.* Palo Alto, Cal.: Pacific Books, 1972.

Gagne, R. M. *The Conditions of Learning.* New York: Holt, Rinehart and Winston, 1965.

_____. "Domains of Learning." *Interchange,* III (1972), pp. 1-8.

_____. "Policy Implications and Future Research. A Response." *Do Teachers Make a Difference?* A Report on Research on Pupil Achievement. U.S. Department of Health, Education and Welfare, Office of Education. Washington, D.C., Government Printing Office, 1970.

Gale, R. *The Psychology of Being Yourself.* Englewood Cliffs, N.J.: Prentice-Hall, 1974.

Gambrill, Eileen D. *Behavior Modification: Handbook of Assessment, Intervention, and Evaluation.* San Francisco: Jossey-Bass, 1977.

Gardner, John. *Self-Renewal: The Individual and the Innovative Society.* New York: Harper and Row, 1963.

Gessner, R. (ed.). *The Democratic Man: Selected Writings of Eduard C. Lindeman.* Boston: Beacon, 1956.

Getzels, J. W., and Jackson, P. W. *Creativity and Intelligence.* New York: Wiley, 1962.

_____, J. M. Lipham, and Campbell, R. F. *Educational Administration As A Social Process.* New York: Harper & Row, 1968.

Glaser, R. (ed.). *Training Research and Education.* Pittsburgh: University of Pittsburgh Press, 1962.

Goble, F. *The Third Force: The Psychology of Abraham Maslow.* New York: Pocket Books, 1971.

Goldstein, K. M., and Blackman, S. *Cognitive Style: Five Approaches and Relevant Research.* New York: Wiley-Interscience, 1978.

Goodlad, J. I. *The Dynamics of Educational Change.* New York: Mc-Graw-Hill, 1975.

Gordon, Ira J. *Criteria for Theories of Instruction.* Washington, D.C.: Association for Supervision and Curriculum Development, N.E.A., 1968.

Gould, Samuel, chairman, Commission on Nontraditional Study. *Diversity By Design.* San Francisco: Jossey-Bass, 1973.

Goulet, L. R., and Baltes, P. B. *Life-Span Developmental Psychology.* New York: Academic Press, 1970.

Gowan, J. C., et al. *Creativity: Its Educational Implications.* New York: John Wiley & Sons, 1967.

_____, and Associates. *Preparing Educators of Adults.* San Francisco: Jossey-Bass, 1981.

Grabowski, S. M. (ed.). *Adult Learning and Instruction.* Syracuse: ERIC Clearinghouse on Adult Education, 1970.

_____, and Mason, Dean W. *Learning for Aging.* Washington, D.C.: Adult Education Association of the U.S.A., 1974.

Granick, S. and Patterson, R. D. *Human Aging II.* U.S. Department of Health, Education, and Welfare, National Institute of Mental Health. (HSM 71-9037). Washington, D.C., Government Printing Office, 1971.

Grant, G., et al. *On Competence.* San Francisco: Jossey-Bass, 1979.

Greiner, L. E. (ed.). *Organizational Change and Development.* Homewood, Ill.: Irwin, 1971.

Griffiths, D. E. (ed.). *Behavioral Science and Educational Administration.* Sixty-Third Yearbook of the National Society for the Study of Education. Chicago: NSSE, 1964.

Gross, Ronald. *The Lifelong Learner: A Guide to Self-Development.* New York: Simon and Schuster, 1977.

_____. *Invitation to Lifelong Learning.* Chicago: Follett Publishing Co., 1982.

Guba, E. G., and Lincoln, Y. S. *Effective Evaluation.* San Francisco: Jossey-Bass, 1981.

Gubrium, Jaber F. (ed.). *Time, Roles, and Self in Old Age.* New York: Human Sciences Press, 1976.

_____, and Buckholdt, D. R. *Toward Maturity: the Social Processing of Human Development.* San Francisco: Jossey-Bass, 1977.

Haggard, E. A. "Learning A Process of Change." *Readings in Human Learning*. Edited by L. D. and A. Crow. New York: McKay, 1963, pp. 19-27.

Hall, G. E., and Jones, H. L. *Competency-Based Education: A Process for the Improvement of Education*. Englewood Cliffs, N.J.: Prentice-Hall, 1976.

Handy, H. W., and Hussain, K. M. *Network Analysis for Educational Management*. Englewood Cliffs, N.J.: Prentice-Hall, 1968.

Hare, Paul. *Handbook of Small Group Research*. New York: Free Press of Glencoe, 1962.

————. *Small Group Process*. New York: Macmillan, 1969.

Hare, Van Court, Jr. *Systems Analysis. A Diagnostic Approach*. New York: Harcourt, Brace, and World, 1967.

Harrington, Fred H. *The Future of Adult Education*. San Francisco: Jossey-Bass, 1977.

Harris, P. R., and Moran, R. T. *Managing Cultural Differences*. Houston: Gulf Publishing Co., 1979.

Harris, T. L., and Schwahn, W. E. *Selected Readings on the Learning Process*. New York: Oxford University Press, 1961.

Hartley, H. J. *Educational Planning-Programming-Budgeting A Systems Approach*. Englewood Cliffs, N.J.: Prentice-Hall, 1968.

Havighurst, Robert. *Developmental Tasks and Education*. 2nd ed. New York: David McKay, 1970.

Hefferlin, J. B. L. *Dynamics of Academic Reform*. San Francisco: Jossey-Bass, 1969.

Heffernan, J. M., Macy, F. L., and Vickers, D. F. *Educational Brokering: A New Service for Adult Learners*. Washington, D.C.: National Center for Educational Brokering, 1976.

Herzberg, Frederick. *Work and the Nature of Man*. Cleveland: The World Publishing Co., 1966.

————, et al. *The Motivation to Work*. New York: John Wiley & Sons, 1959.

Hesburgh, T. M., Miller, P. A., and Wharton, C. R. Jr. *Patterns for Lifelong Learning*. San Francisco: Jossey-Bass, 1973.

Heyman, Margaret M. *Criteria and Guidelines for the Evaluation of Inservice Training*. Washington, D.C.: Social and Rehabilitation Service, Department of Health, Education and Welfare, 1967.

Hilgard, E. R., and Bower, G. H. *Theories of Learning.* New York: Appleton-Century-Crofts, 1966.

Hill, J. E., and Nunney, D. N. *Personalizing Educational Programs Utilizing Cognitive Style Mapping.* Bloomfield Hills, Mich.: Oakland Community College, 1971.

Horney, Karen. *Feminine Psychology.* New York: W. W. Norton, 1967.

Hornstein, H. A., et al. *Social Intervention: A Social Science Approach.* New York: The Free Press, 1971.

Hospital Continuing Education Project. *Training and Continuing Education.* Chicago: Hospital Research and Educational Trust, 1970.

Houle, Cyril O. *Continuing Your Education.* New York: McGraw-Hill, 1964.

_____. *The Design of Education.* San Francisco: Jossey-Bass, 1972.

_____. *The Effective Board.* New York: Association Press, 1960.

_____. *The External Degree.* San Francisco: Jossey-Bass, 1973.

_____. *The Inquiring Mind.* Madison: University of Wisconsin Press, 1961.

_____. *Continuing Learning in the Professions.* San Francisco: Jossey-Bass, 1980.

Howe, M. J. A. *Adult Learning: Psychological Research and Applications.* New York: John Wiley & Sons, 1977.

Hultsch, D. F., and Deutsch, F. *Adult Development and Aging: A Life Span Perspective.* New York: McGraw-Hill, 1981.

Hunt, Morton. *The Universe Within: A New Science Explores the Human Mind.* New York: Simon & Schuster, 1982.

Hunkins, Francis P. *Involving Students in Questioning.* Boston: Allyn and Bacon, 1975.

Ickes, W., and Knowles, E. S. *Personality, Roles, and Social Behavior.* New York: Springer-Verlag, 1982.

Illich, Ivan. *Deschooling Society.* New York: Harper and Row, 1970.

_____. *Tools for Conviviality.* New York: Harper and Row, 1973.

Ingalls, John. *Human Energy: The Critical Factor for Individuals and Organizations.* Reading, Mass.: Addison-Wesley, 1976.

Ingalls, J. D., and Arceri, J. M. *A Trainers Guide to Andragogy.* Social and Rehabilitation Service. U.S. Department of Health, Education, and Welfare. (SRS 72-05301). Washington, D.C., Government Printing Office, 1972.

Iscoe, I., and Stevenson, W. W. (eds.). *Personality Development in Children.* Austin, Texas: University of Texas Press, 1960.

Jensen, G., Liveright, A. A., and Hallenbeck, W. *Adult Education: Outlines of an Emerging Field of University Study.* Washington, D.C.: Adult Education Association, 1964.

Johnson, D. W., and Johnson, F. P. *Learning Together and Alone: Co-operation, Competition, and Individualization.* Englewood Cliffs, N.J.: Prentice-Hall, 1975.

Johnstone, J. W. C., and Rivera, William. *Volunteers for Learning: A Study of the Educational Pursuits of American Adults.* Chicago: Aldine, 1965.

Jones, G. Brian, et al. *New Designs and Methods for Delivering Human Developmental Services.* New York: Human Sciences Press, 1977.

Jones, H. E. "Intelligence and Problem Solving." *Handbook of Aging and the Individual.* Edited by J. E. Birren. Chicago: University of Chicago Press, 1959, pp. 700-738.

Jones, R. M. *Fantasy and Feeling in Education.* New York: New York University Press, 1968.

Jourard, S. M. "Fascination. A Phenomenological Perspective on Independent Learning." *The Psychology of Open Teaching and Learning.* Edited by M. L. Silberman, et al. Boston: Little, Brown, 1972, pp. 66-75.

Joyce, Bruce, and Weil, Marsha. *Models of Teaching.* Englewood Cliffs, N.J.: Prentice-Hall, 1972.

Jung, Carl. *The Nature of the Psyche.* Trans. by R. F. C. Hull. Bollingen Series XX, Vol. 8. Princeton, N.J.: Princeton University Press, 1969.

Kagan, J. (ed.). *Creativity and Learning.* Boston: Houghton-Mifflin, 1967.

_____, and Moss, H. A. *Birth to Maturity: A Study in Psychological Development.* New York: John Wiley & Sons, 1962.

Kaplan, Abraham. *The Conduct of Inquiry.* San Francisco: Chandler, 1964.

Kast, F. E., and Rozenzweig, J. E. *Organization and Management: A Systems Approach*. New York: McGraw-Hill, 1970.

Kastenbaum, Robert (ed.). *New Thoughts on Old Age*. New York: Springer Publishing Co., 1964.

_____. *Contributions to the Psycho-Biology of Aging*. New York: Springer Publishing Co., 1965.

Katz, D., and Kahn, R. L. *The Social Psychology of Organizations*. New York: Wiley, 1966.

Kaufman, R. *Educational System Planning*. Englewood Cliffs, N.J.: Prentice-Hall, 1972.

Keeton, Morris T., et al. *Experiential Learning: Rationale, Characteristics, and Assessment*. San Francisco: Jossey-Bass, 1976.

Kelly, G. S. *The Psychology of Personal Constructs*. New York: W. W. Norton, 1955.

Kempfer, H. H. *Adult Education*. New York: McGraw-Hill, 1955.

Kidd, J. R. *How Adults Learn*. New York: Association Press, 1959, 1973.

Kingsley, H. L., and Garry, R. *The Nature and Conditions of Learning*. 2nd ed. Englewood Cliffs, N.J.: Prentice-Hall, 1957.

Kirkpatrick, Donald L. *Evaluating Training Programs*. Madison, Wis.: American Society for Training and Development, 1975.

_____. *A Practical Guide for Supervisory Training and Development*. Reading, Mass.: Addison-Wesley, 1971.

Knowles, Malcolm S. *The Adult Education Movement in the United States*. 2nd ed. Huntington, N.Y.: Krieger Publishing Co., 1977.

_____. *Self-Directed Learning: A Guide for Learners and Teachers*. New York: Association Press, 1975.

_____. *Informal Adult Education*. New York: Association Press, 1950.

_____. *The Modern Practice of Adult Education: Andragogy versus Pedagogy*. New York: Association Press, 1972, 1980.

_____ and Hulda, F. *Introduction to Group Dynamics*. Chicago: Follett, 1973.

Knox, Alan B. *Adult Development and Learning*. San Francisco: Jossey-Bass, 1977.

_____, and Associates. *Developing, Administering, and Evaluating Adult Education*. San Francisco: Jossey-Bass, 1980.

Kolb, D. A. *The Learning Style Inventory*. Boston: McBer, 1976.

Kreitlow, B. W., and Associates. *Examining Controversies in Adult Education.* San Francisco: Jossey-Bass, 1981.

Laughary, J. W., and Rippley, T. M. *Helping Others Help Themselves.* New York: McGraw-Hill, 1979.

Leagans, J. P., Copeland, H. G., and Kaiser, G. E. *Selected Concepts from Educational Psychology and Adult Education for Extension and Continuing Educators.* Syracuse: University of Syracuse Press, 1971.

Lefcourt, Herbert M. *Locus of Control: Current Trends in Theory and Research.* New York: John Wiley & Sons, 1976.

Lengrand, Paul. *An Introduction to Lifelong Education.* Paris: UNESCO, 1970.

Lenning, Frank W., and Many, W. A. (eds.). *Basic Education for the Disadvantaged Adult: Theory and Practice.* Boston: Houghton Mifflin, 1966.

Leonard, G. B. *Education and Ecstasy.* New York: Delacorte, 1968.

Levinson, H., et al. *Men, Management, and Mental Health.* Cambridge, Mass.: Harvard University Press, 1963.

Lewin, Kurt. *Field Theory in Social Science.* New York: Harper, 1951.

Leypoldt, M. M. *Forty Ways to Teach in Groups.* Valley Forge, Penn.: Judson Press, 1967.

Likert, R. *The Human Organization: Its Management and Value.* New York: McGraw-Hill, 1967.

_____. *New Patterns of Management.* New York: McGraw-Hill, 1961.

Lindeman, Eduard C. *The Meaning of Adult Education.* New York: New Republic, 1926.

Lippitt, G. L. *Organization Renewal.* New York: Appleton-Century-Crofts, 1969.

_____. *Visualizing Change.* Somerset, N.J.: John Wiley & Sons, 1978.

_____, and R. Lippitt. *The Consulting Process In Action.* La Jolla, CA: University Associates, 1978.

Loevenger, J. *Ego Development: Concepts and Theories.* San Francisco: Jossey-Bass, 1976.

Long, Huey B. *Are They Ever Too Old to Learn?* Englewood Cliffs, N.J.: Prentice-Hall, 1971.

_____. *The Psychology of Aging: How It Affects Learning.* Englewood Cliffs, N.J.: Prentice-Hall, 1972.

_____., et al. *Changing Approaches to Studying Adult Education.* San Francisco: Jossey-Bass, 1980.

Lumsden, D. B., and Sherron, R. H. *Experimental Studies in Adult Learning and Memory.* New York: John Wiley & Sons, 1975.

McClelland, D. C. *Power: The Inner Experience.* New York: McGraw-Hill, 1960.

_____, Atkinson, J. W., Clark, R. A., and Lowell, E. I. *The Achievement Motive.* New York: Appleton-Century-Crofts, 1953.

McDonald, F. J. "The Influence of Learning Theories on Education." *Theories of Learning and Instruction.* Sixty-third Yearbook of the National Society for the Study of Education, Part I. Edited by E. R. Hilgard. Chicago: University of Chicago Press, 1964, pp. 1-26.

McGregor, D. *The Human Side of Enterprise.* New York: McGraw-Hill, 1960.

_____. *Leadership and Motivation.* Cambridge, Mass.: The Massachusetts Institute of Technology Press, 1967.

McKenzie, L. *The Religious Education of Adults.* Birmingham, Ala.: Religious Education Press, 1982.

Mager, R. F. *Preparing Instructional Objectives.* Palo Alto, Cal.: Fearon, 1962.

_____. *Goal Analysis.* Palo Alto, Cal.: Fearon, 1972.

_____, and Pipe, P. *Analyzing Performance Problems,* Palo Alto, Cal.: Fearon, 1970.

Mangham, I. *Interactions and Interventions in Organizations.* New York: John Wiley & Sons, 1948.

Marrow, A. J., Bowers, D. G., and Seashore, S. E. *Management By Participation.* New York: Harper and Row, 1968.

Martorana, S. V., and Kuhns, E. *Managing Academic Change.* San Francisco: Jossey-Bass, 1975.

Maslow, A. H. *Motivation and Personality.* New York: Harper and Row, 1970.

_____. "Defense and Growth." *The Psychology of Open Teaching and Learning.* Edited by M. L. Silberman, et al. Boston: Little, Brown, 1972, pp. 43-51.

Messick, S., et al. *Individuality in Learning.* San Francisco: Jossey-Bass, 1976.

Michael, Donald. *On Learning to Plan and Planning to Learn: The Social Psychology of Changing Toward Future-Responsive Societal Learning.* San Francisco: Jossey-Bass, 1973.

Miles, M. W., and Charters, W. W., Jr. *Learning in Social Settings.* Boston: Allyn and Bacon, 1970.

Millenson, J. R. *Principles of Behavioral Analysis.* New York: Macmillan, 1967.

Miller, H. L. *Teaching and Learning in Adult Education.* New York: Macmillan, 1964.

Millett, J. D. *Decision-Making and Administration in Higher Education.* Kent, Ohio: Kent State University Press, 1968.

Millhollan, Frank, and Forisha, B. E. *From Skinner to Rogers.* Lincoln, Nebraska: Professional Educators Publications, 1972.

Moran, R. T., and Harris, P. R. *Managing Cultural Synergy.* Houston: Gulf Publishing Co., 1982.

Moustakas, C. *Finding Yourself, Finding Others.* Englewood Cliffs, N.J.: Prentice-Hall, 1974.

Nadler, Leonard, and Nadler, Zeace. *The Conference Book.* Houston: Gulf Publishing Co., 1977.

_____. *Developing Human Resources.* Houston: Gulf Publishing Co., 1970.

_____. *Designing Training Programs: The Critical Events Model.* Reading, Mass.: Addison-Wesley, 1982.

Neugarten, Bernice L. (ed.). *Personality in Middle and Later Life.* New York: Atherton Press, 1964.

_____. *Middle Age and Aging.* Chicago: University of Chicago Press, 1968.

Optner, S. *Systems Analysis for Business and Industrial Problem Solving,* Englewood Cliffs, N.J.: Prentice-Hall, 1965.

Osborn, Ruth H. *Developing New Horizons for Women.* New York: McGraw-Hill, 1977.

Parsons, T. *The Social System.* New York: Free Press of Glencoe, 1951.

Patton, M. Q. *Creative Evaluation.* Beverly Hills, CA.: Sage Publications, 1981.

_____. *Practical Evaluation.* Beverly Hills, CA. Sage Publications, 1982.

_____. *Qualitative Evaluation*. Beverly Hills, CA.: Sage Publications, 1980.

Peters, J. M., and Associates. *Building an Effective Adult Education Enterprise*. San Francisco: Jossey-Bass, 1980.

Pfeiffer, William J., and Jones, John E. *A Handbook of Structured Experiences for Human Relations Training*. Vols. I, II, III, IV, V. San Diego: University Associates Press, 1969-1976.

Phillips, J. J. *Handbook of Training Evaluation and Measurement Methods*. Houston: Gulf Publishing Co., 1983.

Piaget, Jean. *Science of Education and the Psychology of the Child*. New York: Viking, 1970.

Pittenger, O. E., and Gooding, C. T. *Learning Theories in Educational Practice*. New York: Wiley, 1971.

Pollack, O. *Human Behavior and the Helping Professions*. New York: John Wiley & Sons, 1976.

Postman, N., and Weingartner, C. *Teaching as a Subversive Activity*. New York: Dell, 1969.

Pressey, S. L., and Kuhlen, R. G. *Psychological Development Through the Life Span*. New York: Harper and Row, 1957.

Raths, Louis, et al. *Teaching for Learning*. Columbus, Ohio: Charles E. Merrill, 1967.

_____, Harmin, H., and Simon, Sidney. *Values and Teaching*. Columbus, Ohio: Charles E. Merrill, 1966.

Reese, H. W., and Overton, W. F. "Models of Development and Theories of Development." *Life-Span Developmental Psychology*. Edited by L. R. Goulet and P. B. Baltes. New York: Academic Press, 1970, pp. 115-145.

ROCOM. *Intensive Coronary Care Multimedia System Program Coordinator's Manual*. Nutley, N. J.: Hoffman-LaRoche, 1971.

Rogers, C. R. *Client-Centered Therapy*. Boston: Houghton-Mifflin, 1951.

_____. *On Becoming a Person*. Boston: Houghton-Mifflin, 1961.

_____. *Freedom to Learn*. Columbus, Ohio: Merrill, 1969.

_____. *A Way of Being*. Boston: Houghton Mifflin, 1980.

Rosenshine, B. "Enthusiastic Teaching. A Research Review." *School Review*, LXXVIII (1970), pp. 499-514.

Rosenthal, R. and Jacobson, L. *Pygmalian in the Classroom*. New York: Holt, Rinehart & Winston, 1968.

Rossi, P. H., and Biddle, B. J. *The New Media and Education*. Chicago: Aldine, 1966.

Rudwick, B. H. *Systems Analysis for Effective Planning*. New York: Wiley, 1969.

Runkel, P., Harrison, R., and Runkel, M. *The Changing College Classroom*. San Francisco: Jossey-Bass, 1969.

Schein, E. *Process Consultation. Its Role in Organization Development*. Reading, Mass.: Addison-Wesley, 1969.

————, and Bennis, W. G. *Personal and Organizational Change through Group Methods*. New York: Wiley, 1965.

Schindler-Rainman, Eva, and Lippitt, Ronald. *The Volunteer Community: Creative Use of Human Resources*. Washington, D.C.: Center for a Voluntary Society, 1971.

Schlossberg, N. K., et al. *Perspectives on Counseling Adults*. Monterey, CA: Brooks/Cole, 1965.

Schon, Donald A. *Beyond the Stable State*. San Francisco: Jossey-Bass, 1971.

Schuttenberg, E. "The Development of a General Purpose Organizational Output Instrument and Its Use in Analysis of an Organization." Unpublished doctral diss. Boston University School of Education, 1972.

Schwab, J. J. "The Practical: Arts of Eclectic." *School Review*, LXXIX (August, 1971), pp. 493-542.

Seay, Maurice F., et al. *Community Education: A Developing Concept*. Midland, Mich.: Pendell Publishing Co., 1974.

Seiler, J. A. *Systems Analysis in Organizational Behavior*. Homewood, Ill.: Irwin and Dorsey, 1967.

Shaw, N. (ed.). *Administration of Continuing Education*. Washington, D.C.: National Association for Public and Continuing Education, N.E.A., 1969.

Sheehy, Gail. *Passages: Predictable Crises of Adult Life*. New York: E. P. Dutton, 1974.

Silberman, C. E. *Crisis in the Classroom*. New York: Vintage, 1971.

Silberman, M. L., Allender, J. S., and Yanoff, J. M. *The Psychology of Open Teaching and Learning. An Inquiry Approach*. Boston: Little, Brown, 1972.

Simon, H. A. *Administrative Behavior.* New York: Macmillan, 1961.

Simon, Sydney, Howe, L. W., and Kirschenbaum, H. *Values Clarification.* New York: Hart Publishing Co., 1972.

Skinner, B. F. *The Technology of Teaching.* New York: Appleton-Century-Crofts, 1968.

Smith, Maury. *A Practical Guide to Value Clarification.* La Jolla, Cal.: University Associates, 1977.

Smith, R. M., Aker, G. F., and Kidd, J. R. (eds.). *Handbook of Adult Education.* New York: Macmillan, 1970.

Smith, R. M. *Learning How to Learn: Applied Theory for Adults.* Chicago: Follett, 1982.

Solomon, L., and Berzon, B. (eds.) *New Perspectives on Encounter Groups.* San Francisco: Jossey-Bass, 1972.

Sorenson, Herbert. *Adult Abilities.* Minneapolis: University of Minnesota Press, 1938.

Srinivasan, Lyra. *Perspectives on Nonformal Adult Learning.* New York: World Education, 1977.

Steele, Sara M., and Brack, Robert E. *Evaluating the Attainment of Objectives: Process, Properties, Problems, and Projects.* Syracuse: Syracuse University Publications in Continuing Education, 1973.

Stephens, J. M. *The Process of Schooling.* New York: Holt, Rinehart and Winston, 1967.

Stevens-Long, J. Adult Life: *Developmental Processes.* Palo Alto, CA: Mayfield Publishing Co., 1979.

Stokes, Kenneth (ed.). *Faith Development in the Adult Life Cycle.* New York: William H. Sadlier, 1983.

Storey, W. D. *Orientation to Your Career Development Program.* Ossining, N.Y.: General Electric Company Management Development Institute, 1972.

Suchman, Edward A. *Evaluative Research: Principles and Practice in Public Service and Social Action Programs.* New York: Russell Sage Foundation, 1967.

Suchman, J. R. "The Child and the Inquiry Process." *The Psychology of Open Teaching and Learning.* Edited M. L. Silberman, et al. Boston: Little, Brown, 1972, pp. 147-159.

Taba, H. *Curriculum Development Theory and Practice.* New York: Harcourt, Brace and World, 1962.

Taylor, Bernard, and Lippitt, Gordon L. *Management Development and Training Handbook.* New York: McGraw-Hill, 1975.

Tedeschi, J. T. (ed.). *The Social Influence Process.* Chicago: Aldine-Atherton, 1972.

Thayer, Louis (ed.). *Affective Education: Strategies for Experiential Learning.* La Jolla, Cal.: University Associates, 1976.

Thompson, J. R. "Formal Properties of Instructional Theory for Adults." *Adult Learning and Instruction.* Edited by S. M. Grabowski. Syracuse: ERIC Clearing House on Adult Education, 1970, pp. 28-45.

Thorndike, Edward L. *Adult Interests.* New York: Macmillan, 1935.

_____. *Adult Learning.* New York: Macmillan, 1928.

Toffler, A. (ed.). *Learning for Tomorrow: The Role of the Future in Education.* New York: Random House, 1974.

Tough, A. *The Adult's Learning Projects.* Toronto: Ontario Institute for Studies in Education, 1971, 1979.

_____. *Learning Without a Teacher.* Toronto: Ontario Institute for Studies in Education, 1967.

_____. *Intentional Changes: A Fresh Approach to Helping People Change.* Chicago: Follett, 1982.

Torshen, K. P. *The Mastery Approach to Competency-Based Education.* New York: Academic Press, 1977.

Tracey, William R. *Managing Training and Development Systems.* New York: American Management Associations, 1974.

Trecker, H. B. *Citizen Boards at Work.* New York: Association Press, 1970.

Tyler, L. *Individuality: Human Possibilities and Personal Choice in the Psychological Development of Men and Women.* San Francisco: Jossey-Bass. 1978.

Tyler, R. W. *Basic Principles of Curriculum and Instruction.* Chicago: University of Chicago Press, 1950.

Van Maanen, J., and Dabbs, J. M. *Varieties of Qualitative Research.* Beverly Hills, CA: Sage Publications, 1982.

Vermilye, Dyckman W. (ed.). *Lifelong Learners—A New Clientele for Higher Education.* San Francisco: Jossey-Bass, 1974.

Verner, C. *A Conceptual Scheme for the Identification and Classification of Processes.* Washington, D.C.: Adult Education Association, 1962.

_____, and Booth, Alan. *Adult Education.* New York: Center for Applied Research in Education, 1964.

Von Bertalanffy, L. *General System Theory.* New York: Braziller, 1968.

Waetjen, W. B., and Leeper, R. R. (eds.). *Learning and Mental Health in the School.* Washington, D.C.: Association for Supervision and Curriculum Development, N.E.A., 1966.

Walberg, Herbert J. (ed.). *Evaluating Educational Performance: A Sourcebook of Methods, Instruments, and Examples.* Berkeley, Cal.: McCutchan, 1974.

Watson, G. (ed.). *Concepts for Social Change.* Washington, D.C.: National Training Laboratories Institute for Applied Behavioral Science, N.E.A., 1967.

_____. "What Do We Know About Learning?" *Teachers College Record,* 1960-61, pp. 253-257.

Weiler, Nicholas W. *Reality and Career Planning: A Guide for Personal Growth.* Reading, Mass.: Addison-Wesley, 1977.

White, R. H. "Motivation Reconsidered. The Concept of Competence." *Psychological Review,* LXVI (1959), pp. 297-333.

Willems, E. P., and Rausch, H. L. (eds.). *Naturalistic Viewpoints in Psychological Research.* New York: Holt, Rinehart and Winston, 1969.

Woodruff, Diana S., and Birren, J. E. (eds.). *Aging.* New York: D. Van Nostrand Co., 1975.

Zadeh, L. *Systems Theory.* New York: McGraw-Hill, 1969.

Zahn, J. C. *Creativity Research and Its Implications for Adult Education.* Syracuse: Library of Continuing Education, Syracuse University, 1966.

Zander, A. *Groups at Work.* San Francisco: Jossey-Bass, 1977.

_____. *Making Groups Effective.* San Francisco: Jossey-Bass, 1982.

Zurcher, L. A. *The Mutable Self: A Concept for Social Change.* Beverly Hills, CA: Sage, 1977.

Author Index

Subject Index

through modeling, 93–96
modes, 89
principles, 64–96
theories 64–96
theories, applied to human
resources development,
106–136
traditional, Dewey's criticism,
85–86
Techniques, transmittal vs
experiential, 56–57
Technology, behavioral, 142
Telectures, 119
Television, 119
Terminal behavior, 127
Tests of intelligence, 165–167
Theories, behaviorist, 17–20
of change, 96–103, 122
cognitive, 14, 65–66, 113,
127–128, 135
conditioning, 14
control-oriented, 67–75
coping with, 106–114
criteria for choosing, 106–115
interpreters, 12–13
of learning, *See* Learning
theories.
of learning and teaching applied
to human resources
development, 106–115
mechanistic, 17–21
modeling, 15
organismic, 15–17, 21–26
reinforcement, criticism, 93
stimulus-response, learning,
17–21, 67–69, 93–96
teaching, 64–96
Theory of adult learning, 28
of behavioral settings, 103
cognitive, 14, 65–66, 113,
127–128, 135
of consultation, 122
definition, 2–5, 106–115
field, 15, 23–24, 96–135
instruction, 25, 88–93
intervention, 229–231
personality, 66
systematic behavior, 20

systems, 96–99, 121
X and Y, 107–108
Therapy, as learning process,
41–42
Thinking, productive, 93
stages in development, 25
Third force psychology, 23, 39–42
See also Humanistic psychology.
Time, perception, 44, 162–163
personality change through, 157
Traces, 22
Traditional education, 29–30, 33,
52–53, 85–86, 98
criticism, 85–86
Trainer. *See* Adult educator,
Consultant, Human resources
developer.
Training, change, role in, 228–234
definition of, 111–112, 145
human relations, 99
individual vs organizational, 114,
228–234
organization development,
228–234
teacher, 133–134, 185–186
vs education 111–112, 145
Training Project, Inquiry, 92–93
Transfer of learning, 93–94, 114
Tutoring, 224–249
Types of learning,
objectives, 127–128
theories of learning, 14–15

V–W

UNESCO, 93
Valence, 23
Values, in organization
development, 231–232
See Affective objectives.
Variable, intervening, learners as,
in stimulus-response formula,
157–160
Verbal association, 71
Westinghouse Electric Corporation,
201–218
Will to learn, 88
Work and learning, 32